Assessments Handbook

Hampton-Brown

EDGE

Reading, Writing & Language

Acknowledgments

Grateful acknowledgment is given to the authors, artists, photographers, museums, publishers, and agents for permission to reprint copyrighted material. Every effort has been made to secure the appropriate permission. If any omissions have been made or if corrections are required, please contact the Publisher.

Photographic Credits

Cover: Ancient Eye, Arches National Park, Utah, USA, Marsel van Oosten. Photograph © Marsel van Oosten/ squiver.com.

T1 ©James P. Blair/National Geographic Stock; ©Robert Rostma/First Light/Getty Images; ©Mike Bueno/My Shot/ National Geographic Stock; ©Marsel van Oosten. **1** ©Mike Bueno/My Shot/National Geographic Stock; ©Scala/ Art Resources. **17** ©Bettmann/CORBIS; ©Bettmann/ CORBIS. **18** ©Rudolph Burckhardt/Sygma/CORBIS; ©Oleg Golovnev/Shutterstock; ©Peter Will/Getty Images; ©Rudolph Burckhardt/Sygma/CORBIS. **22** ©Michael Ochs Archives/CORBIS. **29** ©Roy Ooms/Masterfile. **32** ©Noel Powell/Shutterstock; Accounts Table with cueiform script, c.2400 BC (terracotta), Mesopotamian/Louvre, Paris, France/©The Bridgeman Art Library. **68** ©Jack Moebes/ CORBIS. **77** ©Rogelio Solis/AP Images. **94** ©Florian Werner/Getty Images. **97** Portrait of Emily Dickinson (1830-86) as a Child, from the 'Letters of Emily Dickinson', 1951 (litho) by English School, (20th century); Private Collection; English/©The Bridgeman Art Library; ©Carol Lollis-The Daily Hampshire Gazette/AP Photo.

For product information and technology assistance, contact us at
Customer & Sales Support, 888-915-3276

For permission to use material from this text or product, submit all requests online at **www.cengage.com/permissions**
Further permissions questions can be emailed to
permissionrequest@cengage.com

National Geographic Learning | Cengage Learning
1 Lower Ragsdale Drive
Building 1, Suite 200
Monterey, CA 93940

Cengage Learning is a leading provider of customized learning solutions with office locations around the globe, including Singapore, the United Kingdom, Australia, Mexico, Brazil, and Japan. Locate your local office at **www.cengage.com/global**.

Visit National Geographic Learning online at **ngl.cengage.com**
Visit our corporate website at **www.cengage.com**

Printed in the USA.
RR Donnelley, Harrisonburg, VA

ISBN: 978-12854-43782

Printed in the United States of America
14 15 16 17 18 19 20 21 22
10 9 8 7 6 5 4 3

Contents

EDGE Level C

Contents

Program Goals

Hampton-Brown Edge offers instruction based on the Common Core State Standards in reading. The program is carefully designed for struggling high school readers and English language learners to accelerate their growth in literacy and language.

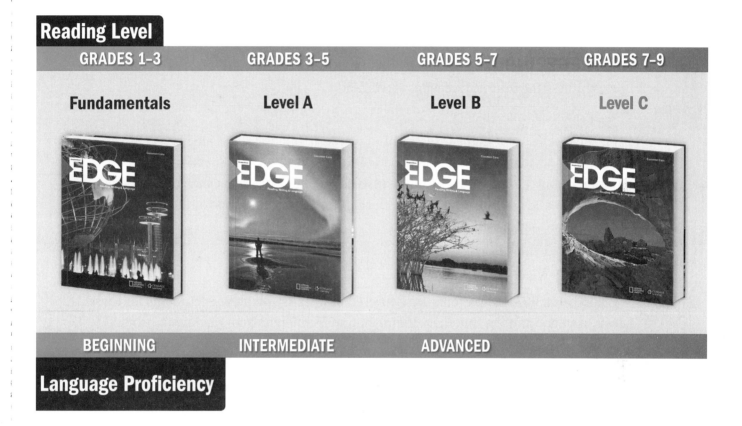

The assessment tools in this Assessments Handbook are aligned with instruction in the major skill strands of the program and the focus of the Common Core State Standards.

Multiple measures and a range of assessment strategies are incorporated into the *Edge* assessment plan to account for the various learning outcomes involved in language and literacy learning. Performance assessments and tests are accompanied with rubrics and answer keys to help teachers gather data and inform instruction, reteaching, or acceleration. For students in need of basic or advanced phonics instruction, a complete array of diagnostic and progress monitoring assessments is provided in *Inside Phonics*. The array of measures effectively addresses the range of skills and learners that comprise today's diverse classrooms and students.

Assessing the Common Core State Standards

The instruction and assessment in *Edge* has been designed to align with the major instructional and assessment shifts that were instituted with the Common Core State Standards and carried through in the development specifications for the Partnership for Assessment of Readiness for College and Careers (PARCC) and the Smarter Balanced Assessment Consortium (SBAC). These standards and assessments present new foci both for the content of assessment and for testing format. Content shifts include:

- a balance of complex and authentic literature and informational texts,
- synthesizing information across texts, and
- a focus on text evidence.

Additional elements such as the assessment of research, integration of media, listening and speaking, and other shifts are described in further detail in the specific test preparation resources and reflected in the instruction and assessment included in *Edge*. The instruction and assessment in *Edge* reflects these shifts and supports students and teachers in achieving success.

Addressing New Test Formats

Both PARCC and SBAC assessments are delivered online. As you prepare students for these new tests, it's important to note that reading online is different from reading in print. Responding to technology-enhanced test items also requires knowledge and comfort with computers and computer software. Keyboarding skills and typing speed are also a factor when completing responses to constructed-response items or completing writing composition tests online. To build confidence and focus for online testing, it is important that students have multiple opportunities to read on computers, tablets, and other digital devices.

To prepare students for computer-based tests, *Edge* includes a range of digital reading options—**eEditions, Comprehension Coach**, and tablet-friendly **eBooks**—that allow students to engage in online reading. Multiple-choice and constructed-response items are available in both the *Edge* **eAssessment** and **ExamView** offerings.

Addressing New Test Content

Regardless of whether tests are administered in print or on computers, the content of the tests in this handbook was designed in accordance with the specifications released by SBAC and PARCC. Major content shifts are reflected in the new assessments and include the following key features:

Literature & Informational Texts The assessments in *Edge* reflect the appropriate balance of literary and informational texts to ensure that students have opportunities to learn and demonstrate understanding of comprehension and textual analysis skills across a variety of genres.

Synthesizing Across Texts PARCC and SBAC include thematically related pairs or larger collections of texts that facilitate opportunities for students to make text-to-text connections. Similarly, the texts in *Edge* instruction and assessments are aligned around consistent themes and items to help focus students on synthesizing information in the range of texts they encounter.

Text Evidence PARCC and SBAC incorporate evidence-centered assessment designs. Students must not only select or write responses to questions, but they must also demonstrate the ability to cite evidence from the passage to support their responses. The focus on citing text evidence is reflected in both multiple-choice and constructed response items in *Edge* Cluster Tests and Unit Tests. Students are directed to cite text evidence in short constructed-response items.

23 The authors of this article and the article "Advertising and Your Emotions" would both argue that

A   advertisements do more good than harm.

B   the main reason to watch television is for information.

C   advertisers want to help people make good decisions.

D   people should really think while watching television.

Edge gives students multiple opportunities to develop literacy skills and demonstrate knowledge of the Common Core State Standards. Instruction and assessments in *Edge* are designed to facilitate transfer to the high-stakes tests they encounter at the end of each school year. Enabling students to gain familiarity and comfort with the formats, in addition to building reading and writing skills and knowledge, accelerates the achievement of striving readers and English language learners and helps promote the goal of having all students—including those who may need extra support – become college and career ready.

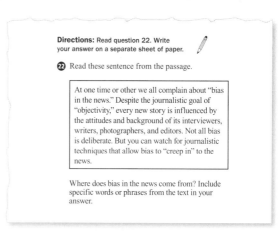

Directions: Read question 22. Write your answer on a separate sheet of paper.

22 Read these sentence from the passage.

> At one time or other we all complain about "bias in the news." Despite the journalistic goal of "objectivity," every new story is influenced by the attitudes and background of its interviewers, writers, photographers, and editors. Not all bias is deliberate. But you can watch for journalistic techniques that allow bias to "creep in" to the news.

Where does bias in the news come from? Include specific words or phrases from the text in your answer.

Assessment Goals and Design

Edge is a core reading intervention program designed for English language learners and students reading below grade level. It prepares students for success on exit exams and moves them to graduation and a promising future. *Edge* has been designed so that frequent, varied assessment informs instruction every step of the way.

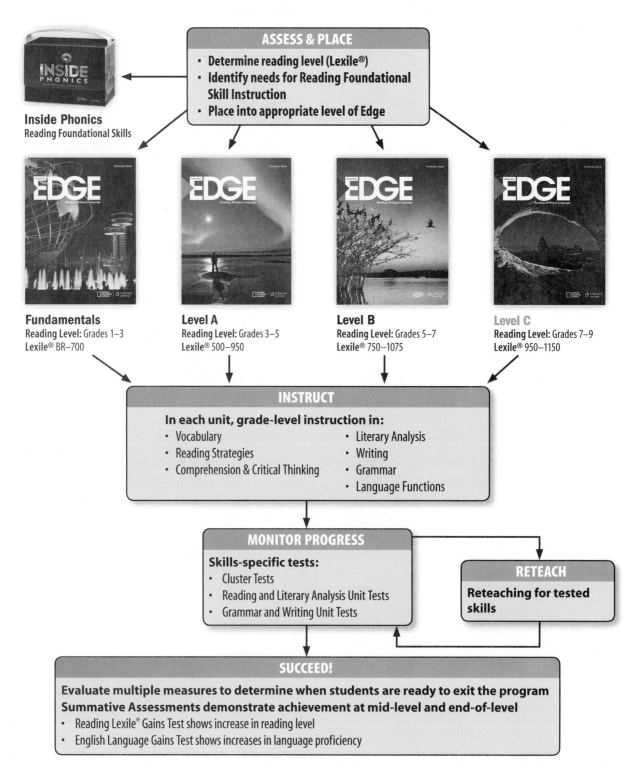

Inside Phonics
Reading Foundational Skills

ASSESS & PLACE
- **Determine reading level (Lexile®)**
- **Identify needs for Reading Foundational Skill Instruction**
- **Place into appropriate level of Edge**

Fundamentals
Reading Level: Grades 1–3
Lexile® BR–700

Level A
Reading Level: Grades 3–5
Lexile® 500–950

Level B
Reading Level: Grades 5–7
Lexile® 750–1075

Level C
Reading Level: Grades 7–9
Lexile® 950–1150

INSTRUCT
In each unit, grade-level instruction in:
- Vocabulary
- Reading Strategies
- Comprehension & Critical Thinking
- Literary Analysis
- Writing
- Grammar
- Language Functions

MONITOR PROGRESS
Skills-specific tests:
- Cluster Tests
- Reading and Literary Analysis Unit Tests
- Grammar and Writing Unit Tests

RETEACH
Reteaching for tested skills

SUCCEED!
Evaluate multiple measures to determine when students are ready to exit the program
Summative Assessments demonstrate achievement at mid-level and end-of-level
- Reading Lexile® Gains Test shows increase in reading level
- English Language Gains Test shows increases in language proficiency

Assessment Tools

Assessment Purpose	Test Type	Printed Components	PDFs on myNGconnect	eAssessment	Exam View
Placement and Gains	**Reading Placement and Gains Test** Places students into the appropriate level of the program by reading level. Three parallel forms report Lexile® measures.	•	Placement Test	•	
	Language Gains Test Three parallel forms report out Beginning, Intermediate, or Advanced proficiency level.	•	Placement Test	•	
Progress Monitoring	**Cluster Tests** These weekly tests allow you to provide immediate feedback and reteaching of the week's instruction in literary analysis, vocabulary, and comprehension and critical thinking. Each test includes a Reader Reflection form that allows input from students on their own progress.	•	•	•	•
	Oral Reading Fluency Measures students' progress toward their words correct per minute goal (wcpm).	•	•	Comprehension Coach	
Performance Assessment	**Language Acquisition Rubrics** Assess the movement of English learners through the stages of language acquisition.	•	•		
	Unit Project Rubrics Holistic assessment of students' performance on the unit project, including key unit skills.	•	•		
Summative Assessments	**Unit Reading and Literary Analysis Tests** Measure students' performance in the targeted unit skills: vocabulary strategies, key vocabulary, literary analysis, and comprehension and critical thinking.	•	•	•	•
	Unit Grammar and Writing Tests Measure students' performance in the targeted unit skills: grammar, traits of good writing, revising and editing for written conventions, and written composition.	•	•	•	•
Reteaching	**Reteaching Prescriptions** include suggestions for re-presenting the skill (from Cluster and Unit Tests), guided practice, and application.		•	•	
Affective and Metacognitive Measures	**Surveys, Reflection Forms, Self- and Peer-Assessments** Help students make personal connections and get committed to their own learning through reflection and metacognition.	•	•		

Reader Reflections

The **Reader Reflections** are self-assessments targeted to the instruction and reading in each instructional cluster. They help students make a personal connection with what they learned and read in the cluster, and provide teachers with valuable insight into student thoughts and attitudes toward learning and content. Students respond to questions about the literature and reading strategy instruction in the cluster and how this will help them in the future. Students also tell what they liked and disliked about each reading selection, and which types of reading they would like to do more of in the future. Reader Reflections are particularly well-suited for intrapersonal learners and help all learners develop metacognitive habits of mind.

Cluster Tests

Purpose and Description

At levels A-C, a Cluster Test is available for each of the three clusters in a Unit, for a total of 21 Cluster Tests per level. Constructed-response and selected-response items are included. Cluster Tests are formative evaluations designed to measure Key Vocabulary, Literary Analysis, and Comprehension with 22 items (20 multiple-choice and 2 constructed-response items). Basic and high-level comprehension is assessed in each Cluster Test. Each Cluster Test focuses on the specific literary skills and instructional-level reading selections within the cluster. They check student progress and provide an early indicator when reteaching or additional instruction may be necessary.

Administering the Tests

Administer the test for each cluster after instruction. Before administering the Cluster Test, you may wish to have students complete the Reader Reflection for the cluster. Make a copy of the test for each student. Provide paper for the constructed responses. Also distribute a copy of the answer sheet on page 164 to each student. This answer sheet provides a one-page record of multiple-choice test answers for convenient hand scoring. Students may use their books to read the selections during the test.

Scoring the Tests and Using the Results

Score Cluster Tests with the Answer Keys and Scoring Guides at the back of this handbook. Use the Student Profile: Cluster Tests to determine if students need reteaching. If you are using eAssessment, multiple choice items are automatically scored. Scores for constructed response items can be easily entered into the system. The reports in eAssessment summarize performance and provide access to reteaching resources.

Reader Reflection, Level B

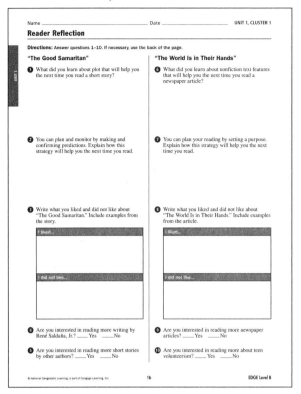

Name _____ Date _____ UNIT 1, CLUSTER 1
Reader Reflection

Directions: Answer questions 1–10. If necessary, use the back of the page.

"The Good Samaritan"

1 What did you learn about plot that will help you the next time you read a short story?

2 You can plan and monitor by making and confirming predictions. Explain how this strategy will help you the next time you read.

3 Write what you liked and did not like about "The Good Samaritan." Include examples from the story.

I liked...

I did not like...

4 Are you interested in reading more writing by René Saldaña, Jr.? ____ Yes ____ No

5 Are you interested in reading more short stories by other authors? ____ Yes ____ No

"The World Is in Their Hands"

6 What did you learn about nonfiction text features that will help you the next time you read a newspaper article?

7 You can plan your reading by setting a purpose. Explain how this strategy will help you the next time you read.

8 Write what you liked and did not like about "The World Is in Their Hands." Include examples from the article.

I liked...

I did not like...

9 Are you interested in reading more newspaper articles? ____ Yes ____ No

10 Are you interested in reading more about teen volunteerism? ____ Yes ____ No

© National Geographic Learning, a part of Cengage Learning, Inc.   1b   EDGE Level B

Cluster Test: Key Vocabulary, Level B

Name _____ Date _____ UNIT 1, CLUSTER 1
"The Good Samaritan" and "The World Is in Their Hands" 📕 Closed Book

Directions: Read each question and choose the best answer.

KEY VOCABULARY

1 To affect something is to
  Ⓐ sell it.
  Ⓑ change it.
  Ⓒ produce it.
  Ⓓ connect it.

2 Conflict means that people
  Ⓐ forgive each other.
  Ⓑ control each other.
  Ⓒ talk with each other.
  Ⓓ disagree with each other.

3 When people contribute, they
  Ⓐ copy others.
  Ⓑ confuse others.
  Ⓒ fight with others.
  Ⓓ share with others.

4 To show disrespect means to be
  Ⓐ sick.
  Ⓑ rude.
  Ⓒ foolish.
  Ⓓ confused.

5 People of the same generation
  Ⓐ are about the same age.
  Ⓑ speak the same language.
  Ⓒ belong to the same family.
  Ⓓ come from the same country.

6 Motivation is a
  Ⓐ reason for an action.
  Ⓑ special type of motion.
  Ⓒ way to persuade people.
  Ⓓ clue to help solve a mystery.

7 To receive a privilege means to receive
  Ⓐ a valuable prize.
  Ⓑ extra assistance.
  Ⓒ a second chance.
  Ⓓ special treatment.

8 If a person is responsible, it means the person
  Ⓐ listens carefully.
  Ⓑ insists on fairness.
  Ⓒ can be depended upon.
  Ⓓ is fun to spend time with.

GO ON ➤

© National Geographic Learning, a part of Cengage Learning, Inc.   1c   EDGE Level B

Cluster Test: Main Selection, Level B

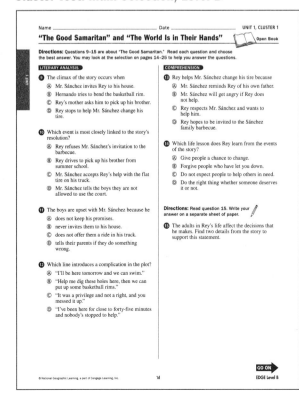

Name _____ Date _____ UNIT 1, CLUSTER 1
"The Good Samaritan" and "The World Is in Their Hands" 📖 Open Book

Directions: Questions 9–15 are about "The Good Samaritan." Read each question and choose the best answer. You may look at the selection on pages 14–25 to help you answer the questions.

LITERARY ANALYSIS

9 The climax of the story occurs when
  Ⓐ Mr. Sánchez invites Rey to his house.
  Ⓑ Hernando tries to bend the basketball rim.
  Ⓒ Rey's mother asks him to pick up his brother.
  Ⓓ Rey stops to help Mr. Sánchez change his tire.

10 Which event is most closely linked to the story's resolution?
  Ⓐ Rey refuses Mr. Sánchez's invitation to the barbecue.
  Ⓑ Rey drives to pick up his brother from summer school.
  Ⓒ Mr. Sánchez accepts Rey's help with the flat tire on his truck.
  Ⓓ Mr. Sánchez tells the boys they are not allowed to use the court.

11 The boys are upset with Mr. Sánchez because he
  Ⓐ does not keep his promises.
  Ⓑ never invites them to his house.
  Ⓒ does not offer them a ride in his truck.
  Ⓓ tells their parents if they do something wrong.

12 Which line introduces a complication in the plot?
  Ⓐ "I'll be here tomorrow and we can swim."
  Ⓑ "Help me dig these holes here, then we can put up some basketball rims."
  Ⓒ "It was a privilege and not a right, and you messed it up."
  Ⓓ "I've been here for close to forty-five minutes and nobody's stopped to help."

COMPREHENSION

13 Rey helps Mr. Sánchez change his tire because
  Ⓐ Mr. Sánchez reminds Rey of his own father.
  Ⓑ Mr. Sánchez will get angry if Rey does not help.
  Ⓒ Rey respects Mr. Sánchez and wants to help him.
  Ⓓ Rey hopes to be invited to the Sánchez family barbecue.

14 Which life lesson does Rey learn from the events of the story?
  Ⓐ Give people a chance to change.
  Ⓑ Forgive people who have let you down.
  Ⓒ Do not expect people to help others in need.
  Ⓓ Do the right thing whether someone deserves it or not.

Directions: Read question 15. Write your answer on a separate sheet of paper.

15 The adults in Rey's life affect the decisions that he makes. Find two details from the story to support this statement.

GO ON ➤

© National Geographic Learning, a part of Cengage Learning, Inc.   1d   EDGE Level B

Cluster Test: Adjunct Selection, Level B

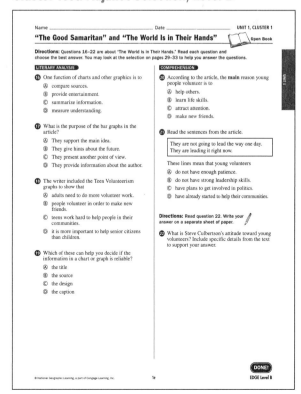

Name _____ Date _____ UNIT 1, CLUSTER 1
"The Good Samaritan" and "The World Is in Their Hands" 📖 Open Book

Directions: Questions 16–22 are about "The World Is in Their Hands." Read each question and choose the best answer. You may look at the selection on pages 29–33 to help you answer the questions.

LITERARY ANALYSIS

16 One function of charts and other graphics is to
  Ⓐ compare sources.
  Ⓑ provide entertainment.
  Ⓒ summarize information.
  Ⓓ measure understanding.

17 What is the purpose of the bar graphs in the article?
  Ⓐ They support the main idea.
  Ⓑ They give hints about the future.
  Ⓒ They present another point of view.
  Ⓓ They provide information about the author.

18 The writer included the Teen Volunteerism graphs to show that
  Ⓐ adults need to do more volunteer work.
  Ⓑ people volunteer in order to make new friends.
  Ⓒ teens work hard to help people in their communities.
  Ⓓ it is more important to help senior citizens than children.

19 Which of these can help you decide if the information in a chart or graph is reliable?
  Ⓐ the title
  Ⓑ the source
  Ⓒ the design
  Ⓓ the caption

COMPREHENSION

20 According to the article, the **main** reason young people volunteer is to
  Ⓐ help others.
  Ⓑ learn life skills.
  Ⓒ attract attention.
  Ⓓ make new friends.

21 Read the sentences from the article.

They are not going to lead the way one day. They are leading it right now.

These lines mean that young volunteers
  Ⓐ do not have enough patience.
  Ⓑ do not have strong leadership skills.
  Ⓒ have plans to get involved in politics.
  Ⓓ have already started to help their communities.

Directions: Read question 22. Write your answer on a separate sheet of paper.

22 What is Steve Culbertson's attitude toward young volunteers? Include specific details from the text to support your answer.

DONE!

© National Geographic Learning, a part of Cengage Learning, Inc.   1e   EDGE Level B

Language Acquisition Rubrics

Purpose and Description

Edge is designed for integrated instruction and assessment. Each unit contains numerous opportunities for students to use language as they participate in authentic communicative activities. You can observe students during these activities to assess their progress in language acquisition. Performance assessments also provide structured assessment opportunities targeted to learning outcomes.

Conducting the Performance Assessment

Each unit offers three performance assessment opportunities in Language Development. During these performance assessments, work with pairs and small groups of students so that the assessment process is manageable. Follow these steps:

1. As the directions indicate, provide time for students to prepare before they begin each activity.

2. Observe pairs or small groups of students.

3. Look for how well students perform the language function as described in the "What to look for" section.

4. Refer to the Language Function Rubric.

5. Circle a score for each student based on how well he or she performs the language function.

Using the Results

After working through a number of units in *Edge,* you will have accumulated several language assessments for each student. As you review the scores over time, you should begin to see a pattern emerge. For example, for students who are clearly at the beginning stage of English language development, you will find that scores 1 and 2 are usually circled for most of the assessments. This will enable you to tailor instruction to students' individual levels of language proficiency.

As a student makes progress in language development, you will begin to note that you are circling scores 3 and 4 more frequently. Once the assessments begin to indicate increased proficiency for a student, you may wish to consider evaluating that student against the criteria designated by your school or district for exit from the ESL program. In addition, use the results from the English Language Gains test to measure language development and assess potential level adjustment or program exit.

Language Acquisition Rubics, Level B

Name _Anna Park_   Date _10/8, 10/22, 11/4_   UNIT 1: CHOICES

Language Acquisition Rubics

UNIT 1

DIRECTIONS

Provide time for students to prepare before they begin each activity. Then observe pairs or small groups.

Cluster 1

ASK AND ANSWER QUESTIONS

Role Play ▶ page 36

Directions: Pair students. Give them a few moments to review the selections and decide on their roles. Partners should take turns acting out the conversation between the characters in the selection.

Language Function   ①   2   3   4

What to look for:
how well the student asks and answers *Who*, *What*, *When*, *Where*, *How*, and *Why* questions during their character role plays.

Cluster 2

EXPRESS IDEAS AND OPINIONS

Group Talk ▶ page 60

Directions: Group students. Give them a few moments to review the selection. After students discuss what they think happened to Roger, encourage them to share their opinions about the characters.

Language Function   1   ②   3   4

What to look for:
how well the student expresses ideas and opinions about the characters and their actions. Student should use opinion words and phrases, such as *I think*, *I believe*, *In my opinion*, *should*, and *ought to*. Student should give reasons for their opinions.

Cluster 3

EXPRESS FEELINGS AND INTENTIONS

Role Play ▶ page 88

Directions: Pair students. Have them take notes about what Monsieur and Madame Loisel are like. Then as partners take turns role playing, they can use their notes to tell what they want to do and how they feel about it.

Language Function   1   2   ③   4

What to look for:
how well the student expresses feelings and intentions in the character's role. Student should use specific words to describe feelings and begin statements of intention with *I want to*, *I plan to*, *I am going to*, and *I will*.

WHAT TO LOOK FOR

Look for how well a student performs the language function as described in this section.

	Language Function Rubric
4	Student effectively performs the function.
3	Student performs the function.
2	Student does not adequately perform the function.
1	Student makes no attempt or offers a non-verbal response.

   1o   EDGE LEVEL B

LANGUAGE FUNCTION RUBRIC

Circle a score for each student based on how well he or she performs the language function as described under the "What to look for" section.

   T9   EDGE Level C

Reading and Literary Analysis Unit Tests

Purpose and Description

A **Reading and Literary Analysis Unit Test** is available for each Unit. In the Unit Tests, students apply the key concepts and skills learned throughout the Unit, across all three Clusters, to new reading selections and material. Key domains include Vocabulary Strategies, Key Vocabulary, Literary Analysis, and Comprehension and Critical Thinking. In addition to measuring the key skills taught within the Unit, Unit Tests are designed to be rigorous and thereby familiarize students with Common Core test formats. All tests include a focus on using text evidence. Reading and Literary Analysis Unit Tests include multiple-choice and constructed-response items.

Administering the Tests

Administer the test for each Unit after instruction. Before administering the Reading and Literary Analysis Unit Test, you may wish to have students complete the Self-Assessment for the Unit. Make a copy of the test for each student. Provide paper for the constructed responses. Also distribute a copy of the answer sheet on page 164 to each student. Students may not use their books during the test. If you are using eAssessment, follow the on-screen instructions for assigning tests.

Scoring the Tests and Using the Results

Score Reading and Literary Analysis Unit Tests with the Answer Keys and Scoring Guides at the back of this handbook. Use the Student Profile: Unit Tests to determine if students need reteaching in Vocabulary Strategies, Key Vocabulary, Literary Analysis, or Comprehension and Critical Thinking. If you are using eAssessment, multiple choice items are automatically scored. Scores for constructed response items can be easily entered into the system. The reports in eAssessment summarize performance and provide access to reteaching resources.

Vocabulary, Level B

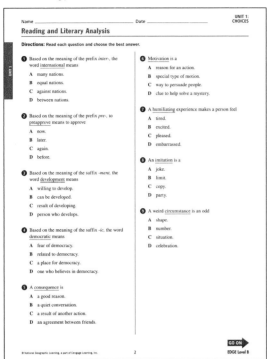

Name _____ Date _____

UNIT 1: CHOICES

Reading and Literary Analysis

Directions: Read each question and choose the best answer.

❶ Based on the meaning of the prefix *inter-*, the word *international* means

A many nations.
B equal nations.
C against nations.
D between nations.

❷ Based on the meaning of the prefix *pre-*, to *preapprove* means to approve

A now.
B later.
C again.
D before.

❸ Based on the meaning of the suffix *-ment*, the word *development* means

A willing to develop.
B can be developed.
C result of developing.
D person who develops.

❹ Based on the meaning of the suffix *-ic*, the word *democratic* means

A fear of democracy.
B related to democracy.
C a place for democracy.
D one who believes in democracy.

❺ A *consequence* is

A a good reason.
B a quiet conversation.
C a result of another action.
D an agreement between friends.

❻ *Motivation* is a

A reason for an action.
B special type of motion.
C way to persuade people.
D clue to help solve a mystery.

❼ A *humiliating* experience makes a person feel

A tired.
B excited.
C pleased.
D embarrassed.

❽ An *imitation* is a

A joke.
B limit.
C copy.
D party.

❾ A weird *circumstance* is an odd

A shape.
B number.
C situation.
D celebration.

© National Geographic Learning, a part of Cengage Learning, Inc.   2

GO ON

EDGE Level B

One Long Reading Selection, Level B

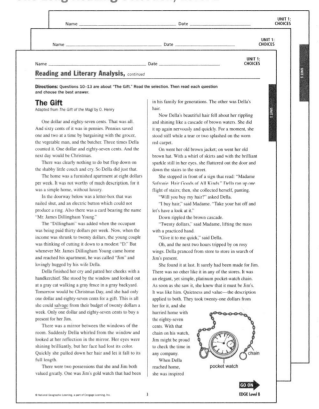

Name _____ Date _____

UNIT 1: CHOICES

Reading and Literary Analysis, *continued*

Directions: Questions 10–13 are about "The Gift." Read the selection. Then read each question and choose the best answer.

The Gift
Adapted from *The Gift of the Magi* by O. Henry

One dollar and eighty-seven cents. That was all. And sixty cents of it was in pennies. Pennies saved one and two at a time by bargaining with the grocer, the vegetable man, and the butcher. Three times Della counted it. One dollar and eighty-seven cents. And the next day would be Christmas.

There was clearly nothing to do but flop down on the shabby little couch and cry. So Della did just that.

The home was a furnished apartment at eight dollars per week. It was not worthy of much description, for it was a simple home, without luxury.

In the doorway below was a letter-box that was nailed shut, and an electric button which could not produce a ring. Also there was a card bearing the name "Mr. James Dillingham Young."

The "Dillingham" was added when the occupant was being paid thirty dollars per week. Now, when the income was shrunk to twenty dollars, the young couple was thinking of cutting it down to a modest "D." But whenever Mr. James Dillingham Young came home and reached his apartment, he was called "Jim" and lovingly hugged by his wife Della.

Della finished her cry and patted her cheeks with a handkerchief. She stood by the window and looked out at a gray cat walking a gray fence in a gray backyard. Tomorrow would be Christmas Day, and she had only one dollar and eighty-seven cents for a gift. This is all she could *salvage* from their budget of twenty dollars a week. Only one dollar and eighty-seven cents to buy a present for her Jim.

There was a mirror between the windows of the room. Suddenly Della whirled from the window and looked at her reflection in the mirror. Her eyes were shining brilliantly, but her face had lost its color. Quickly she pulled down her hair and let it fall to its full length.

There were two possessions that she and Jim both valued greatly. One was Jim's gold watch that had been in his family for generations. The other was Della's hair.

Now Della's beautiful hair fell about her rippling and shining like a cascade of brown waters. She did it up again nervously and quickly. For a moment, she stood still with a tear or two splashed on the worn red carpet.

On went her old brown jacket; on went her old brown hat. With a whirl of skirts and with the brilliant sparkle still in her eyes, she fluttered out the door and down the stairs to the street.

She stopped in front of a sign that read: "Madame Sofronie. Hair Goods of All Kinds." Della ran up one flight of stairs; then, she collected herself, panting.

"Will you buy my hair?" asked Della.

"I buy hair," said Madame. "Take your hat off and let's have a look at it."

Down rippled the brown cascade.

"Twenty dollars," said Madame, lifting the mass with a practiced hand.

"Give it to me quick," said Della.

Oh, and the next two hours tripped by on rosy wings. Della pranced from store to store in search of Jim's present.

She found it at last. It surely had been made for Jim. There was no other like it in any of the stores. It was an elegant, yet simple, platinum pocket-watch chain. As soon as she saw it, she knew that it must be Jim's. It was like him. Quietness and value—the description applied to both. They took twenty-one dollars from her for it, and she hurried home with the eighty-seven cents. With that chain on his watch, Jim might be proud to check the time in any company.

When Della reached home, she was inspired

chain

pocket watch

© National Geographic Learning, a part of Cengage Learning, Inc.   3

GO ON

EDGE Level B

Two Short Reading Selections, Level B

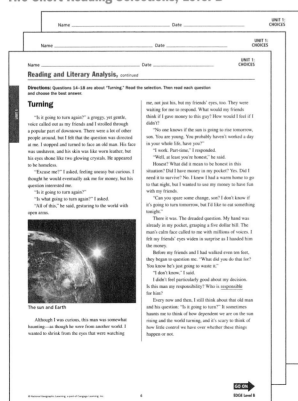

Name _____ Date _____

UNIT 1: CHOICES

Reading and Literary Analysis, *continued*

Directions: Questions 14–18 are about "Turning." Read the selection. Then read each question and choose the best answer.

Turning

"Is it going to turn again?" a groggy, yet gentle, voice called out as my friends and I strolled through a popular part of downtown. There were a lot of other people around, but I felt that the question was directed at me. I stopped and turned to face an old man. His face was unshaven, and his skin was like worn leather, but his eyes shone like two glowing crystals. He appeared to be homeless.

"Excuse me?" I asked, feeling uneasy but curious. I thought he would eventually ask me for money, but his question interested me.

"Is it going to turn again?" I asked.

"Is what going to turn again?" I asked.

"All of this," he said, gesturing to the world with open arms.

The sun and Earth

Although I was curious, this man was somewhat haunting—as though he were from another world. I wanted to shrink from the eyes that were watching

me, not just his, but my friends' eyes, too. They were waiting for me to respond. What would my friends think if I gave money to this guy? How would I feel if I didn't?

"No one knows if the sun is going to rise tomorrow, son. You are young. You probably haven't worked a day in your whole life, have you?"

"I work. Part-time," I responded.

"Well, at least you're honest," he said.

Honest? What did it mean to be honest in this situation? Did I have money in my pocket? Yes. Did I need it to survive? No. I knew I had a warm home to go to that night, but I wanted to use my money to have fun with my friends.

"Can you spare some change, son? I don't know if it's going to turn tomorrow, but I'd like to eat something tonight."

There it was. The dreaded question. My hand was already in my pocket, grasping a five dollar bill. The man's calm face called to me with millions of voices. I felt my friends' eyes widen in surprise as I handed him the money.

Before my friends and I had walked even ten feet, they began to question me. "What did you do that for? You know he's just going to waste it."

"I don't know," I said.

I didn't feel particularly good about my decision. Is this man my responsibility? Who is *responsible* for him?

Every now and then, I still think about that old man and his question: "Is it going to turn?" It sometimes haunts me to think of how dependent we are on the sun rising and the world turning, and it's scary to think of how little control we have over whether these things happen or not.

© National Geographic Learning, a part of Cengage Learning, Inc.   6

GO ON

EDGE Level B

Reading, Level B

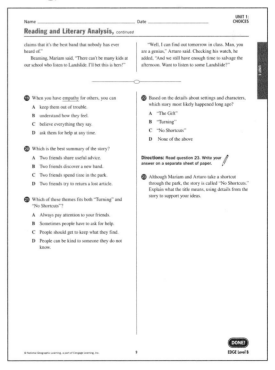

Name _____ Date _____

UNIT 1: CHOICES

Reading and Literary Analysis, *continued*

claims that it's the best band that nobody has ever heard of."

Beaming, Mariam said, "There can't be many kids at our school who listen to Landslide. I'll bet this is hers!"

"Well, I can find out tomorrow in class. Man, you are a genius," Arturo said. Checking his watch, he added, "And we still have enough time to salvage the afternoon. Want to listen to some Landslide?"

❶❾ When you have *empathy* for others, you can

A keep them out of trouble.
B understand how they feel.
C believe everything they say.
D ask them for help at any time.

❷⓿ Which is the best summary of the story?

A Two friends share useful advice.
B Two friends discover a new band.
C Two friends spend time in the park.
D Two friends try to return a lost article.

❷❶ Which of these themes fits both "Turning" and "No Shortcuts"?

A Always pay attention to your friends.
B Sometimes people have to ask for help.
C People should get to keep what they find.
D People can be kind to someone they do not know.

❷❷ Based on the details about settings and characters, which story most likely happened long ago?

A "The Gift"
B "Turning"
C "No Shortcuts"
D None of the above

Directions: Read question 23. Write your answer on a separate sheet of paper.

❷❸ Although Mariam and Arturo take a shortcut through the park, the story is called "No Shortcuts." Explain what the title means, using details from the story to support your ideas.

© National Geographic Learning, a part of Cengage Learning, Inc.   9

DONE!

EDGE Level B

Grammar and Writing Unit Tests

Purpose and Description

A **Grammar and Writing Unit Test** is available for each Unit. Key domains include Common Core Grammar, Revising and Editing, and Written Composition. In addition to measuring the key skills taught within the Unit, Unit Tests are designed to be rigorous and thereby familiarize students with Common Core test formats. To align with the broad range of learning outcomes associated with writing, Grammar and Writing Unit Tests include multiple-choice items and writing prompts.

Administering the Tests

Administer the test for each unit after instruction. Before administering the Grammar and Writing Unit Test, you may wish to have students complete the Self-Assessment for the unit. Make a copy of the test for each students. Provide paper for the written composition. Also distribute a copy of the answer sheet on page 164 to each student. This answer sheet provides a one-page record of multiple-choice test answers for convenient hand scoring. Students may not use their books during the test. If you are using eAssessment, follow the on-screen instructions for assigning tests.

Scoring the Tests and Using the Results

Score the Grammar and Writing Unit Tests with the Answer Keys and Scoring Guides at the back of this handbook. Score the written composition with the Good Writing Traits Rubric on page 122. Use the Student Profile to determine if students need reteaching in Grammar, Revising and Editing, or any of the five Good Writing Traits. If you are using eAssessment, multiple choice items are automatically scored. Rubric scores for writing compositions can be easily entered into the system. The reports in eAssessment summarize performance and provide access to reteaching resources.

Self-Assessments

The **Self-Assessment** helps students evaluate what they have learned in each unit. It is designed to help students monitor their own progress and take responsibility for meeting specific learning goals. Students rate their performance in five key areas: Literary Analysis, Reading Strategies, Vocabulary Strategies, Grammar, and the Good Writing Traits. In addition, students are prompted to explain how one thing they learned from the unit will help them the next time they read or write. This prompt can provide insight into students' progress in metacognitive thinking and problem-solving. Monitor self-assessments to gauge student progress in using skills and strategies without teacher guidance.

Assessment Guidelines

Revising and Editing Passage, Level B

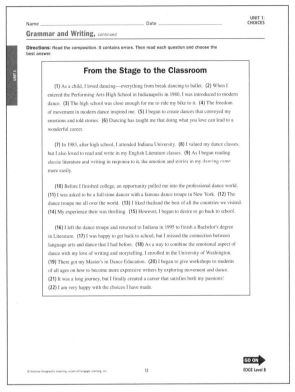

Multiple-Choice Items, Level B

Writing Prompts, Level B

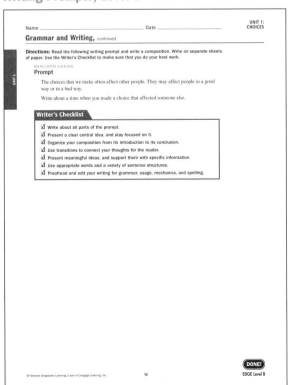

Unit Self-Assessment, Level B

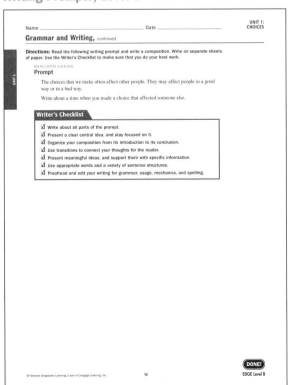

EDGE Level C

Fluency Assessment

Description and Purpose

Oral reading fluency is strongly correlated to reading comprehension. At Levels A–C, *Edge* offers two ways to measure oral reading fluency:

- The program offers 24 passages per level to use in conducting timed readings.
- In addition, the Comprehension Coach records a student's reading of selections from the Student Book and automatically calculates the words read correctly per minute (WCPM). The information for all passages read is collected over time and displayed in line graphs by student and class. Teachers can also access each student's recordings, which are stored in the Comprehension Coach.

Conducting Timed Readings by Hand

If you plan to use the print passages, download a Teacher Copy with word counts and a Student Copy of the fluency passages from 🌐 **myNGconnect.com.**

Give the student a copy of the passage. Place your copy so that the student cannot see what you record. Ask the student to do his or her best reading and start a stopwatch for one minute. Mark a slash (/) through any word that is skipped or mispronounced. (Tell the student to skip a word after 3 seconds.) Stop the student at exactly one minute, and put a bracket after the last word he or she reads aloud. Repeat this process for the remaining two passages.

Using the Scoring Box to Calculate the WCPM

Complete the calculation for words correct per minute (WCPM) by following these steps:

- Count the number of words attempted.
- Subtract the total number of errors.
- The difference is the number of words read correctly per minute (WCPM).

After conducting each timed reading, calculate the average WCPM score. Then, record the results on the student's **Oral Reading Fluency Tracker** (available online). Also record the student's rubric scores for intonation, phrasing, and expression.

Monitor results and identify frequent miscues. If miscues indicate the need for intervention or practice with basic or advanced phonics skills, use the additional Assessments and instruction in **Inside Phonics** to conduct targeted reteaching of specific skills or engage students in systematic, explicit phonics instruction in parallel with reading, writing, and language instruction in the *Edge* Student Book and Teacher's Edition.

Fluency Passage, Level B

Practice Intonation: "The Fashion Show"

Intonation is the rise and fall in the pitch or tone of your voice as you read aloud. Use this passage to practice reading with proper intonation. Print a copy of this passage from myNGconnect.com to help you monitor your progress. To use an Intonation Rubric, see page 748. When listening to a partner read, notice if you can understand the sound of each word. Then listen again to hear how your partner's intonation changes.

I felt torn and confused. I could not take part in the dance, of	14
course, but should I be in the fashion show? I really wanted to do	28
it. I had two beautiful Afghan outfits I could model. But I was also	42
thinking, *My leg is damaged. What if I fall down?*	52
Finally, I said to myself, *Okay, next Wednesday I'll sit in on the practice*	66
session and see what it's like, and then I'll decide.	76
That day the girl who always picked on me came to the practice	89
session, because she was planning to be in the fashion show. The	101
moment she saw me sitting there, she could tell I was thinking of	114
entering the show, too. She didn't tell me to my face that I could not	129
do it, but she immediately called out to the teacher. "Ms. Ascadam,"	141
she said, "when you model clothes at a fashion show, isn't this how	154
you have to walk? Isn't this how models walk on a runway?"	166
Then she began to walk the way she thought a model should	178
walk—with long strides, placing one foot in front of the other in a	192
straight line that made her back end swing from side to side. "Is this	206
the way you should walk?" she said. "If someone can't walk like this,	219
should she be in the fashion show? She would just spoil the whole	232
thing, wouldn't she?" And she kept walking back and forth, swinging	243
from side to side.	247

From "The Fashion Show," page 81

Accuracy and Rate Formula

_____	−	_____	=	_____
words attempted in one minute		number of errors		words correct per minute (wcpm)

Level B · Reading Handbook **753**

T15   **EDGE Level C**

Project Rubrics

Each **Project Rubric** is tailored to a Unit Project but allows analytic scoring across four common domains:

- Planning/Preparation
- Content of Project
- Delivery/Presentation
- Collaboration

Encourage creativity in the projects and review the rubric at the start of the unit to ensure students are aware of how the unit projects will be measured. Display the rubric and review it together as a class. Invite students to ask questions about each part of the rubric. Use the rubric to learn how well your students work together to complete a variety of challenging and engaging projects. Monitor results in Planning/Preparation as you assess student progress in procedural knowledge, principles, and rules. Note that various projects address different learning modalities and encourage group members to clarify roles early in the project planning process. Collaboration measures can be used to gauge progress in Speaking and Listening standards relating to academic discussion. Furthermore, Delivery/Presentation and Content of Project address core Common Core standards in Speaking and Listening.

Project Rubic, Level B

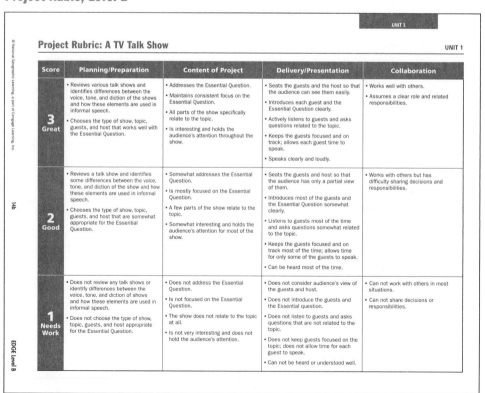

Project Rubric: A TV Talk Show — UNIT 1

Score	Planning/Preparation	Content of Project	Delivery/Presentation	Collaboration
3 Great	• Reviews various talk shows and identifies differences between the voice, tone, and diction of the shows and how these elements are used in informal speech. • Chooses the type of show, topic, guests, and host that works well with the Essential Question.	• Addresses the Essential Question. • Maintains consistent focus on the Essential Question. • All parts of the show specifically relate to the topic. • Is interesting and holds the audience's attention throughout the show.	• Seats the guests and the host so that the audience can see them easily. • Introduces each guest and the Essential Question clearly. • Actively listens to guests and asks questions related to the topic. • Keeps the guests focused and on track; allows each guest time to speak. • Speaks clearly and loudly.	• Works well with others. • Assumes a clear role and related responsibilities.
2 Good	• Reviews a talk show and identifies some differences between the voice, tone, and diction of the show and how these elements are used in informal speech. • Chooses the type of show, topic, guests, and host that are somewhat appropriate for the Essential Question.	• Somewhat addresses the Essential Question. • Is mostly focused on the Essential Question. • A few parts of the show relate to the topic. • Somewhat interesting and holds the audience's attention for most of the show.	• Seats the guests and host so that the audience has only a partial view of them. • Introduces most of the guests and the Essential Question somewhat clearly. • Listens to guests most of the time and asks questions somewhat related to the topic. • Keeps the guests focused and on track most of the time; allows time for only some of the guests to speak. • Can be heard most of the time.	• Works with others but has difficulty sharing decisions and responsibilities.
1 Needs Work	• Does not review any talk shows or identify differences between the voice, tone, and diction of shows and how these elements are used in informal speech. • Does not choose the type of show, topic, guests, and host appropriate for the Essential Question.	• Does not address the Essential Question. • Is not focused on the Essential Question. • The show does not relate to the topic at all. • Is not very interesting and does not hold the audience's attention.	• Does not consider audience's view of the guests and host. • Does not introduce the guests and the Essential question. • Does not listen to guests and asks questions that are not related to the topic. • Does not keep guests focused on the topic; does not allow time for each guest to speak. • Can not be heard or understood well.	• Can not work with others in most situations. • Can not share decisions or responsibilities.

© National Geographic Learning, a part of Cengage Learning, Inc.

14b

EDGE Level B

Affective and Metacognitive Measures

Purpose and Description

Personal interests, learning modalities, and attitudes affect motivation. Motivation is an important factor in reading and writing performance. The **Affective Measures** will help you and your students pursue their interests in and examine their attitudes toward reading and writing.

In this program, metacognitive measures are focused on the mental processes involved in becoming an effective reader and writer. The metacognitive ability to monitor, evaluate, and adjust the processes used while reading and writing is essential. The **Metacognitive Measures** will help you and your students think about and improve the ways they read and write. Metacognitive measures will also require students to identify types of thinking strategies and analyze and evaluate their own thinking.

Administration

There are a range of options for how to administer these inventories and surveys. You may administer them at the beginning of the program to get a feel for students' interests and attitudes toward reading and writing. You may administer them selectively, to engage students in the program. You may also administer them multiple times to compare any changes in interests and attitude over time.

Using the Results

Use individual results as a basis for discussion during teacher-student conferences. For a picture of overall class results, fill out the generic Class Tally Form and tally individual student results. Whether looking at individual or class results, use the information to help engage students and get them reading and writing.

for Reading

What I Do: Vocabulary Strategies

Name _____ Date _____

Directions: Answer questions 1–5.

1. When you read your school assignments, how many of the words do you usually know?

   Check one.

   ☐ all or almost all

   ☐ most

   ☐ about half

   ☐ less than half

   ☐ none or almost none

2. Do you think you would be a better reader if you knew more words? ☐ Yes ☐ No

3. People learn new words in different ways. One person might decide to draw a picture related to a new word. Another person might use the word in a sentence. Someone else might learn the word by saying it out loud over and over again.

   When y...
   remem...

   If yes, ...

4. If you s...

   ☐ I k...

   ☐ So...

   ☐ I t...

© National Geograp...

What Interests Me: Reading Topics

Name _____ Date _____

A. What interests me?

Directions: Put a ✓ next to all the topics that interest you. There are many, many other things that might interest you, of course—too many to list. If your interests are not on the list, write them on the blank lines.

☐ Acting	☐ Electronics	☐ Photography
☐ Animals	☐ Fashion	☐ Poetry
☐ Arts and crafts	☐ Gardening	☐ Politics
☐ Auto mechanics	☐ Golf	☐ Psychology
☐ Auto racing	☐ Hiking	☐ Puzzles
☐ Baseball	☐ Hockey	☐ Rock climbing
☐ Basketball	☐ Languages	☐ Rock collecting
☐ Camping	☐ Math	☐ Sailing
☐ Cheerleading	☐ Motorcycles	☐ Sewing
☐ Chemistry	☐ Mountain biking	☐ Skateboarding
☐ Chess	☐ Movies: watching	☐ Skiing
☐ Coin collecting	☐ Movies: making	☐ Swimming
☐ Computer animation	☐ Music: listening	☐ Travel
☐ Cooking and baking	☐ Music: playing	☐ Video games
☐ Dancing	☐ Nature	☐ Weight lifting
☐ Ecology	☐ Painting/Drawing	☐ Woodworking

Additional interests not included on the list:

_____ _____

_____ _____

_____ _____

Personal Connections to Reading

Name _____ Date _____

Directions: Circle one answer for each question.

How often do you read . . .	Never	Rarely	Sometimes	Often
1. for pleasure?	1	2	3	4
2. to learn how to do something (for example, from a manual or instruction book)?	1	2	3	4
3. to locate information on a schedule or a map?	1	2	3	4
4. to search on the Internet?	1	2	3	4
5. to learn about current events?	1	2	3	4
6. to communicate with friends and family (for example, with letters, notes, or e-mails)?	1	2	3	4
7. in a language other than English?	1	2	3	4

Directions: Put a ✓ next to all of the statements that apply to you.

☐ 8. I sometimes read aloud to family members, such as younger children or grandparents.

☐ 9. If I like what I'm reading, it is easier to understand.

☐ 10. My reading has improved since last year.

☐ 11. I am good at following written instructions.

☐ 12. I only read books when they are assigned at school.

☐ 13. I would rather read an article on the Internet than in a magazine or newspaper.

☐ 14. I have a library card.

GO ON →

---

for Writing

What I Do: Writing Strategies

Name _____ Date _____

Directions: Reflect on the process you used to write your composition titled _____

Prewriting

1. What did you do that helped you brainstorm and plan your composition? _____

2. What will you do differently when you brainstorm and plan your next composition? _____

Drafting

3. What did you do that helped you draft your composition? _____

4. What will you do differently when you draft your next composition? _____

Revising

5. What di...

6. What wi...

Editing a...

7. What di...

8. What wi...

Publishing

9. What di...

10. What wi...

© National Geograp...

What Interests Me: Writing

Name _____ Date _____

A. What interests me?

Directions: Put a ✓ next to all the topics that interest you. If you do not see your interests, add them to the list.

My Self	My Country	My Hobbies
☐ hopes	☐ history	☐ games/sports
☐ dreams	☐ government	☐ cars
☐ strengths	☐ laws	☐ music/dance
☐ personality	☐ states/cities/towns	☐ cooking
☐ other:	☐ other:	☐ other:
My Family	**My World**	**My School**
☐ parents	☐ the environment	☐ teachers
☐ brothers/sisters	☐ travel/exploration	☐ activities
☐ memories	☐ history	☐ classmates
☐ vacations	☐ countries/cultures	☐ classes
☐ other:	☐ other:	☐ other:
My Friends	**My Beliefs**	**My Future**
☐ best friends	☐ values	☐ job/college
☐ funny moments	☐ religion	☐ relationships
☐ helpful friends	☐ philosophy	☐ apartment/house
☐ spending time together	☐ holidays	☐ children
☐ other:	☐ other:	☐ other:
My Community	**My Feelings**	**Add to the List**
☐ the neighborhood	☐ fear	_____
☐ neighborhood people	☐ excitement	_____
☐ doing things together	☐ love	_____
☐ things to improve	☐ wonder	_____
☐ other:	☐ other:	_____

Personal Connections to Writing, *continued*

Name _____ Date _____

Directions: For many people, some stages of the writing process are easier to do than others. Read the list of things people do when they write. Circle the numbers that show how hard or how easy you think each stage is.

	Hard	Somewhat Hard	Somewhat Easy	Easy
1. Deciding what I want to write about	1	2	3	4
2. Organizing my thoughts for writing	1	2	3	4
3. Thinking of enough things to say in my writing	1	2	3	4
4. Getting feedback on my writing from others	1	2	3	4
5. Changing my writing to make it better	1	2	3	4
6. Correcting little mistakes in my writing	1	2	3	4
7. Deciding when my writing is finished	1	2	3	4
8. Sharing my writing with others	1	2	3	4

Directions: Answer questions 9 and 10. If you need more room, use the back of the page.

9. Which stage of the writing process do you think is the easiest? Explain why. _____

10. Which stage of the writing process do you think is the hardest? Explain why. _____

DONE!

(Partial visible text on underlying pages: "e passing", "essional", "out.", "EDGE Level B")

AFFECTIVE & METACOGNITIVE

Good Writing Traits Rubric

The **Good Writing Traits Rubric** is an analytic scoring tool for evaluating any written composition on the five traits of good writing. Assign 1 to 4 points for each of the five traits: Focus and Unity, Organization, Development of Ideas, Voice and Style, and Written Conventions. Measure writing fluency with Write on Demand activities in the program, and use the Good Writing Traits Rubric to measure improvements in writing quality. Use it to evaluate compositions written for the Grammar and Writing Unit Tests and writing projects, or use it to evaluate compositions written to your own class assignments. For additional guidance, the rubric extension offers descriptions of how the five traits of good writing look in common types of writing: narrative, expository, and argument.

Student-Friendly Writing Traits Rubrics

The student-friendly **Writing Trait Rubrics** include a separate rubric for each of the five traits of good writing: Focus and Unity, Organization, Development of Ideas, Voice and Style, and Written Conventions. These rubrics, which are written in accessible language, break down the concept of each writing trait for students. Distribute these rubrics to students for their instructional value or for their use in evaluating Writing Projects.

Good Writing Traits Rubric

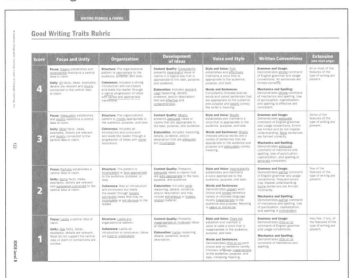

Organization Rubric

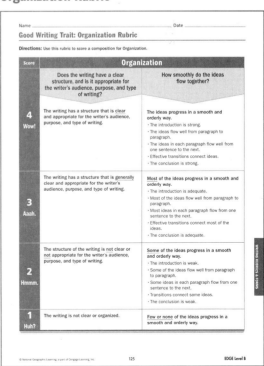

Good Writing Traits Class Profile

The **Good Writing Trait Class Profile** form measures student writing projects and will help you plan instruction. It allows you to see at a glance the writing trait(s) that the majority of your students need to work on. Follow these steps to fill out the form:

1. At the top of the form, record the writing assignment and the date.

2. Write the student's initials in the cell that corresponds to the score he or she received in each trait. Each student's initials will appear in five cells—one for each trait.

3. After you have entered each student's initials, for each trait, find where most students are clustered and draw a dot in that cell. Connect the dots across the five traits to see in which traits your class is strongest and in which traits your class needs work.

INDIVIDUAL SCORES

Don's scores range from a 2 for Voice to a 4 for Organization and Development of Ideas. His performance on each trait is indicated by the initials *DL*.

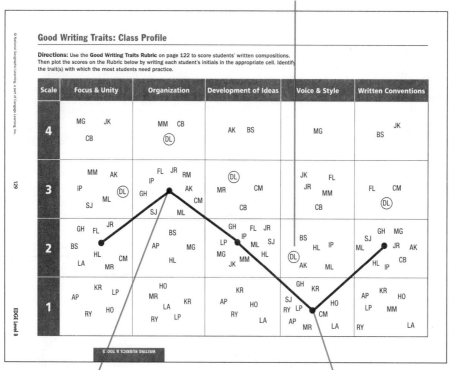

Good Writing Traits: Class Profile

Directions: Use the **Good Writing Traits Rubric** on page 122 to score students' written compositions. Then plot the scores on the Rubric below by writing each student's initials in the appropriate cell. Identify the trait(s) with which the most students need practice.

Scale	Focus & Unity	Organization	Development of Ideas	Voice & Style	Written Conventions
4	MG JK CB	MM CB (DL)	AK BS	MG	JK BS
3	MM AK IP (DL) ML SJ	FL JR RM IP GH AK CM SJ ML	(DL) MR CM CB	JK FL JR MM CB	FL CM (DL)
2	GH FL JR BS HL CM LA MR	BS AP MG HL	GH FL JR LP IP ML SJ MG MM HL JK	BS (DL) HL IP AK ML	SJ GH MG ML JR AK HL IP CB
1	AP KR LP RY HO	HO MR KR LA RY LP	KR AP HO RY LA	GH KR SJ RY LP HO AP CM MR LA	AP KR HO LP MM RY LA

GROUP PERFORMANCE

The dot is drawn here because 9 out of 21 students earned a scale score of 3 on Organization. This is the highest point on the line graph, indicating the class's greatest strength.

MAKING INSTRUCTIONAL DECISIONS

This is the lowest point of the line graph, indicating the area of greatest need. Students will benefit from several weeks of practice activities that focus on this trait.

Writing Portfolio Forms

Portfolios are useful in measuring student writing progress over time. These three forms help teachers and students build a portfolio of Writing Projects for each unit.

Coversheet

The portfolio Coversheet helps students organize their portfolios. The form also encourages students to create and track multiple drafts of their compositions.

Record of Scores

The Record of Scores helps teachers track student projects in each of the five Good Writing Traits across the Writing Projects for each unit. Teachers may keep this as a record for their files and distribute to students for inclusion in their portfolios.

Strengths and Needs Summary

Teachers use this chart to summarize the writing strengths and needs of each student. This information may be useful during student conferences, identifying partners for peer assessments, and instructional planning.

Strengths and Needs Summary

WRITING RUBRICS & TOOLS

Writing Portfolio: Strengths and Needs Summary　　　Name: Sue Smith

Directions: Teachers, use this chart to summarize the strengths and needs of your students. This information will be valuable during student conferences and for instructional planning.

Writing Traits	Consistent Strengths	Some Successes	Greatest Needs
Focus and Unity			tends to wander from topic
Organization		use of transitions is improving	
Development of Ideas		could offer more details and examples	
Voice and Style		should vary sentence structures	
Written Conventions	excellent grammar and mechanics!		

© National Geographic Learning, a part of Cengage Learning, Inc.

132

EDGE Level B

Self- and Peer-Assessments:
Written Composition

The **Self- and Peer-Assessments** for written compositions help students reflect on and evaluate their own writing and the writing of others. These forms can be used with all forms of writing.

The **Self-Assessment** form helps students evaluate drafts of their own writing. Students are prompted to comment on the strengths and weaknesses of their own compositions. The student may then use his or her self-assessment to revise the composition before it is peer-reviewed or scored.

The **Peer-Assessment** form helps students gather feedback on their compositions. Allow students to revise their work based on this feedback before scoring them with the Good Writing Traits Rubric.

Peer-Assessment

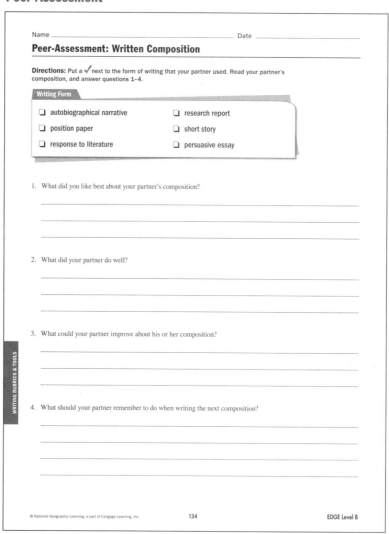

Name _____ Date _____

Peer-Assessment: Written Composition

Directions: Put a ✓ next to the form of writing that your partner used. Read your partner's composition, and answer questions 1–4.

Writing Form

❏ autobiographical narrative   ❏ research report
❏ position paper   ❏ short story
❏ response to literature   ❏ persuasive essay

1. What did you like best about your partner's composition?

2. What did your partner do well?

3. What could your partner improve about his or her composition?

4. What should your partner remember to do when writing the next composition?

© National Geographic Learning, a part of Cengage Learning, Inc.   134   EDGE Level B

Reporting Results

The multiple-choice sections of the Cluster and Unit Tests can be scored electronically. If students take a test through the eAssessment system, their scores will appear in the online reports automatically.

Teachers can also score and report results by hand. Photocopy the hand-scorable answer sheet on page 164 and have students mark their answers on the answer sheet. Use the Answer Keys and Scoring Guides to score the tests. Use the **Student Profiles** to record student scores and report results.

When evaluating Unit Tests, remember to review skills in Cluster Test profiles to ensure sufficient data points and progress across the unit is measured and considered before identifying needs for further reteaching or intervention.

Cluster Test Student Profile, Level B

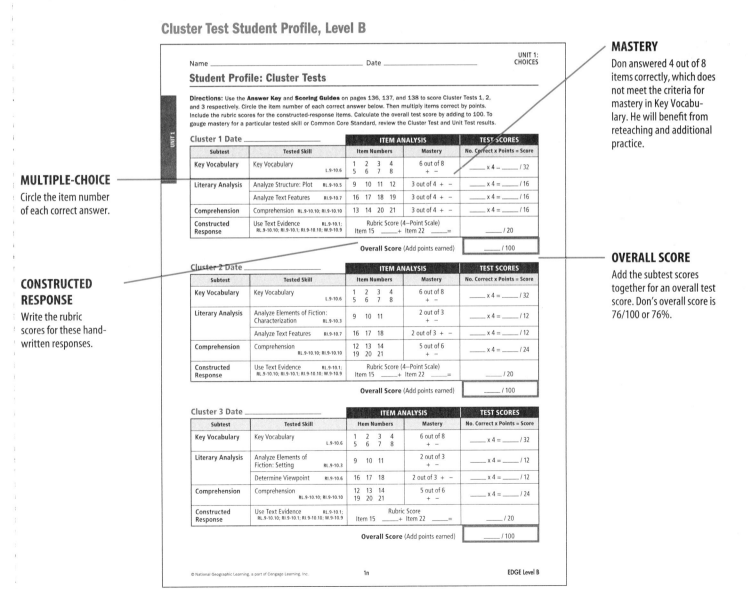

MASTERY
Don answered 4 out of 8 items correctly, which does not meet the criteria for mastery in Key Vocabulary. He will benefit from reteaching and additional practice.

MULTIPLE-CHOICE
Circle the item number of each correct answer.

CONSTRUCTED RESPONSE
Write the rubric scores for these handwritten responses.

OVERALL SCORE
Add the subtest scores together for an overall test score. Don's overall score is 76/100 or 76%.

Unit Test Student Profile, Level B

MULTIPLE-CHOICE

Circle the item number of each correct answer.

CONSTRUCTED RESPONSE

Write the rubric scores for these hand-written responses.

WRITTEN COMPOSITION

Use the Good Writing Traits Rubric on page 120, and write the scores for each of five writing traits of each correct answer.

Name _____ Date _____

UNIT 1: CHOICES

UNIT 1

Student Profile: Unit Tests

Directions: Use the **Answer Key** on page 139 to score the multiple-choice items. Circle the item number of each correct answer below. Calculate test scores by assigning one point for each correct answer. Use the scoring guides on page 139 to score the constructed-response items. Use the Good Writing Traits Rubric on page 122 to score the written composition. Total the scores and calculate the % score or use the conversion chart. To gauge mastery for a particular tested skill or Common Core Standard, review the Cluster Test and Unit Test results.

Reading and Literary Analysis

Category	Tested Skill	ITEM ANALYSIS		TEST SCORES
		Item Numbers	Mastery	Points: Earned / Total
Vocabulary	Use Word Parts: Prefixes, Roots, Suffixes L.9-10.4	1 2 3 4	3 out of 4 + −	_____ / 4
	Key Vocabulary L.9-10.6	5 6 7 8 9 11 16 19	6 out of 8 + −	_____ / 8
Literary Analysis	Analyze Elements of Fiction RL.9-10.3	10 15 17 22	3 out of 4 + −	_____ / 4
	Analyze Theme RL.9-10.2	12 14 20 21	3 out of 4 + −	_____ / 4
Constructed Response	Use Text Evidence RL.9-10.1; RL.9-10.10; W.9-10.9	Rubric Score (4–Point Scale) Item 13 _____ + Item 18 _____ + Item 23 _____ = _____		_____ / 12

Overall Score (Points Earned ÷ Total Points x 100 = %)   _____ ÷ 32 = _____%

Grammar and Writing

Category	Tested Skill	ITEM ANALYSIS		TEST SCORES
		Item Numbers	Mastery	Points: Earned / Total
Grammar	Sentences L.9-10.1	1 11 13 16	3 out of 4 + −	_____ / 4
	Subject-Verb Agreement L.9-10.1	4 5 6 8	3 out of 4 + −	_____ / 4
Revising and Editing	Focus and Unity W.9-10.5	2 3 9 10	3 out of 4 + −	_____ / 4
	Grammar, Mechanics, and Usage L.9-10.2	7 12 14 15	3 out of 4 + −	_____ / 4
Written Composition (Narrative) W.9-10.3; W.9-10.4; W.9-10.10	Focus and Unity	Rubric Scores: _____ / 4		
	Organization	_____ / 4		
	Development of Ideas	_____ / 4 =		_____ / 20
	Voice and Style	_____ / 4		
	Written Conventions	_____ / 4		

Overall Score (Points Earned ÷ Total Points x 100 = %)   _____ ÷ 36 = _____%

14a   **EDGE Level B**

MASTERY

Karen answered 2 out of 4 items correctly, which does not meet the criteria for mastery in Prefixes and Suffixes. She will benefit from reteaching additional practice in this area.

OVERALL SCORE

For an overall score, add the number of points earned and divide it by the total number of points or use the conversion chart on the Answer Keys page.

Diagnostic Assessments

National Geographic Learning provides a complete assessment system that moves from program placement, through progress monitoring, to summative and exit assessment. The Unit Tests for Progress Monitoring provide diagnostic reporting by skill and guide instruction to focused reteaching lessons for those students who need them. In addition to the *Edge* assessment system, we recommend the following diagnostic assessments if you wish to screen students in any of these six technical skill areas: Phonological Awareness, Phonics and Decoding, Oral Reading Fluency, Vocabulary, Reading Comprehension, and Spelling.

	Diagnostic Assessment	Phonological Awareness	Phonics and Decoding	Oral Reading Fluency	Vocabulary	Reading Comprehension	Spelling
Assess Multiple Skill Level	TPRI™	•	•	•	•	•	
	DIBELS	•	•	•			
	ERDA	•	•			•	
	PAT	•	•				
	TOWRE		•	•			
	WIAT III		•		•	•	
	WJ III ACH		•		•	•	
	WRMT™-III		•		•	•	
	GORT-4			•		•	
Assess Single Skill Level	CTOPP-2	•				•	
	LAC-3	•					
	YSTOPS	•				•	
	LSFT					•	
	TWS-5					•	•
	WIST					•	•
	PPVT™-4				•	•	
	TOLD-P:4				•	•	
	TOWK				•	•	
	DRP®					•	

The following tables provide useful information about each diagnostic assessment by technical skill level.

Phonological Awareness

Assessment	Scores	Grade Levels	Administration	Publisher
Texas Primary Reading Inventory (TPRI™)	NRT	K–2	Individual 5 min. screening 20 min. inventory	Texas Education Agency, University of Texas System tpri.org
Dynamic Indicators of Basic Early Literacy Skills (DIBELS)	CRT	K–6	Individual 10–15 min.	Sopris West dibels.uoregon.edu
Early Reading Diagnostic Assessment® (ERDA)	NRT CRT	K–3	Individual 15–20 min./subtest	Pearson Assessment pearsonassessments.com
Phonological Awareness Test 2 (PAT 2)	NRT	K–3	Individual 40 min.	LinguiSystems, Inc. linguisystems.com
Comprehensive Test of Phonological Processing—Second Edition (CTOPP-2)	NRT	K–12	Individual 30 min.	PRO-ED, Inc. proedinc.com
Lindamood Auditory Conceptualization Test-Third Edition (LAC-3)	CRT	Pre K–Adult	Individual 20–30 min.	PRO-ED, Inc. proedinc.com
Yopp-Singer Test of Phoneme Segmentation (YSTOPS)	CRT	K–1	Individual 5–10 min.	The Reading Teacher

Phonics and Decoding

Assessment	Scores	Grade Levels	Administration	Publisher
Texas Primary Reading Inventory (TPRI™)	NRT	K–2	Individual 5 min. screening 20 min. inventory	Texas Education Agency, University of Texas System tpri.org
Dynamic Indicators of Basic Early Literacy Skills (DIBELS)	CRT	K–6	Individual 10–15 min.	Sopris West dibels.uoregon.edu
Early Reading Diagnostic Assessment (ERDA)	NRT CRT	K–3	Individual 15–20 min./subtest	Pearson Assessment pearsonassessments.com
Phonological Awareness Test 2 (PAT 2)	NRT	K–3	Individual 40 min.	LinguiSystems, Inc. linguisystems.com
Test of Word Reading Efficiency—Second Edition (TOWRE-2)	NRT	1-Adult	Individual 5–10 min.	PRO-ED, Inc. proedinc.com
Wechsler Individual Achievement Test—Third Edition (WIAT®-III)	CRT	Pre K–Adult	Individual 45–120 min.	Pearson Assessment pearsonassessments.com
Woodcock-Johnson® III Test of Achievement (WJ III ACH)	NRT	K–12	Individual 5 min./subtest	Riverside Publishing riverpub.com
Woodcock Reading Mastery Tests, Third Edition (WRMT™-III)	NRT	K–12	Individual 40–45 min. total 5-10 min./subtest	Pearson Clinical Assessment psychcorp. pearsonassessments.com
Letter Sound Fluency Test (LSFT)	CRT	K–1	Individual 5 min.	Vanderbilt University

Oral Reading Fluency

Assessment	Scores	Grade Levels	Administration	Publisher
Texas Primary Reading Inventory (TPRI™)	NRT	K–2	Individual 5 min. screening 20 min. inventory	Texas Education Agency, University of Texas System tpri.org
Dynamic Indicators of Basic Early Literacy Skills (DIBELS)	CRT	K–6	Individual 10–15 min.	Sopris West dibels.uoregon.edu
Test of Word Reading Efficiency—Second Edition (TOWRE-2)	NRT	1-Adult	Individual 5–10 min.	PRO-ED, Inc. proedinc.com
Gray Oral Reading Test, Fourth Edition. (GORT-4)	NRT	2-12	Individual 15–30 min.	Pearson Clinical Assessment psychcorp. pearsonassessments.com

Vocabulary

Assessment	Scores	Grade Levels	Administration	Publisher
Texas Primary Reading Inventory (TPRI™)	NRT	K–2	Individual 5 min. screening 20 min. inventory	Texas Education Agency, University of Texas System tpri.org
Wechsler Individual Achievement Test—Third Edition (WIATT®-III)	NRT	Pre K–Adult	Individual 45–120 min.	Pearson Assessment www.pearsonassessments.com
Woodcock-Johnson® III Test of Achievement (WJ III ACH)	NRT	K–12	Individual 5 min./subtest	Riverside Publishing riverpub.com
Woodcock Reading Mastery Tests, Third Edition (WRMT™-III)	NRT	K–12	Individual 40–45 min. total 5–10 min./subtest	Pearson Clinical Assessment psychcorp. pearsonassessments.com
Peabody Picture Vocabulary Tests, Fourth Edition (PPVT™-4)	NRT	Pre K–Adult	Individual 12 min.	Pearson Clinical Assessment psychcorp. pearsonassessments.com
Test of Language Development—Primary, Fourth Edition (TOLD-P:4)	NRT	K–3	Individual 30–60 min.	Pearson Assessment pearsonassessments.com PRO-ED, Inc. proedinc.com
Test of Word Knowledge (TOWK)	NRT	K–12	Individual 30 min. Level 1 60 min. Level 2	Pearson Assessment pearsonassessments.com

Reading Comprehension

Assessment	Scores	Grade Levels	Administration	Publisher
Texas Primary Reading Inventory (TPRI™)	NRT	K–2	Individual 5 min. screening 20 min. inventory	Texas Education Agency, University of Texas System tpri.org
Early Reading Diagnostic Assessment® (ERDA)	NRT CRT	K–3	Individual 15–20 min./subtest	Pearson Assessment pearsonassessments.com
Wechsler Individual Achievement Test—Third Edition (WIAT®-III)	NRT	Pre K–Adult	Individual 45–120 min.	Pearson Assessment pearsonassessments.com
Woodcock-Johnson® III Test of Achievement (WJ III ACH)	NRT	K–12	Individual 5 min./subtest	Riverside Publishing riverpub.com
Woodcock Reading Mastery Tests, Third Edition (WRMT™-III)	NRT	K–12	Individual 40–45 min. total 5–10 min./subtest	Pearson Clinical Assessment psychcorp. pearsonassessments.com
Gray Oral Reading Test, Fourth Edition. (GORT-4)	NRT	2–12	Individual 15–30 min.	Pearson Clinical Assessment psychcorp. pearsonassessments.com
Degrees of Reading Power® (DRP®)	NRT CRT	1–12	Group 45 min.	Questar Assessment, Inc. www.questarai.com

Spelling

Assessment	Scores	Grade Levels	Administration	Publisher
Test of Written Spelling, 5th Edition (TWS-5)	NRT CRT	1–12	Group 15 min.	PRO-ED proedinc.com
Word Identification and Spelling Test (WIST)	NRT CRT	2–12	Individual 40 min.	PRO-ED proedinc.com

 EDGE Level C

Reader Reflection

Directions: Answer questions 1–10. If necessary, use the back of the page.

"The Moustache"

1 What did you learn about conflict that will help you the next time you read a short story?

2 You can plan and monitor by making and confirming predictions. Explain how this strategy will help you the next time you read.

3 Write what you liked and did not like about "The Moustache." Include examples from the short story.

I liked...

I did not like...

4 Are you interested in reading more writing by Robert Cormier? _____ Yes _____ No

5 Are you interested in reading more short stories by other authors? _____ Yes _____ No

"Who We Really Are"

6 What did you learn about news features that will help you the next time you read a news feature?

7 You can also plan your reading by previewing and setting a purpose. Explain how this strategy will help you the next time you read.

8 Write what you liked and did not like about "Who We Really Are." Include examples from the news feature.

I liked...

I did not like...

9 Are you interested in reading more works by Joshunda Sanders? _____ Yes _____ No

10 Are you interested in reading more news features by other writers? _____ Yes _____ No

"The Moustache" and "Who We Really Are"

Directions: Read each question and choose the best answer.

KEY VOCABULARY

1 To characterize something means to
- (A) find out how it works.
- (B) guess what it means.
- (C) tell why it is important.
- (D) describe what it is like.

2 Intensity means
- (A) force.
- (B) love.
- (C) interest.
- (D) success.

3 If a person is lucid, it means the person is
- (A) sick.
- (B) silent.
- (C) sane.
- (D) selfish.

4 To obscure means to
- (A) fix.
- (B) hide.
- (C) grab.
- (D) trade.

5 If a person is pathetic, it means the person makes you feel
- (A) pity.
- (B) hate.
- (C) trust.
- (D) anger.

6 A perspective is a
- (A) point of view.
- (B) perfect ending.
- (C) person who lies.
- (D) problem to solve.

7 Pretense is the act of
- (A) choosing.
- (B) preparing.
- (C) pretending.
- (D) representing.

8 To stigmatize means to
- (A) confuse.
- (B) disgrace.
- (C) surrender.
- (D) apologize.

"The Moustache" and "Who We Really Are"

Open Book

Directions: Questions 9–15 are about "The Moustache." Read each question and choose the best answer. You may look at the selection on pages 14–26 to help you answer the questions.

LITERARY ANALYSIS

9 Which words best describe the conflict between Mike and his mother?

- Ⓐ funny and playful
- Ⓑ routine and familiar
- Ⓒ hurtful and serious
- Ⓓ frustrating and stressful

10 Which of Mike's conflicts is both internal **and** external?

- Ⓐ Should he have a moustache?
- Ⓑ Should he keep a family secret?
- Ⓒ Should he visit his grandmother?
- Ⓓ Should he drive at the speed limit?

11 Mike's main conflict with his grandmother is whether he should

- Ⓐ visit her more often.
- Ⓑ tell her who he really is.
- Ⓒ show her family pictures.
- Ⓓ tell her why his sister could not visit.

12 Mike's grandmother suffers over a conflict that happened

- Ⓐ the last time her daughter visited.
- Ⓑ many years ago when her husband was alive.
- Ⓒ when her granddaughter went away to college.
- Ⓓ during her grandson's visit to the nursing home.

COMPREHENSION

13 Because of his experience with his grandmother, Mike begins to

- Ⓐ wish he could visit her more often.
- Ⓑ wonder about his relationship with his girlfriend.
- Ⓒ wish he could have known his grandfather better.
- Ⓓ wonder about the relationship between his parents.

14 What causes Mike to see who his grandmother really is?

- Ⓐ her surprising strength
- Ⓑ her enjoyment of birds
- Ⓒ his sympathy for her condition
- Ⓓ his glimpse of her personal life

Directions: Read question 15. Write your answer on a separate sheet of paper.

15 The Downtown Cinema has a special Friday night offer—half-price admission for high school couples, seventeen or younger. But the woman in the box office took one look at my moustache and charged me full price. Even when I showed her my driver's license. She charged full admission for Cindy's ticket, too, which left me practically broke and unable to take Cindy out for a hamburger with the crowd afterward. That didn't help matters, because Cindy has been getting impatient recently about things like the fact that I don't own my own car and have to concentrate on my studies if I want to win that college scholarship, for instance. Cindy wasn't exactly crazy about the moustache, either.

Why do some people believe in superstitions? Include specific words or phrases from the text to support your answer.

GO ON

"The Moustache" and "Who We Really Are"

 Open Book

Directions: Questions 16–22 are about "Who We Really Are." Read each question and choose the best answer. You may look at the selection on pages 29–32 to help you answer the questions.

LITERARY ANALYSIS

16 Which sentence from the news **feature** would probably **not** be included in a news **story**?

Ⓐ Fostering Art helps foster youth empower themselves.

Ⓑ Nationally, there are half a million youths in foster care.

Ⓒ Many of them are stigmatized as hardened troublemakers.

Ⓓ Today she is a giddy 17-year-old with perfectly manicured nails.

17 What do the quotations add to the news **feature**?

Ⓐ They give examples of opposite views.

Ⓑ They tell personal thoughts and feelings.

Ⓒ They prove that the numbers in the graph are correct.

Ⓓ They show how many people the author interviewed.

18 Which of these does the caption tell you?

Ⓐ when the exhibit was held

Ⓑ where the exhibit was held

Ⓒ how many students participated

Ⓓ how many photos were in the exhibit

COMPREHENSION

19 The author of the news **feature** wants readers to understand that many foster children

Ⓐ could have careers as photographers.

Ⓑ need a lot of therapy to overcome their problems.

Ⓒ are successful and should be treated as individuals.

Ⓓ are adopted by the foster families after a few years.

20 Tamisha thinks that foster care has given her an opportunity to

Ⓐ live a normal life.

Ⓑ meet new friends.

Ⓒ appear in the news.

Ⓓ learn to take photos.

21 Which of these is a purpose of Fostering Art?

Ⓐ to find good homes for foster youth

Ⓑ to raise money for foster care programs

Ⓒ to educate the community about foster youth

Ⓓ to provide safe places for foster youth to gather

Directions: Read question 22. Write your answer on a separate sheet of paper.

22 Nationally, there are half a million youths in foster care. Many of them are stigmatized as hardened troublemakers. That attitude may keep some adults from adopting youths from foster care, and some foster youths see adoption as an undesirable option. But being adopted was "the best thing that could ever happen to me," Tamisha wrote in a 2004 exhibition at the Zeum children's museum. (The last names of the artists featured in the show were withheld at their request.)

What does the passage tell you about how the author thinks some people perceive the youths in foster care?

DONE!

EDGE Level C

Reader Reflection

Directions: Answer questions 1–10. If necessary, use the back of the page.

"Two Kinds"

1 What did you learn about protagonists and antagonists that will help you the next time you read a short story?

2 You can plan and monitor by clarifying your ideas. Explain how this strategy will help you the next time you read.

3 Write what you liked and did not like about "Two Kinds." Include examples from the short story.

I liked...

I did not like...

4 Are you interested in reading more writing by Amy Tan? _____ Yes _____ No

5 Are you interested in reading more short stories about families? _____ Yes _____ No

"Novel Musician"

6 What did you learn about a nonfiction profile that will help you the next time you read a profile?

7 You can also clarify your ideas using a 5Ws Chart. Explain how this strategy will help you the next time you read a profile.

8 Write what you liked and did not like about "Novel Musician." Include examples from the profile.

I liked...

I did not like...

9 Are you interested in reading more works by Sharon Wooten? _____ Yes _____ No

10 Are you interested in reading more profiles of other authors? _____ Yes _____ No

"Two Kinds" and "Novel Musician"

Directions: Read each question and choose the best answer.

KEY VOCABULARY

1 An <u>accusation</u> is a

Ⓐ feeling that something is about to happen.

Ⓑ reaction to something that someone said.

Ⓒ claim that someone did something wrong.

Ⓓ suggestion about how someone should act.

2 If a person is <u>ambitious</u>, it means the person is

Ⓐ grateful for help.

Ⓑ anxious to leave.

Ⓒ thoughtful of others.

Ⓓ determined to succeed.

3 To <u>assert</u> means to

Ⓐ declare.

Ⓑ thank.

Ⓒ quote.

Ⓓ beg.

4 A <u>discordant</u> sound is

Ⓐ distant.

Ⓑ sudden.

Ⓒ unusual.

Ⓓ unpleasant.

5 An <u>expectation</u> is a

Ⓐ type of exercise.

Ⓑ false statement.

Ⓒ contract between two people.

Ⓓ belief that something will happen.

6 An <u>inevitable</u> event is

Ⓐ fun to remember.

Ⓑ certain to happen.

Ⓒ planned in advance.

Ⓓ attended by many people.

7 A <u>prodigy</u> is a

Ⓐ professor.

Ⓑ child genius.

Ⓒ type of music.

Ⓓ special award.

8 Beyond <u>reproach</u> means beyond

Ⓐ hope.

Ⓑ care.

Ⓒ blame.

Ⓓ reason.

GO ON

"Two Kinds" and "Novel Musician"

Open Book

Directions: Questions 9–15 are about "Two Kinds." Read each question and choose the best answer. You may look at the selection on pages 41–58 to help you answer the questions.

LITERARY ANALYSIS

9 Why are the daughter and mother protagonist and antagonist?

Ⓐ They are both females.

Ⓑ There is a strong family bond.

Ⓒ There is conflict between them.

Ⓓ They were born in different countries.

10 The mother annoys her daughter by pushing her to

Ⓐ become a fashion model.

Ⓑ discover her special talent.

Ⓒ study to be a piano teacher.

Ⓓ learn the names of capital cities.

11 Why does the conflict described in "Two Kinds" happen?

Ⓐ A surprising event occurs.

Ⓑ A character struggles to change.

Ⓒ Two characters disagree about something.

Ⓓ The story takes place in a dangerous setting.

COMPREHENSION

12 During the talent show, the narrator's feelings about performing change from

Ⓐ angry to happy.

Ⓑ nervous to calm.

Ⓒ curious to scared.

Ⓓ excited to ashamed.

13 Which word best describes the narrator?

Ⓐ obedient

Ⓑ generous

Ⓒ independent

Ⓓ responsible

14 Why does the narrator feel proud when she sees the piano in her parents' living room?

Ⓐ She knows that her teacher clapped for her at the talent show.

Ⓑ She still remembers how to play the song from the talent show.

Ⓒ She finally understands that her mother believes she has talent.

Ⓓ She won the argument with her mother about practicing the piano.

Directions: Read question 15. Write your answer on a separate sheet of paper.

15

> And then I saw what seemed to be the prodigy side of me—because I had never seen that face before. I looked at my reflection, blinking so I could see more clearly. The girl staring back at me was angry, powerful. This girl and I were the same. I had new thoughts, willful thoughts, or rather thoughts filled with lots of won'ts. I won't let her change me, I promised myself. I won't be what I'm not.

What does this passage tell you about how the daughter's relationship with her mother is going to change? Cite text evidence in your answer.

GO ON

"Two Kinds" and "Novel Musician"

Directions: Questions 16–24 are about "Novel Musician." Read each question and choose the best answer. You may look at the selection on pages 61–64 to help you answer the questions.

LITERARY ANALYSIS

16 What should a reader expect to find in a profile?

Ⓐ a timeline of a person's life

Ⓑ dialogue between two characters

Ⓒ imaginary stories about a character

Ⓓ entertaining details about a person

17 "Novel Musician" is mostly about Amy Tan's

Ⓐ writing career.

Ⓑ musical hobby.

Ⓒ award-winning books.

Ⓓ childhood music lessons.

18 One of the subheads in this profile is "Two Kinds of Storytelling." What does this subhead help the reader understand about Amy Tan?

Ⓐ She writes two types of stories.

Ⓑ She plays two different instruments.

Ⓒ She listens to rock music while she writes.

Ⓓ She thinks music and stories are connected.

COMPREHENSION

19 According to the profile, how are the members of the Rock Bottom Remainders alike?

Ⓐ They are all authors.

Ⓑ They are all good singers.

Ⓒ They all took piano lessons.

Ⓓ They all wear costumes for performances.

20 Amy Tan thinks that playing with the Rock Bottom Remainders is

Ⓐ just for fun.

Ⓑ a challenging job.

Ⓒ more important than her stories.

Ⓓ what her mother wanted her to do.

21 What kind of information does the chart near the end of the profile show?

Ⓐ who is in the band

Ⓑ where the band performs

Ⓒ what songs the band plays

Ⓓ why people joined the band

Directions: Read question 22. Write your answer on a separate sheet of paper.

22

> Wearing colorful wigs and costumes is part of the fun when Amy Tan sings with the Rock Bottom Remainders.

This is a caption from a photo in "Novel Musician" on page 62. Why does the author include this photo and caption?

Reader Reflection

Directions: Answer questions 1–10. If necessary, use the back of the page.

"Skins"

1 What did you learn about character and theme that will help you the next time you read a short story?

2 Explain how clarifying vocabulary with familiar word parts will help you the next time you read.

3 Write what you liked and did not like about "Skins." Include examples from the short story.

I liked...

I did not like...

4 Are you interested in reading more writing by Joseph Bruchac? _____ Yes _____ No

5 Are you interested in reading more short stories about Native American culture? _____ Yes _____ No

"Nicole"

6 What did you learn about determining viewpoints in personal narratives that will help you the next time you read a personal narrative?

7 Explain how clarifying vocabulary with context clues will help you the next time you read.

8 Write what you liked and did not like about "Nicole." Include examples from the personal narrative.

I liked...

I did not like...

9 Are you interested in reading more works by Rebecca Carroll and Nicole? _____ Yes _____ No

10 Are you interested in reading more personal narratives by teens? _____ Yes _____ No

"Skins" and "Nicole"

Directions: Read each question and choose the best answer.

KEY VOCABULARY

1 Authenticity means that something is

- Ⓐ real.
- Ⓑ sturdy.
- Ⓒ popular.
- Ⓓ expensive.

2 To compel means to

- Ⓐ persuade.
- Ⓑ compare.
- Ⓒ force.
- Ⓓ injure.

3 To discriminate against others means to

- Ⓐ try to change their minds.
- Ⓑ say mean things about them.
- Ⓒ watch them closely to see how they act.
- Ⓓ treat them differently because of prejudice.

4 To eliminate means to

- Ⓐ lose.
- Ⓑ remove.
- Ⓒ replace.
- Ⓓ discover.

5 If a person has potential, it means the person has

- Ⓐ big ideas.
- Ⓑ natural ability.
- Ⓒ strong opinions.
- Ⓓ powerful friends.

6 To predominate means to

- Ⓐ start first.
- Ⓑ make a difference.
- Ⓒ occur most often.
- Ⓓ change completely.

7 Racism is a belief that

- Ⓐ people should honor their ancestors.
- Ⓑ people should be proud of their ancestry.
- Ⓒ people of today are smarter than their ancestors.
- Ⓓ people of certain ancestry are better than others.

8 Tension means

- Ⓐ embarrassment.
- Ⓑ failure.
- Ⓒ stress.
- Ⓓ exhaustion.

Directions: Questions 9–15 are about "Skins." Read each question and choose the best answer. You may look at the selection on pages 73–91 to help you answer the questions.

Open Book

LITERARY ANALYSIS

9 Which sentence from "Skins" best communicates the theme of the story?

- Ⓐ Never interrupt people when they're speaking from their heart.
- Ⓑ They know everything about you, including stuff you wish they'd forget.
- Ⓒ Like Uncle Tommy told me, pain is part of the admission fee for being human.
- Ⓓ You never can tell what's in someone's heart by the way they look on the outside.

GO ON

EDGE Level C

"Skins" and "Nicole"

10 Which detail about Mitchell is most closely related to the theme of the story?

Ⓐ Mitchell dyes his hair black.

Ⓑ Mitchell visited Sweden with his mother.

Ⓒ Mitchell is a kicker on the football team.

Ⓓ Mitchell spends his spare time at Uncle Tommy's house.

11 What is the greatest cause of the tension between Randolph and Jimmy T?

Ⓐ Jimmy T is jealous of Randolph's father's new job as director.

Ⓑ Randolph knows the truth about Jimmy T's family background.

Ⓒ Randolph is part Indian, and Jimmy T wants to be the only Indian at school.

Ⓓ Jimmy T and Randolph were on different teams before they moved to Long Pond.

COMPREHENSION

12 The other students avoid the Whites on their first day of school because of the Whites'

Ⓐ words.

Ⓑ actions.

Ⓒ reputation.

Ⓓ appearance.

13 Why does Jimmy T avoid Mitchell?

Ⓐ He knows that Mitchell is already friends with Randolph.

Ⓑ He thinks that Mitchell should try harder when he plays football.

Ⓒ He feels jealous of Mitchell's friendship with Uncle Tommy.

Ⓓ He worries that Mitchell will find out he is pretending to be Indian.

14 Why does Mitchell want Jimmy T to meet Uncle Tommy? Mitchell thinks Uncle Tommy will

Ⓐ show Jimmy T how to be a real Indian.

Ⓑ help Jimmy T to be proud of who he is.

Ⓒ give Jimmy T a job at the Indian Village.

Ⓓ teach Jimmy T to be a better quarterback.

Directions: Read question 15. Write your answer on a separate sheet of paper.

15

> I heard Jimmy T say the "n" word. It shocked me so much that I turned around to see him staring at Randolph. Randolph was looking back at him.
>
> Then Randolph shook his head. "Better than a faker, pal."

What does this passage reveal about Randolph's personality? How does his reaction help point to the theme of "Skins"? Cite text evidence in your answer.

Directions: Questions 16-22 are about "Nicole." Read each question and choose the best answer. You may look at the selection on pages 95–98 to help you answer the questions.

LITERARY ANALYSIS

16 Which is the best clue that "Nicole" is a personal narrative?

Ⓐ Nicole tells her story without using dialogue.

Ⓑ Nicole is involved in conflicts with other people.

Ⓒ Nicole tries to persuade the reader to share her opinions.

Ⓓ Nicole shares her thoughts and feelings about real events from her life.

GO ON

"Skins" and "Nicole"

 Open Book

17 What viewpoint about racism does Nicole express in her narrative?

Ⓐ She blames her parents.

Ⓑ She thinks racism is stupid.

Ⓒ She does not believe racism exists.

Ⓓ She feels ashamed of her racial identity.

18 The first-person point of view is used throughout this selection because it

Ⓐ has a main character.

Ⓑ is a personal narrative.

Ⓒ expresses strong opinions.

Ⓓ was originally written for children.

19 Nicole wants to be called by her name because she thinks other labels

Ⓐ could be misunderstood.

Ⓑ do not represent her true identity.

Ⓒ could change the way she views herself.

Ⓓ are not accurate about her being biracial.

COMPREHENSION

20 Which word best describes Nicole?

Ⓐ clever

Ⓑ strong

Ⓒ patient

Ⓓ helpful

21 How does Nicole's reaction to racist insults change as she grows older?

Ⓐ She tries to beat up the kids who insult her.

Ⓑ She blames her parents for the insults she receives.

Ⓒ She struggles to ignore the insults and stay positive.

Ⓓ She talks to her teachers and counselors about the insults.

Directions: Read question 22. Write your answer on a separate sheet of paper.

22

> On the census checkoff lists that offer little boxes next to black, white, or other, I refuse to check just one box. I check them all off because I am all of those things. My mother told me that when I was born and she was filling out my birth certificate, the nurse asked her to write in *mulatto*, which my mother did not do.

What does this statement show about Nicole's mother? How does it help you understand the viewpoint expressed in "Nicole"?

DONE!

EDGE Level C

Name _____ Date _____

Student Profile: Cluster Tests

Directions: Use the **Answer Key** and **Scoring Guides** on pages 136, 137, and 138 to score Cluster Tests 1, 2, and 3 respectively. Circle the item number of each correct answer below. Then multiply items correct by points. Include the rubric scores for the constructed-response items. Calculate the overall test score by adding to 100. To gauge mastery for a particular tested skill or Common Core Standard, review the Cluster Test and Unit Test results.

UNIT 1

Cluster 1   Date _____

Subtest	Tested Skill	ITEM ANALYSIS		TEST SCORES
		Item Numbers	Mastery	No. Correct x Points = Score
Key Vocabulary	Key Vocabulary L.9-10.6	1 2 3 4 5 6 7 8	6 out of 8 + –	_____ x 4 = _____ /32
Literary Analysis	Analyze Elements of Fiction: Conflict RL.9-10.3	9 10 11 12	3 out of 4 + –	_____ x 4 = _____ /16
	Analyze Structure: News Feature RI.9-10.5	16 17 18	2 out of 3 + –	_____ x 4 = _____ /12
Comprehension	Comprehension RL.9-10.10; RI.9-10.10	13 14 19 20 21	4 out of 5 + –	_____ x 4 = _____ /20
Constructed Response	Use Text Evidence RL.9-10.1; RL.9-10.10; RI.9-10.1; RI.9-10.10; W.9-10.9	Rubric Scores Item 15 _____ + Item 22 _____ = _____		_____ /20

Overall Score (Add Points Earned)   _____ /100

Cluster 2   Date _____

Subtest	Tested Skill	ITEM ANALYSIS		TEST SCORES
		Item Numbers	Mastery	No. Correct x Points = Score
Key Vocabulary	Key Vocabulary L.9-10.6	1 2 3 4 5 6 7 8	6 out of 8 + –	_____ x 4 = _____ /32
Literary Analysis	Analyze Elements of Fiction: Protagonist and Antagonist RL.9-10.3	9 10 11	2 out of 3 + –	_____ x 4 = _____ /12
	Analyze Structure: Profile RI.9-10.5	16 17 18	2 out of 3 + –	_____ x 4 = _____ /12
Comprehension	Comprehension RL.9-10.10; RI.9-10.10	12 13 14 19 20 21	5 out of 6 + –	_____ x 4 = _____ /24
Constructed Response	Use Text Evidence RL.9-10.1; RL.9-10.10; RI.9-10.1; RI.9-10.10; W.9-10.9	Rubric Scores Item 15 _____ + Item 22 _____ = _____		_____ /20

Overall Score (Add Points Earned)   _____ /100

Cluster 3   Date _____

Subtest	Tested Skill	ITEM ANALYSIS		TEST SCORES
		Item Numbers	Mastery	No. Correct x Points = Score
Key Vocabulary	Key Vocabulary L.9-10.6	1 2 3 4 5 6 7 8	6 out of 8 + –	_____ x 4 = _____ /32
Literary Analysis	Analyze Theme RL.9-10.2	9 10 11	2 out of 3 + –	_____ x 4 = _____ /12
	Determine Viewpoint RI.9-10.6	16 17 18 19	3 out of 4 + –	_____ x 4 = _____ /16
Comprehension	Comprehension RL.9-10.10; RI.9-10.10	12 13 14 20 21	4 out of 5 + –	_____ x 4 = _____ /20
Constructed Response	Use Text Evidence RL.9-10.1; RL.9-10.10; RI.9-10.1; RI.9-10.10; W.9-10.9	Rubric Scores Item 15 _____ + Item 22 _____ = _____		_____ /20

Overall Score (Add Points Earned)   _____ /100

Language Acquisition Rubrics

Cluster 1
EXPRESS IDEAS AND OPINIONS
Pair Talk ▶ page 34

Directions: Pair students. Give them a few moments to review the selection. Partners should take turns sharing their ideas and feelings about the story and Mike's decision.

Language Function | 1 | 2 | 3 | 4 |

What to look for:
how well the student expresses ideas and opinions with words such as *I think, I believe,* and *In my opinion.* Students should also provide reasons for their opinions.

Cluster 2
ASK FOR AND GIVE INFORMATION
Role Play ▶ page 66

Directions: Pair students. Give them a few moments to review the selections and information about the author. Partners should take turns playing Amy Tan and playing the interviewer.

Language Function | 1 | 2 | 3 | 4 |

What to look for:
how well the student asks for information using *Who, What, When, Where, How, Are, Were, Can, Do,* and *Did* questions. Student should ask and answer questions in the same verb tenses, giving facts and details.

Cluster 3
ENGAGE IN DISCUSSION
Group Talk ▶ page 100

Directions: Group students. Give them a few moments to review the selection. Students should take turns discussing the characters and their actions.

Language Function | 1 | 2 | 3 | 4 |

What to look for:
how well the student engages in discussion by asking and answering questions, focusing on the topic, stating his/her point of view and opinions, and respecting the opinions of others.

	Language Function Rubric
4	Student effectively performs the function.
3	Student performs the function.
2	Student does not adequately perform the function.
1	Student makes no attempt or offers a non-verbal response.

Reading and Literary Analysis

Directions: Read each question and choose the best answer.

1 Based on the meaning of the word "judge," the word <u>prejudge</u> means

   A to review the final results of an event.

   B to try in a court of law for the first time.

   C to form an opinion about something beforehand.

   D to arrive at an agreement about something quickly.

2 Based on the meaning of the word "admire," the word <u>admiration</u> means a feeling of

   A thanks.

   B power.

   C respect.

   D warmth.

3 The root word *dem* means "people." Based on this, the word <u>demography</u> means

   A the movement of people.

   B the study of groups of people.

   C people who are experts on a topic.

   D people who show others how to do things.

4 The root word *subter* means "under" or "secret." Based on this, the word <u>subtle</u> means

   A forgotten over time.

   B hard to detect or define.

   C taking the place of another.

   D gathered together in one place.

GO ON

UNIT 1

Reading and Literary Analysis, *continued*

Directions: Questions 5–10 are about "A Coffee Date." Read the selection. Then read each question and choose the best answer.

A Coffee Date

Monique impatiently sat waiting for Todd to arrive. Maybe she should have waited longer before coming into the café. Was she going to seem desperate just waiting like that? Should she order a coffee, or would that be rude? What if he thinks she expects him to buy her a coffee? What if he does not show up at all? Imagine that! He is the best friend of my best friend's boyfriend. She was sure he would at least show up with an excuse to leave early.

She pulled out a poetry book and began to flip through the pages: Pablo Neruda's *Odes to Common Things*. Okay, so it was a conversation piece. It was inevitable that he would ask her what she was reading, and it would give them something to talk about. Plus, she really did like Pablo Neruda's poetry. Todd might even know who Neruda was. It did not really matter. But what if he did? What if they connected right off?

Monique had decided to try going on a blind date a few weeks before. Her best friend had convinced her that she knew someone that she was sure Monique would like. Ever since she had graduated from high school a few months ago, she had grown tired of her small group of friends who always dated the same sorts of people. In fact, she never liked the idea of being asked to go on a date. She hated the idea that just because she was a girl, she was expected to wait for a guy to make the first move.

Without telling her other friends, she agreed to meet this guy her best friend knew. They had exchanged photos, and Monique's friend had arranged a place for them to meet.

An almost familiar face came through the door of the coffee shop. Her heart began to rush, partly because she was nervous and partly because he was more attractive in person than his photo. It was not anything in particular about him. He was simply wearing jeans and an old-looking grey sweater. There was a short growth of hair on his face telling her he had not shaved

this morning. She liked it. He seemed real. He *was real*. It was almost as if she had a part in his creation by taking the steps to meet new people.

"Hi, Monique," he said, smiling as he offered her his hand. What a nice voice!

Half standing, Monique offered a slightly sweaty palm to Todd. "Hi, Todd. It's nice to finally meet you." She tried to make her voice calm, like she did this regularly. She summoned up all her confidence to steady her voice. "You want to grab some coffee?"

"Sure."

As they got in line, a thousand thoughts flooded her mind. What is he thinking? Am I as attractive in person as my picture? I spent days trying to take a good picture of myself. I spent days trying to figure out what to wear this morning. Can he tell? I hope not. Quick! Ask him a question. Do not be shy!

"So, how's your week been?"

"Really busy, actually. I must have put a hundred

Reading and Literary Analysis, *continued*

miles on my car just driving to different clients' homes. And then the paperwork just piled up because I was out of the office so much. I finally got caught up yesterday. How was your week? Have many gigs?"

Gigs? Oh, that's right. Her friend had said she was a singer. And she was; she performed about once a month, and she had a lot of <u>potential</u>. It didn't pay much money, but it seemed more exciting to say she was a singer than to say she worked retail. She never felt like herself at her retail job. It was so boring. In fact, she most often felt like her job sucked the life out of her. With so many rules about how to treat customers, it was impossible to be one's real self. So it did not seem like too much of a <u>pretense</u> for her friend to tell Todd that she was a singer. She did get paid to sing, just not very often.

"Uh, no. Mostly just rehearsing. I'm expecting things to pick up though," she replied a little hesitantly.

"Wow! Do you write your own music? I'd love to hear some of it. I'd love to hear you sing. Your voice is so nice. I can't imagine how good it would sound singing."

Monique could feel herself blush so red she thought her face might melt off at any second. "Thank you," she said, quietly looking down.

"What book is that?" he asked, pointing to the book in her hand.

She passed it to him. "Oh, it's this poetry book I've been reading."

"Pablo Neruda, huh? Never heard of him. I like poetry though. Is it good?"

"Yeah, it's really good," she said, glad to change the subject. "He has an incredible way of describing the most ordinary things. He can make a tomato sound more beautiful than a sunset."

"Really?" he said with a smile. "Maybe I'll check it out. I really like to read books with close friends. It's a good way to connect and not constantly talk about the same old boring stuff. But I have to admit, I haven't had much spare time with work and all. People are dropping like flies."

Huh? What does he mean? Did she miss something? "What do you mean 'dropping like flies'? My friend said you are doing an internship this summer. What kind of internship?" she asked.

Todd's face blushed. He looked a bit nervous for the first time in the conversation. "Ummm, well, I… Right now, I'm selling tiny bits of real estate."

"Like houses?"

"No. Like plots."

"Plots?"

"Yes, like cemetery plots. I'm doing an internship with a mortician. Some people think that is weird, but my family has been in the mortuary business for years."

Monique smiled and then laughed, realizing that they both had been afraid to tell the entire truth about who they were. "You know, I think we have a lot more in common than we thought. I need to tell you a little more about my singing career. Let's get our coffee and sit down."

Reading and Literary Analysis, *continued*

5 Why does Monique have an internal conflict about meeting Todd for the first time?

A She is concerned that he will not like her.

B She fears that her friend will be disappointed with her.

C She is not certain that he will show up for their date.

D She worries that someone she knows might see them.

6 Monique realizes that she and Todd have more in common than she thought because they both

A have jobs selling things.

B like the same kinds of books.

C are nervous about meeting new people.

D are afraid of what others think of them.

7 An <u>inevitable</u> event is

A fun to remember.

B certain to happen.

C planned in advance.

D attended by many people.

8 If a person has <u>potential</u>, or promise, it means the person has

A big ideas.

B natural ability.

C strong opinions.

D powerful friends.

9 <u>Pretense</u> is the act of

A choosing.

B preparing.

C pretending.

D representing.

Directions: Read question 10. Write your answer on a separate sheet of paper.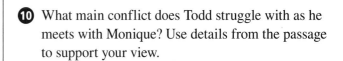

10 What main conflict does Todd struggle with as he meets with Monique? Use details from the passage to support your view.

GO ON

Reading and Literary Analysis, *continued*

Directions: Questions 11–16 are about "Invisible Girl." Read the selection. Then read each question and choose the best answer.

Invisible Girl

I was the kind of person you would find standing in the corner trying to be invisible. It's not that I wanted to be invisible, but I don't much like how I look and I'm smart enough to be teased because of it.

Every day, I felt like a child with my face pressed against the window of a toy store looking at the brightly colored toys inside, full of expectations, but never able to get the door to open. Somehow, I thought that if I could get a foot in that door, a whole new world would open up for me. The trouble was that I had no idea how to make that happen.

I had gathered my courage a few times to talk to the popular girls. It would take me days to work up the nerve to say hello and weeks to get over the inevitable snub that followed. After a while, I gave up trying.

You can imagine how startled I was when Marcy first joined me for lunch—Marcy, who had boys trailing behind her and popular girls wanting to be her friends, and whose rich parents gave her the sun, moon, and stars for breakfast. That Marcy.

She chatted away and pretty soon I felt the <u>tension</u> flow out of me. For the whole week, Marcy introduced

me to her friends and took me under her wing. She and Dana and Janelle turned around my entire way of dressing, fixed my hair, and made me feel as though I had not only gotten into the toy shop, but I was also on my way to owning it.

"We're going shopping this weekend," Marcy said in that way of hers that was both an invitation and an order. "And bring that big purse of yours, Anna. I looooove that purse."

I met up with Marcy and two of her friends, but I still felt awkward around them, like I was the <u>discordant</u> note in an otherwise perfect chord. I had my big, floppy denim purse hanging on my shoulder. Marcy, Dana, and Janelle had cute purses barely big enough for a cell phone, money, and lipstick.

We went into the fanciest department store in town and began to wander along the aisles. Marcy was looking through various kinds of expensive perfume when she edged over close to me, and before I realized what was happening, she stuffed a bottle of perfume into my purse. I stood rooted, totally shocked. She towed me over to the jewelry stands where she and Dana began stuffing jewelry into my bag as well.

"Marcy, what are you doing?!" I made it a hissed

GO ON ▶

Reading and Literary Analysis, *continued*

whisper, but I couldn't help looking around, waiting for the security guards to descend on us.

"Your turn. You pick something," urged Janelle.

"But that's stealing!"

"Yeah, so? Are you in or not?" asked Marcy. It was a challenge. I either went along with what they were doing, or I said good-bye to being in her exalted group.

I didn't understand. Marcy had enough money to buy whatever she wanted. She didn't need to steal. Then I looked into her eyes. They were filled with a bright intensity that told me she was in it for the thrill, and part of that thrill was using me. Making me do what she wanted. Turning me to the Dark Side. Okay, that's

over-the-top maybe, but I knew at that instant that she had no interest in me as a person. She had never really wanted to be my friend. And at the same time, I knew how much that meant to me.

"Distract the sales clerk," I said, coolly. Marcy gave me a sly smile. The three of them got the clerk to the other end of the booth. Fast as I could, I pulled everything out of my purse that Marcy had put there and left it on the counter. I dashed out of the store, leaving them all behind.

I saw a toy store at the far end of the mall and headed for it. Outside, inside…I was going to leave that behind, too. It was time to open my own doors.

---

11 Who is the **main** antagonist in the story?

A Anna

B Dana

C Marcy

D Janelle

12 Both Monique in "A Coffee Date" and Anna in "Invisible Girl" face a personal challenge. What is different about how they respond?

A Monique gives up; Anna always keeps trying.

B Monique hides the truth at first; Anna remains honest.

C Monique finally solves her problem; Anna ignores hers.

D Monique learns about herself; Anna avoids change in the beginning.

13 Tension means

A embarrassment.

B failure.

C stress.

D exhaustion.

14 A discordant, or harsh, sound is

A distant.

B sudden.

C unusual.

D unpleasant.

15 Intensity means

A force.

B love.

C interest.

D success.

Directions: Read question 16. Write your answer on a separate sheet of paper.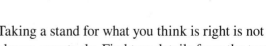

16 Taking a stand for what you think is right is not always easy to do. Find two details from the text to support this statement.

EDGE Level C

Reading and Literary Analysis, *continued*

Directions: Questions 17–23 are about "A Different Kind of Ballplayer." Read the selection. Then read each question and choose the best answer.

A Different Kind of Ballplayer

Taylor loved baseball. He loved the smell of the fresh grass, the crack of the bat meeting the ball, the sight of a fielder diving to snare a base hit, the fast action around the diamond. He loved to watch baseball, and he loved to play.

"So why aren't you on the team?" his cousin Max asked him. The two were in Taylor's backyard, tossing a ball back and forth. "Why haven't you ever tried out for the Lakeville Panthers?"

"Are you kidding?" Taylor asked, stretching to retrieve a ground ball. "The Panthers are for real players, not kids like me."

Max sighed. "You mean kids with a disability?"

Taylor threw the ball back with a hard, angry snap of his right hand. "Yes. That's right." He held up his left hand, which was missing most of the fingers. "In case you haven't noticed." Taylor had spent his whole life feeling that other people <u>stigmatize</u> him as "the kid with the weird hand."

"Actually, I haven't noticed," Max responded. "You're a phenomenal baseball player."

"I'm not good enough to be on the Panthers," Taylor insisted. "Everyone will think I'm <u>pathetic</u>."

Max stopped pitching and walked toward him. "You know very well that there have been baseball players with physical disabilities. The only pathetic thing about you is your attitude," he said angrily. Taylor flushed with embarrassment.

> "You know very well that there have been baseball players with physical disabilities. The only pathetic thing about you is your attitude," he said angrily.

On Friday night, Max called. "There's a wrestling match at my school tomorrow morning. I think you'll like it, and there's someone I want you to meet."

When Max and Taylor walked into the college gymnasium, Taylor saw lots of muscular young men stretching on mats. Max pointed out a young man sitting on a bench. "There's Kyle, and that's my friend Joshua," he said. "They're wrestling against each other tonight. Notice anything different about Joshua?"

Taylor could not believe what he saw. Both of Joshua's arms ended at the elbows.

"You've got to be kidding me," Taylor said. "How can he wrestle?"

"Are you making assumptions based on the way he looks?" Max asked. Taylor didn't answer.

When Joshua's match was called, Taylor watched the young man walk confidently into the ring and face his opponent. Even though Joshua had no lower arms, he quickly managed to pin Kyle to the mat with his powerful upper body and legs.

Afterward, Max introduced Taylor to Joshua. "My cousin wants to join the local baseball team, but he thinks people will judge him by his disability rather than his athletic ability."

Joshua nodded. "When I first started wrestling, people stared at me and made comments about my arms. I didn't waste my time worrying about their expectations. I only worried about my own."

Taylor was speechless. "It's inevitable that people will assume things about you because of the way you look," Joshua said. "That doesn't mean that you can't change their minds."

"Something to think about," Max said as they walked home.

"That's for sure," Taylor agreed. "Are you up for a little more practice?" And he pulled his ever-present baseball out of his jacket pocket and tossed it to Max.

Reading and Literary Analysis, *continued*

17 Which character is the dynamic character in the story?

A Max

B Kyle

C Taylor

D Joshua

18 A theme in both "Invisible Girl" and "A Different Kind of Ballplayer" comes from the fact that both Anna and Taylor

A feel invisible.

B struggle in school.

C want to make friends.

D need more confidence.

19 The themes of "Invisible Girl" and "A Different Kind of Ballplayer" are similar. The main characters in these stories both learn to

A acccpt thcir limitations.

B be honest with other people.

C allow other people to be themselves.

D set their own expectations for themselves.

20 How does a change in setting create a conflict for both Anna in "Invisible Girl" and Taylor in "A Different Kind of Ballplayer"?

A It shows them that they are mistaken about their friends.

B It forces them into an uncomfortable situation.

C It confirms decisions they have made.

D It reminds them of how much they have learned.

21 To <u>stigmatize</u> means to

A confuse.

B disgrace.

C surrender.

D apologize.

22 If a person is <u>pathetic</u>, that person makes you feel

A pity.

B hate.

C trust.

D anger.

Directions: Read question 23. Write your answer on a separate sheet of paper.

23 How does Joshua help Taylor to resolve his conflict? Use details from the passage to support your answer.

EDGE Level C

Grammar and Writing

Directions: Read the composition. It contains errors. Then read each question and choose the best answer.

Headphones

(1) I trudge into Algebra 101 on my first day of ninth grade and sink into my desk. (2) I don't like math that much. (3) Not looking forward to it.

(4) Then, this really weird kid comes in and sits next to me. (5) He walks in listening to heavy metal on his MP3 player. (6) He is dressed entirely in black: a black T-shirt, black leather pants and black boots. (7) His curly, shoulder-length hair swirls around him as he shakes his head to wailing guitar. (8) He takes two pencils out of his pocket and starts pounding the air furiously, as if the pencils are drumsticks.

(9) "This guy looks like trouble," I think to myself.

(10) To make matters worse, the teacher gives us an alphabetical seating arrangement. (11) I am sure he's going to cause all kinds of problems and make the entire semester miserable.

(12) A week later, I are not so sure.

(13) During attendance, I find out his name is Jake. (14) My dad used to have a dog named Jake! (15) To my surprise, when the teacher starts class, Jake turns off his music, puts his headphones away, and stops drumming the air. (16) He does his work and isn't disruptive, so the teacher doesn't pick on him.

(17) One morning over the intercom, the Principal tells everyone that MP3 players are no longer allowed at school. (18) Everyone complains. (19) In algebra, Jake walks in with his headphones still on.

(20) "Hey, man," I say. (21) "Did you hear they banned MP3 players?"

(22) He smiles and shows me the cord of his headphones—plugged into nothing.

(23) "I know," he says. (24) "I just walked right by the principal's office wearing these. (25) I am just so used to having them in my ears. (26) Some lady yelled at me and tried to give me detention. (27) I could tell she really wanted to catch somebody breaking the rules, especially me."

(28) I was relieved and smiled back. (29) Now, we talk about music before and after class. (30) Jake has a band. (31) And says I should check them out.

(32) He's a good guy. (33) I don't think I'll ever wear black leather pants like Jake, but I respect him.

Grammar and Writing, continued

1 Sentence 3 should be changed to

- **A** I not forward to it.
- **B** not looking forward to it.
- **C** I am not looking forward to it.
- **D** No change

2 What change, if any, should be made to sentence 6?

- **A** Change *entirely* to **entirly**
- **B** Change *leather* to **Leather**
- **C** Add a comma after *pants*
- **D** No change

3 Which sentence **best** supports the main idea of paragraph 4?

- **A** I do not like seating charts.
- **B** I hear this teacher is tough.
- **C** I am stuck sitting next to him.
- **D** I do not think algebra is useful.

4 In sentence 12, the word <u>are</u> should be changed to

- **A** am
- **B** be
- **C** is
- **D** No change

5 Which sentence is off topic and should be removed from paragraph 6?

- **A** sentence 13
- **B** sentence 14
- **C** sentence 15
- **D** sentence 16

6 What change, if any, should be made to sentence 17?

- **A** Change *Principal* to **principal**
- **B** Put a comma after *everyone*
- **C** Change *allowed* to **aloud**
- **D** No change

7 In sentence 19, the word <u>walks</u> should be changed to

- **A** walk
- **B** is walk
- **C** walking
- **D** No change

8 Sentences 30 and 31 should be changed to

- **A** Jake has a band. Says check them out.
- **B** Jake has a band, and he says I should check them out.
- **C** Jake has a band; and he says I should check them out.
- **D** No change

GO ON

Grammar and Writing, continued

Directions: Read the composition. It contains errors. Then read each question and choose the best answer.

Windows

(1) When my great-uncle Morrie came to stay with my family, we thought he would take the basement room we had set up for him. (2) When he saw that the room had no windows, he refused to sleep their.

(3) "Sarah wouldn't mind if you took her room," my mother said.

(4) "Sarah," my mother said, looking at me sternly. (5) "Why don't you show Uncle Morrie to your room?" (6) I was so mad.

(7) I took him down the hall, and followed me with his bag.

(8) "This is nice," he said. (9) "You're a lucky kid, you know."

(10) I hoped he wasn't going to launch into some story about how hard life was for him as a kid. (11) I left him there and marched back out to the kitchen.

(12) "Thanks a lot, Mom," I said sarcastically.

(13) "Don't start with me, young lady," she said, tying her apron.

(14) "I just think it's rude of him to tell *us* where he going to sleep."

(15) "Sarah, you knows nothing about this man. (16) You need to cut him some slack. (17) He's had a hard life."

(18) "Fine," I sighed. (19) "What's his problem with no windows?"

(20) "He afraid of enclosed spaces," she muttered.

(21) After dinner, Morrie went to my room to sleep. (22) As I cleared the table, my mom took a book off the shelf and set it on the table. (23) It was *The Diary of Anne Frank*. (24) I have a diary, too.

(25) "It's time you read this," she said.

(26) "Why?" I asked.

(27) My mom explained that it was the diary of a jewish girl who hid from the Nazis in an attic during World War II. (28) She said it would help me understand Uncle Morrie.

(29) "He's afraid of enclosed spaces because of this book?" I asked, surprised.

(30) "No, Sarah. (31) He had to hide just like the girl in this book."

(32) I read the first few pages, and I went to check on Uncle Morrie. (33) The door was open and he was facing the window.

GO ON

Grammar and Writing, continued

9 What change, if any, should be made to sentence 2?

A   Change *windows* to **Windows**

B   Change the comma to a semicolon

C   Change *their* to **there**

D   No change

10 Which sentence should be added after sentence 6 to support the main idea of the paragraph?

A   I am not even sure what a great-uncle is.

B   My mom told me he was born in Europe.

C   I was even grounded once for talking back.

D   Uncle Morrie had a lot of nerve to be so picky.

11 Sentence 7 should be changed to

A   I took him down the hall, and he with his bag.

B   I took him down the hall, he followed me with his bag.

C   I took him down the hall, and he followed me with his bag.

D   No change

12 In sentence 14, the words he going should be changed to

A   he is going

B   he be going

C   he are going

D   No change

13 In sentence 15, the word knows should be changed to

A   know

B   is know

C   knowing

D   No change

14 Sentence 20 should be changed to

A   "Afraid of enclosed spaces," she muttered.

B   "Is afraid of enclosed spaces," she muttered.

C   "He is afraid of enclosed spaces," she muttered.

D   No change

15 Which sentence is off topic and should be removed from the paragraph?

A   sentence 21

B   sentence 22

C   sentence 23

D   sentence 24

16 What change, if any, should be made to sentence 27?

A   Change *jewish* to **Jewish**

B   Put a comma after *girl*

C   Change *attic* to **attick**

D   No change

GO ON

EDGE Level C

Grammar and Writing, *continued*

Directions: Read the following writing prompt, and write a composition. Write on separate sheets of paper. Use the Writer's Checklist to make sure that you do your best work.

Prompt

Write a short story in which a character is treated unfairly or misunderstood by people who do not really know him or her. Draw from your own experiences or from those of someone you know to get ideas for the story.

Writer's Checklist

☑ Write about all parts of the prompt.

☑ Present a clear central idea, and stay focused on it.

☑ Organize your composition from its introduction to its conclusion.

☑ Use transitions to connect your thoughts for the reader.

☑ Present meaningful ideas, and support them with specific information.

☑ Use appropriate words and a variety of sentence structures.

☑ Proofread and edit your writing for grammar, usage, mechanics, and spelling.

DONE!

EDGE Level C

Name _____ Date _____

Student Profile: Unit Tests

Directions: Use the **Answer Key** on page 139 to score the multiple-choice items. Circle the item number of each correct answer below. Calculate test scores by assigning one point for each correct answer. Use the scoring guides on page 139 to score the constructed-response items. Use the Good Writing Traits Rubric on page 122 to score the written composition. Total the scores and calculate the % score or use the conversion chart. To gauge mastery for a particular tested skill or Common Core Standard, review the Cluster Test and Unit Test results.

Reading and Literary Analysis

Category	Tested Skill	ITEM ANALYSIS		TEST SCORES
		Item Numbers	Mastery	Points: Earned / Total
Vocabulary	Use Word Parts: Prefixes, Roots, Suffixes L.9-10.4	1 2 3 4	3 out of 4 + –	_____ / 4
	Key Vocabulary L.9-10.6	7 8 9 13 14 15 21 22	6 out of 8 + –	_____ / 8
Literary Analysis	Analyze Elements of Fiction RL.9-10.3	5 6 11 12 17 20	5 out of 6 + –	_____ / 6
	Analyze Theme RL.9-10.2	18 19	1 out of 2 + –	_____ / 2
Constructed Response	Use Text Evidence RL.9-10.1; RL.9-10.10; W.9-10.9	Rubric Score (4–Point Scale) Item 10 _____ + Item 16 _____ + Item 23 _____ = _____		_____ / 12

Overall Score (Points Earned ÷ Total Points x 100 = %) _____ ÷ 32 = _____%

Grammar and Writing

Category	Tested Skill	ITEM ANALYSIS		TEST SCORES
		Item Numbers	Mastery	Points: Earned / Total
Grammar	Sentences L.9-10.1	1 8 11 14	3 out of 4 + –	_____ / 4
	Subject-Verb Agreement L.9-10.1	4 7 12 13	3 out of 4 + –	_____ / 4
Revising and Editing	Focus and Unity W.9-10.5	3 5 10 15	3 out of 4 + –	_____ / 4
	Grammar, Mechanics, and Usage L.9-10.2	2 6 9 16	3 out of 4 + –	_____ / 4
Written Composition (Narrative) W.9-10.3; W.9-10.4; W.9-10.10	Focus and Unity	Rubric Scores: _____ / 4		
	Organization	_____ / 4		
	Development of Ideas	_____ / 4 =		_____ / 20
	Voice and Style	_____ / 4		
	Written Conventions	_____ / 4		

Overall Score (Points Earned ÷ Total Points x 100 = %) _____ ÷ 36 = _____%

EDGE Level C

Project Rubric: A Sound or Video Recording

Score	Planning/Preparation	Content of Project	Delivery/Presentation	Collaboration
3 Great	• Researches and selects a literary work that addresses the Essential Question. • Determines the best format for recording the literary work and who will read or perform the literary work. • Practices the reading several times before final recording.	• Addresses the Essential Question. • Is interesting and maintains the audience's attention throughout the reading.	• Presents the literary work in the format that best expresses the Essential Question. • The pace of the reading is easy-to-follow and clear. • Speaks clearly and loudly.	• Works well with others. • Assumes a clear role and related responsibilities.
2 Good	• Researches and selects a literary work that somewhat addresses the Essential Question. • Picks a format for recording the literary work and selects who will read or perform the literary work. • Practices the reading once before final recording.	• Somewhat addresses the Essential Question. • Is somewhat interesting and maintains the audience's attention throughout most of the reading.	• Presents the literary work in the format that somewhat expresses the Essential Question. • The pace of the reading is somewhat easy-to-follow and clear but may be too slow or too fast at specific moments. • Can be heard most of the time.	• Works with others but has difficulty sharing decisions and responsibilities.
1 Needs Work	• The literary work selected does not relate to the Essential Question. • Decides on the format but does not select who will read the literary work. • Does not practice before the final recording.	• Does not address the Essential Question. • Is not interesting and does not maintain the audience's attention throughout the reading.	• Does not present the literary work in an appropriate format. • The pace of the reading is hard to follow and is too slow or too fast. • Cannot be heard or understood well.	• Cannot work with others in most situations. • Cannot share decisions or responsibilities.

Name _____ Date _____

Self Assessment

Directions: Circle the numbers that show how much you agree or disagree with each sentence. Then answer the question below. If necessary, use the back of the page.

		Strongly Disagree	Disagree	Agree	Strongly Agree
1	When I read a story, I understand conflict, characterization, and theme.	1	2	3	4
2	When I read a story, I can identify and understand the antagonist and protagonist.	1	2	3	4
3	I understand the features of a news feature, a profile, and an oral history.	1	2	3	4
4	I know how to plan my reading and monitor my comprehension.	1	2	3	4
5	When I find a word I do not know, I look for word parts to help me understand the meaning.	1	2	3	4
6	I know how to write complete sentences, making my subjects and verbs agree.	1	2	3	4
7	I know how to make my writing focused and unified.	1	2	3	4

8 Think of one thing you learned really well in this unit. Tell how you will use this next time you read or write.

_____

_____

_____

_____

_____

_____

_____

_____

_____

_____

Reader Reflection

Directions: Answer questions 1–10. If necessary, use the back of the page.

"La Vida Robot"

1 What did you learn about what nonfiction text features such as photographs, graphs, and charts can add to the text found in a technology article?

2 You can determine importance by identifying main ideas and details. Explain how this strategy will help you the next time you read.

3 Write what you liked and did not like about "La Vida Robot." Include examples from the technology article.

I liked...
I did not like...

4 Are you interested in reading more writing by Joshua Davis? _____ Yes _____No

5 Are you interested in reading more technology articles by other writers? _____ Yes _____No

"Reading, Writing, and . . . Recreation?"

6 What did you learn about the development of ideas in a news feature that will help you the next time you read a news feature?

7 Explain how determining importance by thinking about the "5Ws + H" will help you the next time you read a news feature.

8 Write what you liked and did not like about "Reading, Writing, and . . . Recreation?" Include examples from the news feature.

I liked...
I did not like...

9 Are you interested in reading more works by Nancy C. Rodriguez? _____ Yes _____No

10 Are you interested in reading more news features by other writers? _____ Yes _____No

"La Vida Robot" and "Reading, Writing, and…Recreation?"  Closed Book

Directions: Read each question and choose the best answer.

KEY VOCABULARY

1 To contemplate means to
- Ⓐ control.
- Ⓑ consider.
- Ⓒ continue.
- Ⓓ confuse.

2 To designate means to
- Ⓐ point out.
- Ⓑ question.
- Ⓒ destroy.
- Ⓓ try on.

3 If a person is disciplined, it means the person is
- Ⓐ self-controlled.
- Ⓑ self-confident.
- Ⓒ disappointed.
- Ⓓ dismayed.

4 To implement something means to
- Ⓐ do it.
- Ⓑ plan it.
- Ⓒ break it.
- Ⓓ improve it.

5 If an idea is innovative, it means the idea is
- Ⓐ practical.
- Ⓑ original.
- Ⓒ innocent.
- Ⓓ complicated.

6 Perpetually means
- Ⓐ soon.
- Ⓑ lately.
- Ⓒ always.
- Ⓓ quickly.

7 To procrastinate means to
- Ⓐ delay.
- Ⓑ protect.
- Ⓒ practice.
- Ⓓ educate.

8 If you do something spontaneously, it means you do it
- Ⓐ slowly and carefully.
- Ⓑ quickly and carelessly.
- Ⓒ alone without assistance.
- Ⓓ suddenly without planning.

 **Open Book**

Directions: Questions 9–15 are about "La Vida Robot." Read each question and choose the best answer. You may look at the selection on pages 131–151 to help you answer the questions.

LITERARY ANALYSIS

9 Under which section head will the reader find information about the underwater obstacle course?
- Ⓐ Epilogue
- Ⓑ The Team
- Ⓒ The Results
- Ⓓ The Competition

10 What is the purpose of the captions that are underneath the photographs of the Carl Hayden team members?
- Ⓐ They tell which team member was most important.
- Ⓑ They compare the backgrounds of the team members.
- Ⓒ They describe the main role each team member played.
- Ⓓ They show the order in which the team members were chosen.

GO ON ▶

"La Vida Robot" and "Reading, Writing, and…Recreation?"

 Open Book

11 The "Underwater Task Performance" diagrams show

Ⓐ the size of the MIT team's ROV.

Ⓑ the materials used to build each robot.

Ⓒ how well the Hayden team's ROV was designed.

Ⓓ how well both robots could remove fluid from a drum.

12 What information is provided by the "Competition Results" graphic?

Ⓐ the names of cities hosting robot competitions

Ⓑ the score each team received in each category

Ⓒ the reasons each team excelled in each category

Ⓓ the number of people competing in the championship

COMPREHENSION

13 How did Frank Szwankowski help the Carl Hayden team members?

Ⓐ He contributed money.

Ⓑ He gave them special equipment.

Ⓒ He encouraged them with his words.

Ⓓ He taught them about working as a team.

14 What is the best summary of this article?

Ⓐ Two teachers are determined that their students will succeed at a national robot competition.

Ⓑ Competitors in a national robot competition are surprised to learn that the winners are just teenagers.

Ⓒ A scholarship fund and a movie may help four winners of a national robot competition attend college.

Ⓓ Four teenagers overcome many difficulties to become the unexpected winners of a national robot competition.

Directions: Read question 15. Write your answer on a separate sheet of paper.

15

> By using polyvinyl chloride pipe, or PVC pipe, the team built a robot that was not only cheaper but better. The hollow pipes made the robot lighter and easier to move, trapped air to help it float, and provided waterproof housing for the electrical wiring.

This caption appears in the text feature "Anatomy of a Robot." What information does it provide? How is the caption's information related to information in the numbered labels in the text feature?

Directions: Questions 16–22 are about "Reading, Writing, and…Recreation?" Read each question and choose the best answer. You may look at the selection on pages 153–155 to help you answer the questions.

LITERARY ANALYSIS

16 In a news feature, what idea does the author usually develop by answering the question *who*?

Ⓐ the background of the author

Ⓑ the likely audience for the report

Ⓒ the person or people featured in the report

Ⓓ the importance of the informaton in the report

GO ON

"La Vida Robot" and "Reading, Writing, and...Recreation?"

 Open Book

17 Read this sentence from the news feature.

> Students say they find time for schoolwork during school, after school, and before practice or club meetings.

What question about the topic does this sentence answer?

Ⓐ who

Ⓑ what

Ⓒ when

Ⓓ where

18 The caption under the picture of the basketball players helps to develop an answer to the question

Ⓐ *who.*

Ⓑ *why.*

Ⓒ *when.*

Ⓓ *where.*

COMPREHENSION

19 Courtney Otto and Taylor Distler would probably agree that

Ⓐ extracurricular activities are more important than school.

Ⓑ the best way to overcome one's fear of something is to do it.

Ⓒ clubs started by fellow students are the most interesting ones.

Ⓓ it can be challenging to do extracurricular activities and schoolwork.

20 Which detail shows that Courtney Otto lived up to her potential?

Ⓐ She tutored students during school.

Ⓑ She was accepted into Dartmouth College.

Ⓒ She became captain of a girls' basketball team.

Ⓓ She overcame her fear of public speaking and won an award.

21 The author most likely wrote this news feature in order to

Ⓐ warn students that extracurricular activities take time.

Ⓑ tell about the extracurricular activities of a group of students.

Ⓒ describe different kinds of extracurricular activities for students.

Ⓓ encourage students to become involved in extracurricular activities.

Directions: Read question 22. Write your answer on a separate sheet of paper.

22
> Ashley Brown, a senior at Atherton High School, got involved with the Future Educators of America/Minority Teacher Recruitment club last year. Ashley, who wants to be a special-education teacher, said the club led her to another program that allows her to tutor students during school.

Which of the "five Ws + H" questions are addressed in this paragraph? What main idea does the author use them to develop? What other evidence does the author include to develop that idea?

15e **DONE!** EDGE Level C

Reader Reflection

Directions: Answer questions 1–10. If necessary, use the back of the page.

"My Left Foot"

1 What did you learn about ways in which ideas are developed in autobiographies that will help you the next time you read an autobiography?

2 Explain how determining importance by summarizing will help you the next time you read.

3 Write what you liked and did not like about "My Left Foot." Include examples from the autobiography.

I liked...

I did not like...

4 Are you interested in reading more writing by Christy Brown? ____ Yes ____ No

5 Are you interested in reading more autobiographies by other authors? ____ Yes ____ No

"Success is a Mind-Set"

6 What did you learn about ways of organizing and presenting information that will help you the next time you read an online magazine interview?

7 Explain how summarizing an interview will help you the next time you read an interview.

8 Write what you liked and did not like about "Success Is a Mind-Set." Include examples from the interview.

I liked...

I did not like...

9 Are you interested in reading more about Ben Carson? ____ Yes ____ No

10 Are you interested in reading more interviews with successful people?
____ Yes ____ No

"My Left Foot" and "Success Is a Mind-Set"

 Closed Book

Directions: Read each question and choose the best answer.

1 A <u>consequence</u> means
- (A) a reason.
- (B) an effect.
- (C) an agreement.
- (D) a conversation.

2 To <u>contend</u> is to
- (A) argue that something is true.
- (B) lift something off the ground.
- (C) confuse with something else.
- (D) bend something into a new shape.

3 A <u>conviction</u> is a
- (A) strong belief.
- (B) valuable lesson.
- (C) terrible sickness.
- (D) reasonable suggestion.

4 To <u>dictate</u> means to
- (A) chase.
- (B) control.
- (C) contact.
- (D) cooperate.

5 An <u>endeavor</u> is a
- (A) serious attempt.
- (B) painful memory.
- (C) simple solution.
- (D) personal favor.

6 <u>Momentous</u> means
- (A) finally finished.
- (B) slightly different.
- (C) completely correct.
- (D) extremely important.

7 If a story is <u>profound</u>, it means the story is filled with
- (A) hope.
- (B) humor.
- (C) conflict.
- (D) meaning.

8 A <u>transition</u> is
- (A) a stupid joke.
- (B) a slow change.
- (C) a perfect ending.
- (D) an exciting chance.

Directions: Questions 9–15 are about "My Left Foot." Read each question and choose the best answer. You may look at the selection on pages 165–176 to help you answer the questions.

 Open Book

9 Because this selection is an autobiography, the reader knows that
- (A) Brown wrote the Epilogue.
- (B) Rotunda Hospital is a real place.
- (C) the story has a hero and a villain.
- (D) the thoughts of all characters are revealed.

10 In an autobiography, readers can tell what is important to the writer because of the
- (A) use of a first-person point of view.
- (B) vividness of the writer's descriptions.
- (C) choice and presentation of details by the writer.
- (D) way in which the writer talks about other people.

GO ON

"My Left Foot" and "Success Is a Mind-Set"

 Open Book

11 Which sentence best explains why the events of this autobiography are important to Brown?

Ⓐ It was hard, heartbreaking work, for often all she got from me in return was a vague smile and perhaps a faint gurgle.

Ⓑ After my birth, mother was sent to recuperate for some weeks and I was kept in the hospital while she was away.

Ⓒ In a moment everything was changed, my future life molded into a definite shape, my mother's faith in me rewarded and her secret fear changed into open triumph.

Ⓓ Inside, all the family were gathered round the big kitchen fire that lit up the little room with a warm glow and made giant shadows dance on the walls and ceiling.

COMPREHENSION

12 Which word best describes Brown's mother?

Ⓐ hasty
Ⓑ meek
Ⓒ carefree
Ⓓ determined

13 Brown tells about a time when his mother was reading to him from a storybook. Why did Brown's mother start to cry after they finished the book?

Ⓐ He pulled her hair too hard and hurt her.
Ⓑ He said something that hurt her feelings.
Ⓒ She had hoped he would show that he understood her.
Ⓓ She was happy he was able to communicate with her.

14 When Brown is able to write the letter "A," it shows that he

Ⓐ loves his mother.
Ⓑ can communicate.
Ⓒ knows how to read.
Ⓓ will become a writer.

Directions: Read question 15. Write your answer on a separate sheet of paper.

15
> Suddenly I wanted desperately to do what my sister was doing. Then—without thinking or knowing exactly what I was doing, I reached out and took the stick of chalk out of my sister's hand—*with my left foot.*

What do these autobiographical details reveal about what is important to Christy Brown, the writer? How do you know that these details are important?

Directions: Questions 16–22 are about "Success Is a Mind-Set." Read each question and choose the best answer. You may look at the selection on pages 178–182 to help you answer the questions.

LITERARY ANALYSIS

16 The purpose of an online interview is to

Ⓐ tell a person's life story.
Ⓑ summarize a long article.
Ⓒ get information from a person.
Ⓓ compare different points of view.

GO ON

"My Left Foot" and "Success Is a Mind-Set"

17 When you read an online interview, you expect to see its ideas related through which kind of organization?

Ⓐ chronological order

Ⓑ causes and effects

Ⓒ questions and answers

Ⓓ problems and solutions

18 Which part of "Success Is a Mind-Set" shows why Dr. Carson's life is a good example of "challenging expectations"?

Ⓐ the pictures

Ⓑ the introduction

Ⓒ the sentences in bold print

Ⓓ the explanation of neurosurgery

COMPREHENSION

19 The purpose of the interview is to present Dr. Carson's

Ⓐ family.

Ⓑ career.

Ⓒ thoughts.

Ⓓ ambitions.

20 This interview is mostly about

Ⓐ how to help others.

Ⓑ how to live with limits.

Ⓒ why it is important to be positive.

Ⓓ why it is important to explore choices.

21 A person who thinks of a problem as a fence

Ⓐ changes a plan.

Ⓑ asks others for help.

Ⓒ decides that something is impossible.

Ⓓ questions the reasons for doing something.

Directions: Read question 22. Write your answer on a separate sheet of paper.

22
> . . . We had, in our mother, someone who believed in us and was willing to make sacrifices on our behalf. She encouraged us to believe in ourselves. Success is a mind-set. If you have negative influences coming at you and you allow them to dictate your course in life, you'll never succeed. When you realize that the person with the greatest influence over what happens in your life is you, it makes a huge difference. . . .

How does discussing his mother help Dr. Carson share his ideas about being a successful person? Whom else does he discuss in answering this question from the interviewer?

UNIT 2

DONE!

Reader Reflection

Directions: Answer questions 1–10. If necessary, use the back of the page.

"The Freedom Writers Diary"

1 What did you learn about ways in which diary writers reveal what they consider important that will help you the next time you read a diary?

2 You can determine importance using a Reading Journal. Explain how this strategy will help you the next time you read.

3 Write what you liked and did not like about "The Freedom Writers Diary." Include examples from the diary.

I liked...

I did not like...

4 Are you interested in reading more writing by The Freedom Writers? _____ Yes _____ No

5 Are you interested in reading more diaries by other authors? _____ Yes _____ No

"Strength, Courage, and Wisdom"

6 What did you learn about the importance of word choice in song lyrics that will help you the next time you read song lyrics?

7 Explain how determining what's important in song lyrics will help you the next time you read song lyrics.

8 Write what you liked and did not like about "Strength, Courage, and Wisdom." Include examples from the song lyrics.

I liked...

I did not like...

9 Are you interested in reading more lyrics by India Arie? _____ Yes _____ No

10 Are you interested in reading more song lyrics by other songwriters? _____ Yes _____ No

"Freedom Writers Diary" and "Strength, Courage, Wisdom"  Closed Book

Directions: Read each question and choose the best answer.

KEY VOCABULARY

1 Alienation means
- Ⓐ isolation.
- Ⓑ destruction.
- Ⓒ imagination.
- Ⓓ determination.

2 To commiserate means to
- Ⓐ take somebody's place.
- Ⓑ help somebody to succeed.
- Ⓒ finish somebody else's work.
- Ⓓ share somebody's unhappiness.

3 To empathize means to
- Ⓐ embarrass someone.
- Ⓑ apologize to someone.
- Ⓒ demonstrate you like someone.
- Ⓓ understand how someone feels.

4 Ethnicity refers to
- Ⓐ personal values.
- Ⓑ personal feelings.
- Ⓒ racial background.
- Ⓓ educational background.

5 To integrate means to
- Ⓐ instruct.
- Ⓑ compare.
- Ⓒ mix together.
- Ⓓ follow orders.

6 A perception means
- Ⓐ a reason.
- Ⓑ a purpose.
- Ⓒ an observation.
- Ⓓ an opportunity.

7 Segregation means
- Ⓐ a selfish action.
- Ⓑ the creation of a law.
- Ⓒ a response to unfair treatment.
- Ⓓ the separation of people by race.

8 Tolerance means
- Ⓐ fear of failure.
- Ⓑ hope for the future.
- Ⓒ luck and good fortune.
- Ⓓ respect for different beliefs.

Directions: Questions 9–15 are about "The Freedom Writers Diary." Read each question and choose the best answer. You may look at the selection on pages 191–206 to help you answer the questions.

 **Open Book**

LITERARY ANALYSIS

9 The most common reason a person writes in a diary is to
- Ⓐ make lists of projects and chores.
- Ⓑ relate ideas that are important to him or her.
- Ⓒ keep track of ideas for writing stories and poems.
- Ⓓ persuade readers to agree with his or her beliefs and opinions.

10 People often use diary entries to
- Ⓐ analyze thoughts and feelings.
- Ⓑ develop persuasive arguments.
- Ⓒ communicate with family members.
- Ⓓ distinguish between facts and opinions.

GO ON

"Freedom Writers Diary" and "Strength, Courage, Wisdom"

 Open Book

11 Which sentence from Student Diary Entry 36 includes the best description of the writer's feelings?

Ⓐ To my surprise, I proved myself wrong because the book indeed came to life.

Ⓑ She looked up and said very calmly, "How can you say that?"

Ⓒ The first thing that came to my mind when I finished reading the book was the fact that Ms. G was right.

Ⓓ At the end of the book, I was so mad that Anne died, because as she was dying, a part of me was dying with her.

COMPREHENSION

12 Why does Ms. Gruwell tell about the incident with Sharaud in her first diary entry?

Ⓐ to explain why she disliked her new school

Ⓑ to describe what caused a change in her teaching

Ⓒ to describe a similarity to a story she was teaching

Ⓓ to explain why it was so surprising that he later graduated

13 What idea is common in all of the young people's diary entries?

Ⓐ faith in family

Ⓑ love of country

Ⓒ need for courage

Ⓓ loss of friendship

14 What important idea do all of the student diary entries have in common?

Ⓐ They describe sadness about a family situation.

Ⓑ They show a change of opinion about Ms. Gruwell.

Ⓒ They explain why the war in Sarajevo is still important today.

Ⓓ They show a connection to the writers whose books they read.

Directions: Read question 15. Write your answer on a separate sheet of paper.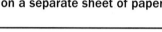

15

I'm beginning to realize that Anne Frank, Zlata Filipovic, and I have a lot in common. We all seem to be trapped in some sort of a cage. Anne's cage was the secret annex she and her family hid in, and the attic where she spent most of her time. Zlata's cage was the basement she had to use for shelter, away from bombs. My cage is my own house.

What important idea do the details in this paragraph from "The Freedom Writers Diary" relate? Support your answer with text evidence.

"Freedom Writers Diary" and "Strength, Courage, Wisdom" Open Book

Directions: Questions 16-22 are about "Strength, Courage, and Wisdom." Read each question and choose the best answer. You may look at the selection on pages 209–210 to help you answer the questions.

LITERARY ANALYSIS

16 Song lyrics are most like

Ⓐ a diary.

Ⓑ a poem.

Ⓒ an interview.

Ⓓ a news report.

17 Word choices that set the tone of a song

Ⓐ determine the song's structure.

Ⓑ express the attitude of the singer.

Ⓒ must be repeated to make their importance clear.

Ⓓ share the same sounds as other words in the song.

18 In the Bridge, the singer repeats the words "Let it be" to create a feeling of

Ⓐ hope.

Ⓑ surprise.

Ⓒ excitement.

Ⓓ cheerfulness.

COMPREHENSION

19 What does the Pre-Chorus describe?

Ⓐ a desire to hide

Ⓑ a need to take risks

Ⓒ a wish to help others

Ⓓ a decision to act on faith

20 The singer's new strength comes from

Ⓐ her music.

Ⓑ her ancestors.

Ⓒ within herself.

Ⓓ members of her community.

21 In this song, the speaker's emotions change from

Ⓐ anger to joy.

Ⓑ fear to triumph.

Ⓒ disgust to desire.

Ⓓ sadness to acceptance.

Directions: Read question 22. Write your answer on a separate sheet of paper.

22
> Inside my head there lives a dream that I want to see in the sun.
> Behind my eyes there lives a me that I've been hiding for much too long.

Think about the word choices in these lyrics from "Strength, Courage, and Wisdom." How does Arie show that there is a difference between the outer world and her inner thoughts?

15m

DONE!

EDGE Level C

Name _____ Date _____

Student Profile: Cluster Tests

Directions: Use the **Answer Key** and **Scoring Guides** on pages 140, 141, and 142 to score Cluster Tests 1, 2, and 3 respectively. Circle the item number of each correct answer below. Then multiply items correct by points. Include the rubric scores for the constructed-response items. Calculate the overall test score by adding to 100. To gauge mastery for a particular tested skill or Common Core Standard, review the Cluster Test and Unit Test results.

Cluster 1   Date _____

Subtest	Tested Skill	Item Analysis		Test Scores
		Item Numbers	**Mastery**	**No. Correct x Points = Score**
Key Vocabulary	Key Vocabulary L.9-10.6	1 2 3 4 5 6 7 8	6 out of 8 + −	_____ x 4 = _____ /32
Literary Analysis	Analyze Text Features RI.9-10.7	9 10 11 12	3 out of 4 + −	_____ x 4 = _____ /16
	Analyze Development of Ideas RI.9-10.3	16 17 18	2 out of 3 + −	_____ x 4 = _____ /12
Comprehension	Comprehension RI.9-10.10	13 14 15 19 20 21	4 out of 5 + −	_____ x 4 = _____ /20
Constructed Response	Use Text Evidence RI.9-10.1; RI.9-10.10; W.9-10.9	Rubric Scores Item 15 _____ + Item 22 _____ = _____		= _____ /20

Overall Score (Add Points Earned)   _____ /100

Cluster 2   Date _____

Subtest	Tested Skill	Item Analysis		Test Scores
		Item Numbers	**Mastery**	**No. Correct x Points = Score**
Key Vocabulary	Key Vocabulary L.9-10.6	1 2 3 4 5 6 7 8	6 out of 8 + −	_____ x 4 = _____ /32
Literary Analysis	Analyze Development of Ideas RI.9-10.3	9 10 11	3 out of 4 + −	_____ x 4 = _____ /16
	Relate Ideas RI.9-10.3	16 17 18	2 out of 3 + −	_____ x 4 = _____ /12
Comprehension	Comprehension RI.9-10.10	12 13 14 19 20 21	4 out of 5 + −	_____ x 4 = _____ /20
Constructed Response	Use Text Evidence RI.9-10.1; RI.9-10.10; W.9-10.9	Rubric Scores Item 15 _____ + Item 22 _____ = _____		= _____ /20

Overall Score (Add Points Earned)   _____ /100

Cluster 3   Date _____

Subtest	Tested Skill	Item Analysis		Test Scores
		Item Numbers	**Mastery**	**No. Correct x Points = Score**
Key Vocabulary	Key Vocabulary L.9-10.6	1 2 3 4 5 6 7 8	6 out of 8 + −	_____ x 4 = _____ /32
Literary Analysis	Relate Ideas RI.9-10.3	9 10 11	2 out of 3 + −	_____ x 4 = _____ /12
	Analyze Style: Word Choice RL.9-10.4	16 17 18	2 out of 3 + −	_____ x 4 = _____ /12
Comprehension	Main Idea and Details RL.9-10.2, RI.9-10.2	12 13 14 19 20 21	5 out of 6 + −	_____ x 4 = _____ /24
Constructed Response	Use Text Evidence RL.9-10.1; RL.9-10.10; RI.9-10.1; RI.9-10.10; W.9-10.9	Rubric Scores Item 15 _____ + Item 22 _____ = _____		= _____ /20

Overall Score (Add Points Earned)   _____ /100

EDGE Level C

UNIT 2

Language Acquisition Rubrics

Cluster 1
DESCRIBE A PROCESS
Pair Talk ▶ page 158

Directions: Pair students. Give them a few moments to consider the task. Partners should then take turns describing an everyday task.

Language Function | 1   2   3   4

What to look for:
how well the student describes a process with words such as *first, next, then, after that,* and *finally.* Student should provide short descriptions and explanations and use precise verbs.

Cluster 2
DESCRIBE PEOPLE AND ACTIONS
Pair Talk ▶ page 184

Directions: Pair students. Give them a few moments to review the selections and write down notes. Partners should then take turns describing characters and guessing which character is being described.

Language Function | 1   2   3   4

What to look for:
how well the student describes people and actions using details, descriptive adjectives, action verbs, comparisons, and sensory words.

Cluster 3
ELABORATE IN A DESCRIPTION
Group Share ▶ page 212

Directions: Group students. Give each student a few moments to choose a person from the selection. As each student describes the person, the group should help elaborate on the description.

Language Function | 1   2   3   4

What to look for:
how well the student elaborates by adding details and using adjectives, examples, and clauses with words such as *because, since, after, before,* and *although.* Student should also use relative pronouns such as *that, which, who, whom,* and *whose.*

	Language Function Rubric
4	Student effectively performs the function.
3	Student performs the function.
2	Student does not adequately perform the function.
1	Student makes no attempt or offers a non-verbal response.

UNIT 2

Reading and Literary Analysis

Directions: Read each question and choose the best answer.

1 Read the sentences.

> Lisa was despondent about moving to a new city, and her best friend felt miserable about it, too. It was the worst thing that could have happened.

Based on clues in the sentences, what does despondent mean?

A sad

B angry

C excited

D surprised

2 Read the sentences.

> Aunt Jo was an eccentric dresser. For example, she mixed and matched colors and styles in a way that most people found odd.

Based on clues in the sentences, what does eccentric mean?

A fancy

B casual

C unusual

D expensive

3 Read the sentences.

> The musician did not brag or boast about her many awards for playing the piano. Instead, she was rather shy and demure.

Based on clues in the sentences, what does demure mean?

A sure

B bored

C modest

D delighted

4 Read the sentences.

> A dog that barks all the time, begs for food at the table, and jumps on guests can exasperate its owner. In other words, the dog can cause the owner to lose all patience.

Based on clues in the sentences, what does exasperate mean?

A train

B annoy

C excuse

D appreciate

GO ON

Reading and Literary Analysis, *continued*

Directions: Questions 5–10 are about "What Makes a Genius?" Read the selection. Then read each question and choose the best answer.

What Makes a Genius?

Questioning Genius

What makes a genius? Is it something people are born with? Is it a really high score on an intelligence test? I have often wondered what makes someone a genius. Sometimes I have even fantasized about being a genius. In fact, I think that fantasizing about being a genius taught me something of its true nature. Genius is a characteristic applied to a person by other people.

This is easy to see with scientific inventions. If the invention affects society in a <u>profound</u> way, people view the inventor as a genius. It is the usefulness of the Internet, printing press, and light bulb that make them, and their creators, so great.

Communicating Genius

But some ideas are more abstract. For example, when Nicolaus Copernicus came up with his model of the solar system and claimed that the earth revolves around the sun rather than the sun revolving around the earth, he had a lot of explaining to do because his theory

Copernicus proposed the idea of a heliocentric universe in the 16th century, and Galileo was criticized for the same ideas in the 17th century.

challenged thousands of years of scientific knowledge. It may have been a hard idea to convey at the time, but it is now seen as a <u>momentous</u> scientific discovery.

Unfortunately, sometimes more abstract ideas carry consequences. Galileo Galilei, who believed in Copernicus's astronomical ideas, was ordered by the church not to teach or defend his theories about the sun. Galileo stuck to his convictions and wrote a book about sun-centered astronomy. He had to stand trial, he was put under house arrest, and his book was banned. Galileo was not seen as a genius until enough people understood his ideas. Genius is largely dependent on the ability to effectively communicate ideas. And the ideas do not have to be complex.

Painting Genius

I see this all the time in art. Take Jackson Pollock, one of America's most famous painters, for example. I remember traveling to New York and going to The Museum of Modern Art just after I graduated from high school. There I stood in front of this gigantic Pollock painting densely covered in colorful drips and splatters. It seemed beautiful to me. I wondered what would possess someone to create a painting like that.

"What a bunch of garbage!" The voice startled me. Next to me was a man about forty years old. "My five-year-old daughter could do that," he claimed. "I should put some of her paintings up on a wall and charge millions of dollars for them."

Hmmm, I thought to myself. Clearly, I saw more technique in Pollock's paintings than the guy standing next to me saw. But the guy had a point. It was just a bunch of paint deliberately splattered on a big canvas. And even though I liked it, I still wondered to myself: Why had he made such a painting? How had he come up with the idea?

I thought about it more. Pollock is called an abstract expressionist. He is not the only one. He was part of an artistic movement in the mid-twentieth century called Abstract Expressionism. Many of the famous painters

Reading and Literary Analysis, *continued*

knew each other. In fact, Pollock's wife, Lee Krasner, was one of them. I imagined what they must have talked about at dinner.

I ruled out the possibility that Pollock and all of his friends were simply crazy. There were too many of them for that. And people took this art seriously. Here it was in a museum! *Somebody* thought it was important. Why? Why had painters become famous for paintings that had no objects in them? If the paintings were about emotions, what made one better than the next?

Researching Genius

This was going to require research. I found out that abstract painting began in the early 1900s with the Russian painter Wassily Kandinsky. A lot of art historians talked about the invention of the camera as having a huge impact on painters. You see, painters

Jackson Pollock at work.

used to make a living painting portraits and landscapes. But once the camera was invented, people didn't need painters to make portraits. Cameras were faster. They produced results that were more realistic.

In some ways, painters reacted by making art that was less realistic. They still tried to represent things, but rather than trying to represent a tree or a face, they focused on painting emotions and thoughts. That's why it is called abstract painting rather than representational painting.

So, Pollock was part of a *tradition* of painters. This seemed important, and he made more sense to me once I understood this. I started to think more about history. The Abstract Expressionists created a certain kind of art at a certain time in history. Pollock was seen as a genius, but only in relation to what he was reacting to at that particular moment. The idea is only important as long as it can be communicated to the public.

Recognizing Genius

In some cases, the public will not recognize a genius. An example of this is the man next to me in the museum who thought his daughter could do what Pollock did. In truth, she couldn't. Her art was not a part of historical events the way Pollock's was. But who knows? Maybe she will be a future genius. I don't know what the future will bring. Maybe in a hundred years everyone will understand that Pollock was a genius in the same way that everyone now understands that Copernicus and Galileo were geniuses. I do know that it's a collective decision though. It can't be made by just one person. Genius is about more than the individual.

Art Timeline

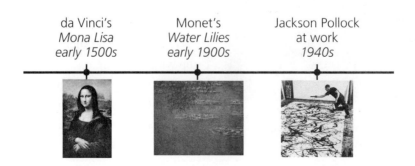

da Vinci's
Mona Lisa
early 1500s

Monet's
Water Lilies
early 1900s

Jackson Pollock
at work
1940s

GO ON

Reading and Literary Analysis, *continued*

5 The author develops and relates ideas in this selection primarily to

A tell the life story of a genius.

B describe how to act like a genius.

C compare a genius to another person.

D discuss what it means to be a genius.

6 Which paragraph shows that the ideas in this selection are developed through a first-person point of view?

A paragraph 1

B paragraph 2

C paragraph 3

D paragraph 4

7 The art timeline in the selection suggests that over time, artists became

A more interested in painting pictures of people.

B more interested in painting scenes from nature.

C less interested in painting with different colors.

D less interested in painting things to appear real.

8 Why does the author include a photo of Jackson Pollock working on one of his paintings?

A to help readers understand what Abstract Expressionism is

B to show the influence that Lee Krasner had on Jackson Pollock

C to support the idea that the best paintings are ones that show emotion instead of objects

D to support the idea that most people prefer representational painting over abstract painting

9 If a story is <u>profound</u>, it means the story is filled with

A hope.

B humor.

C conflict.

D meaning.

10 <u>Momentous</u> means

A finally finished.

B slightly different.

C extremely important.

D lasting only a short time.

Directions: Read question 11. Write your answer on a separate sheet of paper.

11 People often are slow to accept the ideas of a genius. Find two examples from the text to support this statement.

UNIT 2

GO ON

EDGE Level C

Reading and Literary Analysis, *continued*

Directions: Questions 12–16 are about "Acting Called to Her." Read the selection. Then read each question and choose the best answer.

Acting Called to Her
Though she could not hear, she answered back.

Maybe my way of communicating through sign language made me more in tune with my body and how it moved. Who knows? I just know that when I saw a stage for the first time, I wanted to be on it.

Every one of us is different in some way. Those of us who are more different have to put more effort into convincing the less different that we can do the same thing they can, just differently. Everybody's got a job to do. I do mine as best I can.

—Marlee Matlin
Academy-Award winning actress, who is deaf

At eighteen months old, Marlee Matlin contracted a fever caused by *roseola*, a form of measles. She has been deaf ever since and has no memory of what it is like to hear a sound. "In my own mind, I really have no sense of what you can hear. Hearing is something that I am really not familiar with," she said in an interview.

Despite the silence of her world, Matlin accomplished something that had never been done before. She became a prominent actress and has worked steadily in film and television for over twenty-five years.

At the age of twenty-one, she won the Academy Award for Best Actress for her performance in *Children of a Lesser God*. It was her film debut, portraying a distraught young deaf woman. Her character did not speak a single word.

No one achieves the impossible alone. Matlin has often expressed her tremendous gratitude for the support that helped her challenge expectations. Her parents were with her every step of the way. They learned sign language and raised her with an understanding that she could do everything everyone else could do. She believed them.

Matlin's parents enrolled her in a local public school rather than <u>contemplate</u> sending her away to a special school for the deaf. For the most part, Matlin "mainstreamed" well, though she admits it was sometimes difficult to integrate with hearing children. She didn't have many people to talk to in sign language. But she was taught to let no difficulty become an obstacle. During times of loneliness in the first or second grade, she acted out different characters in the bathroom mirror, using sign language. Her strong, young spirit already held the conviction that self-expression and creative communication were her birthright.

Then, when Matlin was seven years old, she had a momentous experience. She went onstage for the first time, at summer camp, and discovered she loved making people laugh. After camp, she walked boldly into an audition for *The Wizard of Oz* in a children's theater at the Chicago Center on Deafness. The director cast her as Dorothy. She went on to participate in many more plays at the Center. Then in 1977, when she was thirteen, she was "discovered."

Actress Marlee Matlin in *Children of a Lesser God,* 1986.

A television actor named Henry Winkler, who was well known at that time, saw her perform. He was so moved by her performance that he went backstage to encourage her to pursue a career in acting. Matlin recounts, "I told Henry Winkler I wanted to act. He said, 'Do it, and don't let anyone stand in your way.'" Along the road ahead, she had to <u>contend</u> with many naysayers who said her dream of acting in television and film was not possible. But Matlin went on to build a trailblazing career.

She has starred in numerous films and television shows as characters who could hear as well as characters who could not. She has graced the covers of top magazines and performed the National Anthem at the Super Bowl in sign language. She played tough,

GO ON ➡

Reading and Literary Analysis, *continued*

tenacious, street-smart characters contrary to the Hollywood stereotype that disabled people are vulnerable and powerless. She even started her own production company, Solo One Productions, and has been the executive producer for several TV movies. Matlin has enjoyed a magnificent career as an actress and blasted down barriers for other deaf actors in Hollywood.

She also works with many charities that benefit people in the deaf community, and she is very much an advocate for their success. "I hope that through my example I can help change attitudes on deafness and prove that we can really do everything, except hear," she says. Marlee Matlin inspires every person, hearing and non-hearing, by her sheer will and profound gifts.

⸻⚬⸻

12 The author develops and relates ideas in this selection primarily to

  A tell the life story of an actor.

  B persuade readers to try acting.

  C share the secrets of good acting.

  D describe a meeting with an actor.

13 Which is the best summary of this quote?

> *Every one of us is different in some way. Those of us who are more different have to put more effort into convincing the less different that we can do the same thing they can, just differently. Everybody's got a job to do. I do mine as best I can.*

  A Some people are just different.

  B People who work hard deserve success.

  C A person feels less different with a job to do.

  D Each person succeeds in his or her own way.

14 To <u>contemplate</u> means to

  A control.

  B consider.

  C continue.

  D confuse.

15 To <u>contend</u> is to

  A argue that something is true.

  B lift something off the ground.

  C confuse with something else.

  D bend something to a new shape.

Directions: Read question 16. Write your answer on a separate sheet of paper.

16 The author concludes by claiming that Marlee Matlin is an inspiration because of "her sheer will and profound gifts." Assess whether this is a valid, well-supported claim. Provide details from the text to support your ideas.

GO ON

Reading and Literary Analysis, *continued*

Directions: Questions 17–25 are about "A Jazz Legend." Read the selection. Then read each question and choose the best answer.

A Jazz Legend

Jazz music is difficult to play for two specific reasons. First, jazz is technically difficult. One must be an expert at his or her instrument. Perhaps more important, one must have an individual sound. In order to succeed, jazz musicians have to find ways to be original. What makes it really difficult is that when you play music, you still have to communicate with people. You can't be such an extreme individual that no one understands you. A jazz musician has to balance being an individual with being aware of what the audience expects. In many ways, John Coltrane's music and life represent this balance perfectly.

Coltrane was born in North Carolina in 1926, and he had a happy childhood until seventh grade when his father died. His mother had to support the family by going to work. Soon after this, Coltrane began playing the saxophone. Even at an early age, he was very <u>disciplined</u> and practiced <u>perpetually</u>. When he was sixteen, his family moved to Philadelphia and soon after that he was drafted into the Navy. He played in the Navy band and was exposed to cutting-edge jazz music. Although he had mastered the saxophone by this time, he still did not have his own sound.

After getting out of the Navy, Coltrane made a living playing music. He still practiced a lot and studied with different teachers. He sounded really good, but there was nothing distinct about his playing. Finally, in 1955 a famous trumpet player named Miles Davis heard Coltrane and decided to hire him to play in his band.

Davis was considered a natural. He had played with some of the most well-known jazz musicians by the time he was eighteen. However, Coltrane was almost thirty years old before he got into the Miles Davis group. Part of what makes him so inspiring is that Coltrane got into one of the best jazz bands because he was so dedicated to practicing. As part of the Miles Davis band, Coltrane developed his own voice and became known as one of the most <u>innovative</u> players in jazz.

Saxophones come in different pitches or tones such as soprano, alto, tenor, and baritone. Coltrane made the soprano sax popular with jazz players.

Unfortunately, during this time, Coltrane also started using drugs. As a <u>consequence</u>, his playing suffered, and he got fired from the band for being irresponsible. Coltrane's feelings were really hurt by getting fired, so he decided to quit all drugs and focus on music. He studied with a great piano player named Thelonious Monk, and he began listening to all kinds of music from all over the world.

After this, Coltrane made a record called *Giant Steps*. On *Giant Steps*, his saxophone playing was so strong that people regarded him as the best saxophone player in the world. He knew so much about music by this time that other players sometimes had a hard time keeping up with him.

In 1960, he recorded a version of the popular song

GO ON ▶

Reading and Literary Analysis, continued

"My Favorite Things" from *The Sound of Music*. But Coltrane's version didn't sound anything like the musical. There was no singing and he used musical ideas from India. In spite of the unusual sounds, the record was a hit, and it made him popular even with people who didn't usually listen to jazz.

Because Coltrane was so popular and innovative, many people were interested in what he was going to do next. He continued to integrate new musical ideas with what he knew. His band was considered one of the best in jazz. Still, he continued to practice nonstop. He explored new sounds, and sometimes critics and audiences didn't understand what he was doing. But even in the face of criticism, Coltrane was such a strong musician that he continued to explore. He was very interested in younger players and tried to understand their musical ideas too. His unending desire to learn everything he could about music continued until he died of cancer in 1967.

Even though he was only forty when he died, John Coltrane is one of the most important figures in all of jazz music. He balanced technical skill with an individual sound. His dedication to practicing and learning and his ability to overcome life's struggles make him an inspiration to musicians and music lovers everywhere.

---

17 Which fact about the selection is the **best** clue that it is nonfiction biography?

A   The topic has to do with jazz music.

B   The details help to support the main idea.

C   The author relates both facts and opinions.

D   The events are related in the order they happened.

18 According to the author, what important idea does John Coltrane help to illustrate about jazz?

A   To enjoy jazz, you have to ignore what other people think.

B   To understand jazz, you have to study the history of music.

C   To play jazz well, you must have skill and an original sound.

D   To be a jazz success, you must play with other jazz players.

19 Look at the picture of John Coltrane in the selection. The caption suggests that the soprano saxophone was

A   what Coltrane had played as a young boy.

B   just invented when Coltrane began to play.

C   used by Coltrane because of its roots in jazz.

D   one of the new sounds Coltrane brought to jazz.

20 Which important idea from the passage does the picture of Coltrane **best** help develop?

A   Coltrane played many kinds of music.

B   Coltrane took playing the saxophone very seriously.

C   Coltrane had to overcome many obstacles throughout his lifetime.

D   Coltrane became popular even with people who did not like jazz.

GO ON

Reading and Literary Analysis, *continued*

21 If a person is <u>disciplined</u>, it means the person is

   A self-controlled.

   B self-confident.

   C disappointed.

   D dismayed.

22 <u>Perpetually</u> means

   A soon.

   B lately.

   C always.

   D quickly.

23 If an idea is <u>innovative</u>, it means the idea is

   A practical.

   B original.

   C innocent.

   D complicated.

24 A <u>consequence</u> means

   A a reason.

   B an effect.

   C an agreement.

   D a conversation.

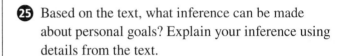

Directions: Read question 25. Write your answer on a separate sheet of paper.

25 Based on the text, what inference can be made about personal goals? Explain your inference using details from the text.

Grammar and Writing

Directions: Read the composition. It contains errors. Then read each question and choose the best answer.

The Purple Heart Battalion

(1) During World War II, when the United States was at war with Germany and Japan, many Americans were suspicious of people of German or Japanese descent. **(2)** Many Americans, including those in the government, thought that people whose parents had come from Germany or Japan sympathized with the countries of their parents' birth. **(3)** Unfortunately, president Franklin D. Roosevelt forced Japanese Americans to move from their homes into camps for the rest of the war. **(4)** We had to give up their jobs and homes simply because other people thought they could not or would not be loyal American citizens.

(5) Ironically, Japanese Americans fought for the United States in World War II. **(6)** Not only did they prove themselves to be loyal, they rocked the battlefield. **(7)** Their story began when the Japanese attacked Pearl Harbor, Hawaii. **(8)** These second generation Japanese Americans, called Nisei, lost their jobs because of the climate of suspicion. **(9)** However, they saw themselves as loyal Americans, and they volunteered for military service. **(10)** They were assigned to the 442nd Regimental Combat Team. **(11)** A second Nisei unit, the 100th Battalion, was largely formed from members of the Hawaiian National Guard. **(12)** The 100th Battalion was later merged into the 442nd.

(13) General Dwight D. Eisenhower, who became president after the war, was offered the Nisei units for his army. **(14)** He didn't want them, so they wound up under the command of General Clark. **(15)** General Clark's army was preparing to invade Italy, where they would be fighting the Germans. **(16)** The Nisei fought so well and so bravely, General Clark asked the army to send as many Nisei as possible!

(17) The Nisei sacrificed a lot for their country. **(18)** Some made the ultimate sacrifice—their lives. **(19)** Their bravery in battle won them respect from their commanders and a legendary reputation. **(20)** People revere the 442nd Regimental Combat Team along with the 100th Battalion as one of the most decorated units in military history. **(21)** Sometimes, the 100th Battalion is referred to as the "Purple Heart Battalion," named after the medal soldiers receive when they are wounded. **(22)** Daniel Inouye, who lost an arm fighting with the 442nd, is now a United States Senator from the state of Hawaii. **(23)** Today, there be a monument in Los Angeles to their courageous service.

Grammar and Writing, *continued*

1 What change, if any, should be made to sentence 3?

A Change the comma to a semicolon

B Change *president* to **President**

C Change *to* to **too**

D No change

2 In sentence 4, the word <u>We</u> should be changed to

A I

B He

C They

D No change

3 To match the tone of the composition, the underlined words in sentence 6 should be changed to

A were really good soldiers

B fought bravely for their country

C showed everyone what they could do

D No change

4 Which sentence has the most appropriate style to begin the third paragraph?

A Still, people doubted them.

B Still, they kind of freaked people out.

C Still, people were hung up about their race.

D Still, some people felt uptight around them.

5 In sentence 14, the word <u>He</u> should be changed to

A I

B We

C They

D No change

6 What change, if any, should be made to sentence 18?

A Change *sacrifice* to **Sacrifice**

B Remove the dash

C Change *their* to **there**

D No change

7 In sentence 20, the word <u>revere</u> should be changed to

A reverse

B reveres

C revering

D No change

8 In sentence 23, the word <u>be</u> should be changed to

A is

B am

C are

D No change

Grammar and Writing, *continued*

Directions: Read the composition. It contains errors. Then read each question and choose the best answer.

Sports Car

(1) One day, my dad buys an old sports car. (2) The idea is that <u>they</u> and my brothers are going to restore it. (3) My dad says my brothers can drive it to school and use it on dates—if they help.

(4) "I want to help, too," I said. (5) I am the only girl and the youngest child. (6) They think of me as the baby.

(7) "It's too dangerous for you, honey," says my dad. (8) "It's going to be really dirty, nasty work."

(9) "There are lots of heavy car <u>things</u> to pick up. (10) You can't help us," says Jake, the youngest of my two brothers.

(11) "But I want to drive the car, too," I protest.

(12) "Mandy, you're twelve," says my mom. (13) "You won't be able to do that for a while."

(14) I know that's not fair. (15) So when my dad and brothers work on the car, <u>I</u> hang around by the garage, hoping they'll ask me to help. (16) I ask if I can get tools for them.

(17) "Go in the house," my brothers complain. (18) When I don't, my mom gets involved.

(19) "Mandy, go in the house now." (20) She is always <u>tell</u> me to stay out of their way.

(21) One day, my mom, dad, and older brother Justin leave to run errands. (22) My Dad tells Jake not to work on the car until he finishes his homework. (23) Jake is mad because he doesn't want to wait to put the new wheels on the car. (24) When my dad and Justin leave, I hear Jake go outside, and I follow him.

(25) "Your going to get in trouble," I say.

(26) "Leave me alone, Mandy!" he shouts.

(27) So I go back inside. (28) A few minutes later, screams are <u>coming</u> from the garage. (29) I race out and find Jake partially trapped under the car. (30) One of the jacks holding the car up had slipped. (31) Without even thinking about it, I slid the jack back into place and raised the car. (32) It was hard to work the jack handle, but I was able to get the car high enough for Jake to roll out.

(33) Now, they let me help with the car, but it takes more than muscle to get the job done.

GO ON

EDGE Level C

Grammar and Writing, *continued*

9 Which sentence has the most appropriate style to begin the story?

   A Cars are way cool.

   B My dad and my brothers love working on cars.

   C This is a story about how I am stronger than people think.

   D I will now describe how I saved my brother from serious injury.

10 In sentence 2, the word they should be changed to

   A I

   B he

   C we

   D No change

11 In sentence 9, which word is the **best** way to express the meaning of the word things?

   A parts

   B pieces

   C chunks

   D engines

12 In sentence 15, the word I should be changed to

   A we

   B she

   C they

   D No change

13 In sentence 20, the word tell should be changed to

   A toll

   B tells

   C telling

   D No change

14 What change, if any, should be made to sentence 22?

   A Change *Dad* to **dad**

   B Put a comma after *Jake*

   C Change *homework* to **home work**

   D No change

15 What change, if any, should be made to sentence 25?

   A Change *Your* to **You're**

   B Put the comma after the quotation marks

   C Change *I* to **i**

   D No change

16 In sentence 28, the word coming should be changed to

   A came

   B comes

   C come

   D No change

UNIT 2

GO ON

Grammar and Writing, *continued*

Directions: Read the following writing prompt and write a composition. Write on separate sheets of paper. Use the Writer's Checklist to make sure that you do your best work.

Prompt

Sometimes other people help us overcome obstacles.

Write about a time when another person's help made a difference to you.

Writer's Checklist

- ☑ Write about all parts of the prompt.
- ☑ Present a clear central idea, and stay focused on it.
- ☑ Organize your composition from its introduction to its conclusion.
- ☑ Use transitions to connect your thoughts for the reader.
- ☑ Present meaningful ideas, and support them with specific information.
- ☑ Use appropriate words and a variety of sentence structures.
- ☑ Proofread and edit your writing for grammar, usage, mechanics, and spelling.

DONE!

EDGE Level C

Student Profile: Unit Tests

Directions: Use the **Answer Key** on page 143 to score the multiple-choice items. Circle the item number of each correct answer below. Calculate test scores by assigning one point for each correct answer. Use the scoring guides on page 143 to score the constructed-response items. Use the Good Writing Traits Rubric on page 122 to score the written composition. Total the scores and calculate the % score or use the conversion chart. To gauge mastery for a particular tested skill or Common Core Standard, review the Cluster Test and Unit Test results.

Reading and Literary Analysis

Category	Tested Skill	Item Analysis		Test Scores
		Item Numbers	Mastery	Points: Earned / Total
Vocabulary	Use Context Clues L.9-10.4	1 2 3 4	3 out of 4 + −	_____ / 4
	Key Vocabulary L.9-10.6	9 10 14 15 21 22 23 24	6 out of 8 + −	_____ / 8
Literary Analysis	Analyze Development of Ideas RI.9-10.3	5 6 12 17	3 out of 4 + −	_____ / 4
	Analyze Text Features RI.9-10.7	7 8 19 20	3 out of 4 + −	_____ / 4
Comprehension	Comprehension RI.9-10.10	13 18	1 out of 2 + −	_____ / 2
Constructed Response	Use Text Evidence RI.9-10.1; RI.9-10.10; W.9-10.9	Rubric Score Item 11 _____ + Item 16 _____ + Item 25 _____ = _____		_____ / 12

Overall Score (Points Earned ÷ Total Points x 100 = %)   _____ ÷ 34 = _____%

Grammar and Writing

Category	Tested Skill	Item Analysis		Test Scores
		Item Numbers	Mastery	Points: Earned / Total
Grammar	Subject Pronouns L.9-10.1	2 5 10 12	3 out of 4 + −	_____ / 4
	Subject-Verb Agreement L.9-10.1	7 8 13 16	3 out of 4 + −	_____ / 4
Revising and Editing	Voice and Style W.9-10.5	3 4 9 11	3 out of 4 + −	_____ / 4
	Grammar, Mechanics, and Usage L.9-10.2	1 6 14 15	3 out of 4 + −	_____ / 4
Written Composition (Narrative) W.9-10.3; W.9-10.4; W.9-10.10	Focus and Unity	Rubric Scores: _____ / 4		_____ / 20
	Organization	_____ / 4		
	Development of Ideas	_____ / 4 =		
	Voice and Style	_____ / 4		
	Written Conventions	_____ / 4		

Overall Score (Points Earned ÷ Total Points x 100 = %)   _____ ÷ 36 = _____%

UNIT 2

Project Rubric: A Press Conference

Score	Planning/Preparation	Content of Project	Delivery/Presentation	Collaboration
3 Great	• Reviews a variety of different press conferences on TV or on the Internet to learn more about the form. • Chooses a famous person who has obvious relevance to the Essential Question.	• Questions and answers are thoughtful and clearly address the Essential Question. • Answers are true to the personality of the person being interviewed. • Reporters ask a variety of different questions.	• The famous person is believable to the audience. • The press conference runs within the allotted amount of time. • All group members participate in the press conference.	• Works well with others. • Assumes a clear role and related responsibilities.
2 Good	• Reviews a few press conferences on TV or on the Internet to learn more about the form. • Chooses a famous person who has some relevance to the Essential Question.	• Questions and answers are mostly thoughtful and somewhat address the Essential Question. • Answers are somewhat true to the personality of the person being interviewed. • Reporters ask a few different types of questions.	• The famous person is somewhat believable to the audience. • The press conference runs nearly within the allotted amount of time. • Most group members participate in the press conference.	• Works with others most of the time. • Sometimes has difficulty sharing decisions and responsibilities.
1 Needs Work	• Reviews one or no press conferences on TV or on the Internet to learn more about the form. • Chooses a famous person who has no relevance to the Essential Question.	• Questions and answers are not thoughtful and do not address the Essential Question. • Answers are not at all true to the personality of the person being interviewed. • Reporters ask the same types of questions over and over again.	• The famous person is not at all believable to the audience. • The press conference does not run anywhere near the allotted amount of time. • Only one or two group members participate in the press conference.	• Cannot work with others in most situations. • Cannot share decisions or responsibilities.

Self-Assessment

Directions: Circle the numbers that show how much you agree or disagree with each sentence. Then answer the question below. If necessary, use the back of the page.

	Not Yet	With Help	Most of the Time	Very Well
1 When I read narrative nonfiction, I understand the author's purpose and point of view.	1	2	3	4
2 When I read nonfiction, I understand the diagrams, captions, and other text features.	1	2	3	4
3 I understand the features of an interview, a news feature, and song lyrics.	1	2	3	4
4 I know how to determine importance by relating main ideas and details and by summarizing.	1	2	3	4
5 When I find a word I do not know, I look for context clues to help me understand the meaning.	1	2	3	4
6 I know how to write using subject pronouns and present tense verbs.	1	2	3	4
7 I know how to revise my writing for voice and style.	1	2	3	4

8 Think of one thing you learned really well in this unit. Tell how you will use this the next time you read or write.

_____

_____

_____

_____

_____

_____

_____

_____

_____

_____

EDGE Level C

Reader Reflection

Directions: Answer questions 1–10. If necessary, use the back of the page.

"Amigo Brothers"

1 What did you learn about author's style, specifically in word choice, that will help you the next time you read a short story?

2 Explain how making inferences will help you the next time you read short stories.

3 Write what you liked and did not like about "Amigo Brothers." Include examples from the short story.

I liked...

I did not like...

4 Are you interested in reading more writing by Piri Thomas? _____ Yes _____ No

5 Are you interested in reading more short stories about loyalty? _____ Yes _____ No

"Lean on Me"

6 What did you learn about rhyme scheme that will help you the next time you read song lyrics?

7 Explain how making inferences will help you the next time you read song lyrics.

8 Write what you liked and did not like about "Lean on Me." Include examples from the song lyrics.

I liked...

I did not like...

9 Are you interested in reading more lyrics by Bill Withers? _____ Yes _____ No

10 Are you interested in reading more lyrics by other songwriters? _____ Yes _____ No

"Amigo Brothers" and "Lean on Me"

Closed Book

Directions: Read each question and choose the best answer.

KEY VOCABULARY

1 An acknowledgment is something done to express
- Ⓐ thanks.
- Ⓑ surprise.
- Ⓒ amazement.
- Ⓓ disappointment.

2 Devastating means
- Ⓐ doubtful.
- Ⓑ desirable.
- Ⓒ destructive.
- Ⓓ demanding.

3 To dispel means to
- Ⓐ scatter.
- Ⓑ support.
- Ⓒ discuss.
- Ⓓ discover.

4 To evade means to
- Ⓐ insist.
- Ⓑ avoid.
- Ⓒ annoy.
- Ⓓ invade.

5 To improvise means to
- Ⓐ make a wish.
- Ⓑ improve a lot.
- Ⓒ figure out by yourself.
- Ⓓ create without planning.

6 To have an opponent means to have a
- Ⓐ neighbor.
- Ⓐ brother.
- Ⓒ buddy.
- Ⓓ rival.

7 Pensively means
- Ⓐ angrily.
- Ⓑ playfully.
- Ⓒ privately.
- Ⓓ thoughtfully.

8 To surge means to
- Ⓐ end quickly.
- Ⓑ suddenly get stronger.
- Ⓒ practice over and over.
- Ⓓ say something you do not mean.

Directions: Questions 9–15 are about "Amigo Brothers." Read each question and choose the best answer. You may look at the selection on pages 245–260 to help you answer the questions.

Open Book

LITERARY ANALYSIS

9 In a short story, the narrator's word choices
- Ⓐ create a formal or informal style.
- Ⓑ are the same for every character.
- Ⓒ are closely tied to the theme of the story.
- Ⓓ matter only when the story has a first-person point of view.

10 What words best describe the writing style of Piri Thomas in "Amigo Brothers"?
- Ⓐ detailed and formal
- Ⓑ cheerful and amusing
- Ⓒ colorful and full of feeling
- Ⓓ mysterious and suspenseful

GO ON

"Amigo Brothers" and "Lean on Me"

11 Which of these is part of the author's style in "Amigo Brothers"?

Ⓐ street dialogue

Ⓑ complex sentences

Ⓒ first-person point of view

Ⓓ formal sentence structure

COMPREHENSION

12 Felix and Antonio have different boxing styles because

Ⓐ they are mentally different.

Ⓑ they are physically different.

Ⓒ they have different training schedules.

Ⓓ they have different goals for competition.

13 Why do Felix and Antonio begin to train in separate gyms?

Ⓐ They need to watch special training films.

Ⓑ They hired new trainers at different gyms.

Ⓒ They want to treat each other as strangers.

Ⓓ They wish to keep their new fighting styles secret.

14 How are the Amigo Brothers loyal to each other?

Ⓐ They help each other get ready for the fight.

Ⓑ They remain friends before and after the fight.

Ⓒ They try not to hurt each other during the fight.

Ⓓ They ask friends to cheer for both of them during the fight.

Directions: Read question 15. Write your answer on a separate sheet of paper.

15

> He walked up some dark streets, deserted except for small pockets of wary-looking kids wearing gang colors. Despite the fact that he was Puerto Rican like them, they eyed him as a stranger to their turf. Felix did a fast shuffle, bobbing and weaving, while letting loose a torrent of blows that would demolish whatever got in its way. It seemed to impress the brothers, who went about their own business.
>
> Finding no takers, Felix decided to split to his aunt's. Walking the streets had not relaxed him, neither had the fight flick. All it had done was to stir him up. He let himself quietly into his Aunt Lucy's apartment and went straight to bed, falling into a fitful sleep with sounds of the gong for Round One.

Think about the narrator's word choices in this passage. How would you describe the style? What do the word choices help you understand about Felix? Give examples from the passage to support your answer.

GO ON

UNIT 3

"Amigo Brothers" and "Lean on Me"

Open Book

Directions: Questions 16–22 are about "Lean on Me." Read each question and choose the best answer. You may look at the selection on pages 262–263 to help you answer the questions.

LITERARY ANALYSIS

16 Rhyme scheme helps give a poem structure because it is based on a pattern of

Ⓐ how words sound.

Ⓑ what words mean.

Ⓒ how many letters are in a word.

Ⓓ whether letters are repeated in a word.

17 How many lines in the Chorus rhyme with the first line of the Chorus?

Ⓐ 1

Ⓑ 2

Ⓒ 3

Ⓓ 4

18 Which of these is true about the song lyrics?

Ⓐ Different verses have different rhyme schemes.

Ⓑ An internal rhyme scheme appears only in the verses.

Ⓒ The rhyme scheme of the verses and the chorus is the same.

Ⓓ The chorus has both an end rhyme scheme and an internal rhyme scheme.

COMPREHENSION

19 What is the message of the Chorus?

Ⓐ The future is full of hope.

Ⓑ Time is short so use it well.

Ⓒ We should depend on each other.

Ⓓ Friends are even more important than family.

20 Read this part of the lyrics.

> Please swallow your pride
> If I have things you need to borrow,
> For no one can fill those of your needs
> That you won't let show.

What do these lines mean?

Ⓐ Choose friends who can help fill your needs.

Ⓑ It is best to hide your feelings, even from your friends.

Ⓒ Friends cannot help if they do not know what you need.

Ⓓ People who have too much pride cannot find happiness.

21 What does the songwriter encourage people to do?

Ⓐ accept support

Ⓑ care for themselves

Ⓒ return things they borrow

Ⓓ spend time with their family

Directions: Read question 22. Write your answer on a separate sheet of paper.

22
> Sometimes in our lives we all have pain,
> We all have sorrow,
> But if we are wise
> We know that there's always tomorrow.

What end rhymes create the rhyme scheme of these lines? What is the rhyme scheme? How does it help structure this verse?

UNIT 3

DONE!

Reader Reflection

Directions: Answer questions 1–10. If necessary, use the back of the page.

"My Brother's Keeper"

1 What did you learn about author's style, specifically sentence structure, that will help you the next time you read a short story?

2 Explain how making inferences using a chart will help you the next time you read.

3 Write what you liked and did not like about "My Brother's Keeper." Include examples from the short story.

I liked...

I did not like...

4 Are you interested in reading more writing by Jay Bennett? _____ Yes _____ No

5 Are you interested in reading more short stories about family? _____ Yes _____ No

"What Price Loyalty?"

6 What did you learn about a writer's viewpoint that will help you the next time you read a news commentary?

7 Explain how making inferences to determine a writer's viewpoint will help you the next time you read a news commentary.

8 Write what you liked and did not like about "What Price Loyalty?" Include examples from the news commentary.

I liked...

I did not like...

9 Are you interested in reading more works by Gerald Pomper? _____ Yes _____ No

10 Are you interested in reading more news commentaries by other writers? _____ Yes _____ No

"My Brother's Keeper" and "What Price Loyalty?"

 Closed Book

Directions: Read each question and choose the best answer.

1 Abstract means

Ⓐ a feeling of regret.

Ⓑ an idea that is not concrete.

Ⓒ an ability to lead other people.

Ⓓ a response that is not appropriate.

2 To adhere to a plan means to

Ⓐ create it.

Ⓑ change it.

Ⓒ stick with it.

Ⓓ give up on it.

3 To advocate means to

Ⓐ allow.

Ⓑ locate.

Ⓒ rescue.

Ⓓ support.

4 To do something deliberately means to do it

Ⓐ alone.

Ⓑ on time.

Ⓒ for money.

Ⓓ on purpose.

5 Desolately means

Ⓐ sadly.

Ⓑ softly.

Ⓒ slowly.

Ⓓ secretly.

6 A dilemma is

Ⓐ a quality other people admire in you.

Ⓑ punishment for a crime you did not commit.

Ⓒ a situation that requires you to make a difficult choice.

Ⓓ the chance to do something over again to make it right.

7 Ethical means

Ⓐ loyal.

Ⓑ moral.

Ⓒ natural.

Ⓓ personal.

8 To reinforce means to

Ⓐ replace.

Ⓑ question.

Ⓒ introduce.

Ⓓ strengthen.

Directions: Questions 9–15 are about "My Brother's Keeper." Read each question and choose the best answer. You may look at the selection on pages 273–291 to help you answer the questions.

 Open Book

9 An author chooses a certain sentence structure in order to

Ⓐ create a style.

Ⓑ develop characters.

Ⓒ state the main idea.

Ⓓ express an opinion.

10 The author's use of questions in this story focuses the reader on the characters'

Ⓐ traits.

Ⓑ faults.

Ⓒ inner conflicts.

Ⓓ physical appearances.

GO ON ➤

EDGE Level C

"My Brother's Keeper" and "What Price Loyalty?"

Open Book

11 The author's use of short sentences helps to create a feeling of

Ⓐ fury.

Ⓑ caring.

Ⓒ tension.

Ⓓ jealousy.

COMPREHENSION

12 How are Ted and Jamie alike?

Ⓐ They are gentle and loving.

Ⓑ They are lost without their parents.

Ⓒ They are tired of each other's problems.

Ⓓ They are willing to do anything for their careers.

13 What event leads up to Ted's telephone call?

Ⓐ a bar fight

Ⓑ a hit-and-run accident

Ⓒ a football championship

Ⓓ a problem with the police

14 Why does Ted react by running away?

Ⓐ He is a coward with no concern for others.

Ⓑ He is worried about his future as an athlete.

Ⓒ He wants to hide the fact that he has been drinking.

Ⓓ He knows somebody else will help the injured man.

Directions: Read question 15. Write your answer on a separate sheet of paper.

15

> And all the time Jamie waited.
> Waited.
> For his older brother to tell him.
> And then he heard it.
> "I'm in trouble, Jamie."

Think about the sentence structure in this passage. How would you describe the author's style at this point? What feeling does this style create? Refer to other text details to support your answer.

UNIT 3

"My Brother's Keeper" and "What Price Loyalty?"

 Open Book

Directions: Questions 16–22 are about "What Price Loyalty?" Read each question and choose the best answer. You may look at the selection on pages 294–296 to help you answer the questions.

LITERARY ANALYSIS

16 What is the main purpose of a news commentary?

Ⓐ to provide a viewpoint about an event or issue

Ⓑ to tell an interesting story about something historic

Ⓒ to present the positive and negative sides of a story

Ⓓ to provide several viewpoints about something important

17 Which of these sentences uses opinionated language?

Ⓐ Often these loyalties reinforce each other.

Ⓑ In the Civil War, Northerners swore fealty to the federal union.

Ⓒ In the abstract, loyalty is a virtue; nobody advocates disloyalty.

Ⓓ We should be suspicious of glib claims of loyalty to principle.

18 Which of these statements expresses a viewpoint, or opinion, of the author?

Ⓐ Loyalty has been a concern throughout American history.

Ⓑ That is appropriate conduct for thinking men and women in a free land.

Ⓒ The Declaration of Independence was an act of disloyalty toward the British Crown.

Ⓓ Dissenters such as Martin Luther King, Jr., have been accused of disloyalty because they disobeyed the law.

19 The historical information in the commentary supports the author's viewpoint that

Ⓐ many heroes from history were actually disloyal.

Ⓑ loyalty to freedom is the most important form of loyalty.

Ⓒ there are many types of loyalty that must all be honored.

Ⓓ loyalties are complicated and must be examined in context.

COMPREHENSION

20 "What Price Loyalty?" examines

Ⓐ the role of loyalty in society.

Ⓑ what causes people to be disloyal.

Ⓒ why individuals should value loyalty.

Ⓓ why people should follow loyalty blindly.

21 According to Pomper, what should people do when their loyalties conflict?

Ⓐ stand by their friends

Ⓑ stick to their principles

Ⓒ determine what is lawful behavior

Ⓓ examine the consequences of each decision

Directions: Read question 22. Write your answer on a separate sheet of paper.

22

> We may get closer to resolving these conflicts if we recall a famous statement of loyalty—naval commander Stephen Decatur's toast, "Our country, right or wrong." Fifty-five years later, Carl Schurz, a United States general and United States senator, provided a better rule: "Our country, right or wrong. When right, to be kept right; when wrong, to be put right." That is appropriate conduct for thinking men and women in a free land.

What viewpoint does Pomper express in this paragraph? Use text evidence to explain how he makes that viewpoint clear.

UNIT 3

DONE!

EDGE Level C

Reader Reflection

Directions: Answer questions 1–9. If necessary, use the back of the page.

"The Hand of Fatima"

1 What did you learn about viewpoint in fiction that will help you the next time you read a short story?

2 Explain how making inferences and confirming with text evidence will help you the next time you read.

3 Write what you liked and did not like about "The Hand of Fatima." Include examples from the short story.

I liked...

I did not like...

4 Are you interested in reading more writing by Elsa Marston? _____ Yes   _____ No

"Old Ways, New World"

5 What did you learn about viewpoint in nonfiction that will help you the next time you read a news report?

6 Explain how making inferences using your own words to describe others' opinions will help you the next time you read a news report.

7 Write what you liked and did not like about "Old Ways, New World." Include examples from the news report.

I liked...

I did not like...

8 Are you interested in reading more works by Joseph Berger? _____ Yes   _____ No

9 Are you interested in reading more news reports by other writers? _____ Yes   _____ No

"The Hand of Fatima" and "Old Ways, New World"

Directions: Read each question and choose the best answer.

KEY VOCABULARY

1 To abolish something means to
Ⓐ get rid of it.
Ⓑ celebrate it.
Ⓒ learn from it.
Ⓓ try to forget it.

2 To admonish means to
Ⓐ admit.
Ⓑ scold.
Ⓒ break.
Ⓓ vanish.

3 Coherent means
Ⓐ long.
Ⓑ clear.
Ⓒ interesting.
Ⓓ necessary.

4 Conscientious means
Ⓐ sensitive and caring.
Ⓑ realistic and practical.
Ⓒ deserving and worthy.
Ⓓ careful and responsible.

5 To be controversial means to
Ⓐ affect many people.
Ⓑ contribute to society.
Ⓒ cause disagreement.
Ⓓ release from a promise.

6 Naive means
Ⓐ simple.
Ⓑ natural.
Ⓒ foreign.
Ⓓ positive.

7 To pursue means to
Ⓐ fight.
Ⓑ reply.
Ⓒ seek.
Ⓓ prefer.

8 Subdued means
Ⓐ quiet.
Ⓑ small.
Ⓒ careful.
Ⓓ sudden.

UNIT 3

GO ON

"The Hand of Fatima" and "Old Ways, New World"

Open Book

Directions: Questions 9–15 are about "The Hand of Fatima." Read each question and choose the best answer. You may look at the selection on pages 305–324 to help you answer the questions.

LITERARY ANALYSIS

9 What does viewpoint in a story communicate?

Ⓐ the theme

Ⓑ the conflicting traits of characters

Ⓒ the setting in which characters interact

Ⓓ the attitudes of the characters, narrator, and author

10 Which word best describes the narrator's viewpoint in "The Hand of Fatima"?

Ⓐ exciting

Ⓑ humorous

Ⓒ mysterious

Ⓓ understanding

11 How do we know the author likes Aneesi?

Ⓐ She describes how beautiful Aneesi is.

Ⓑ She shows only Aneesi's good qualities.

Ⓒ She shows Aneesi as honest and selfless.

Ⓓ She puts Aneesi in situations where she will succeed.

12 The way that Sitt Zeina talks to other characters in the story suggests that the author views her as

Ⓐ bossy.

Ⓑ hateful.

Ⓒ cautious.

Ⓓ easygoing

COMPREHENSION

13 How does Aneesi feel about her family?

Ⓐ She is upset by their traditional values.

Ⓑ She is proud of all they have accomplished.

Ⓒ She is dedicated to helping them meet challenges.

Ⓓ She is embarrassed by their poverty and lack of education.

14 Why does her father's arrival cause Aneesi conflict?

Ⓐ She has adjusted to living in Lebanon, but now she begins to miss Syria.

Ⓑ She is happy to see him again, but it will be difficult to live with him in the house.

Ⓒ She has been studying hard, but he asks that she give it up to make more money.

Ⓓ She likes her independent life, but he tells her someone has asked to marry her.

Directions: Read question 15. Write your answer on a separate sheet of paper.

15

> Although almost too excited to eat, Aneesi soon felt hunger pangs again and settled down to a plate of leftovers. She was chewing the last piece of broiled chicken when Sitt Zeina came into the kitchen to prepare coffee. Swallowing quickly, Aneesi spoke up with uncustomary boldness. "Sitt Zeina, I couldn't help hearing something—I didn't mean to, but I was just leaving the dining room—"
>
> "Yes? What is it, Aneesi? As you can see, I'm busy."

What does this passage show about Aneesi and Sitt Zeina's viewpoints regarding each other? What does it suggest about the narrator's viewpoint? Use text details to support your answer.

GO ON

EDGE Level C

"The Hand of Fatima" and "Old Ways, New World"

Open Book

Directions: Questions 16–22 are about "Old Ways, New World." Read each question and choose the best answer. You may look at the selection on pages 327–330 to help you answer the questions.

LITERARY ANALYSIS

16 Good reporters want readers to

Ⓐ know how the reporter feels about the topic.

Ⓑ get information to make their own decisions.

Ⓒ be influenced by the tone of the news report.

Ⓓ be entertained by the way the news is presented.

17 How do careful reporters remain unbiased in their viewpoint?

Ⓐ They avoid controversial subjects.

Ⓑ They present only positive viewpoints.

Ⓒ They choose their words carefully to avoid favoring one side.

Ⓓ They provide their own opinions as well as the opinions of others.

18 The facts presented in the report show that it is difficult to

Ⓐ leave home to study abroad.

Ⓑ balance old and new customs.

Ⓒ find a good marriage partner.

Ⓓ get a job if you are an immigrant.

COMPREHENSION

19 How are the Afghan and Indian women who live in America different from those who live in the homeland?

Ⓐ They pursue careers.

Ⓑ They disobey their parents.

Ⓒ They leave their customs behind.

Ⓓ They choose their own husbands.

20 Why do the women mentioned in the news report agree to arranged marriages?

Ⓐ to obey the law

Ⓑ to gain personal wealth

Ⓒ to support their careers

Ⓓ to respect their families

21 What is the basis of the conflict experienced by many Afghan and Indian immigrants in the United States?

Ⓐ the pursuit of wealth

Ⓑ the search for the perfect mate

Ⓒ the desire for personal freedom

Ⓓ the high cost of a college education

Directions: Read question 22. Write your answer on a separate sheet of paper.

22

> For Afghan and Indian immigrants in the United States, dating and marriage present special challenges. Ashrat Khwajazadah and Naheed Mawjzada are in many ways modern American women, spurning the headscarves and modest outfits customarily worn by Afghan women.
>
> Both in their early twenties, they have taken a route still controversial for Afghan women living in America: going to college to pursue professions. And both defy the ideal of submissive Afghan womanhood. Mawjzada speaks up forcefully when men talk politics at the dinner table.

Does Joseph Berger, the reporter, mask his viewpoint in this passage? Explain how you can tell.

UNIT 3

Student Profile: Cluster Tests

Directions: Use the **Answer Key** and Scoring Guides on pages 144, 145, and 146 to score Cluster Tests 1, 2, and 3 respectively. Circle the item number of each correct answer below. Then multiply items correct by points. Include the rubric scores for the constructed-response items. Calculate the overall test score by adding to 100. To gauge mastery for a particular tested skill or Common Core Standard, review the Cluster Test and Unit Test results.

Cluster 1   Date _____

Subtest	Tested Skill	ITEM ANALYSIS		TEST SCORES
		Item Numbers	Mastery	No. Correct x Points = Score
Key Vocabulary	Key Vocabulary L.9-10.6	1 2 3 4 5 6 7 8	6 out of 8 + −	_____ x 4 = _____ /32
Literary Analysis	Analyze Style: Language RL.9-10.4	9 10 11	2 out of 3 + −	_____ x 4 = _____ /12
	Analyze Structure: Rhyme Scheme RL.9-10.5	16 17 18	2 out of 3 + −	_____ x 4 = _____ /12
Comprehension	Comprehension RL.9-10.10, RI.9-10.10	12 13 14 19 20 21	5 out of 6 + −	_____ x 4 = _____ /24
Constructed Response	Use Text Evidence RL.9-10.1; RL.9-10.10; RI.9-10.1; RI.9-10.10; W.9-10.9	Rubric Scores Item 15 _____ + Item 22 _____ = _____		= _____ /20

Overall Score (Add Points Earned) | _____ /100 |

Cluster 2   Date _____

Subtest	Tested Skill	ITEM ANALYSIS		TEST SCORES
		Item Numbers	Mastery	No. Correct x Points = Score
Key Vocabulary	Key Vocabulary L.9-10.6	1 2 3 4 5 6 7 8	6 out of 8 + −	_____ x 4 = _____ /32
Literary Analysis	Analyze Style: Sentence Structure RL.9-10.5	9 10 11	2 out of 3 + −	_____ x 4 = _____ /12
	Determine Viewpoint RI.9-10.6	16 17 18 19	3 out of 4 + −	_____ x 4 = _____ /16
Comprehension	Comprehension RL.9-10.10; RI.9-10.10	12 13 14 20 21	4 out of 5 + −	_____ x 4 = _____ /20
Constructed Response	Use Text Evidence RL.9-10.1; RL.9-10.10; RI.9-10.1; RI.9-10.10; W.9-10.9	Rubric Scores Item 15 _____ + Item 22 _____ = _____		= _____ /20

Overall Score (Add Points Earned) | _____ /100 |

Cluster 3   Date _____

Subtest	Tested Skill	ITEM ANALYSIS		TEST SCORES
		Item Numbers	Mastery	No. Correct x Points = Score
Key Vocabulary	Key Vocabulary L.9-10.6	1 2 3 4 5 6 7 8	6 out of 8 + −	_____ x 4 = _____ /32
Literary Analysis	Analyze Viewpoint RL.9-10.6	9 10 11 12	3 out of 4 + −	_____ x 4 = _____ /16
	Determine Viewpoint RI.9-10.6	16 17 18	2 out of 3 + −	_____ x 4 = _____ /12
Comprehension	Comprehension RL.9-10.10; RI.9-10.10	13 14 19 20 21	4 out of 5 + −	_____ x 4 = _____ /20
Constructed Response	Use Text Evidence RL.9-10.1; RL.9-10.10; RI.9-10.1; RI.9-10.10; W.9-10.9	Rubric Scores Item 15 _____ + Item 22 _____ = _____		= _____ /20

Overall Score (Add Points Earned) | _____ /100 |

Language Acquisition Rubrics

Cluster 1
RETELL A STORY
Pair Talk ▶ page 266

Directions: Pair students. Give them a few moments to review the selection. Partners should then take turns retelling their favorite parts of the story.

Language Function | 1 | 2 | 3 | 4

What to look for:
how well the student retells the story or parts of the story by introducing the characters and setting, and stating the problem, main events, and resolution. Student should include details to make his/her retelling of the story interesting.

Cluster 3
COMPARE AND CONTRAST
Pair Talk ▶ page 332

Directions: Pair students. Give them a few moments to review the selections. Partners should take turns discussing the characters' similarities and differences.

Language Function | 1 | 2 | 3 | 4

What to look for:
how well the student compares and contrasts aspects of the two characters using comparatives and words such as *and, all, both, too, alike, same, similar* (for comparisons) and *but, unlike, however,* and *while* (for contrasts).

Cluster 2
MAKE COMPARISONS
Group Talk ▶ page 298

Directions: Give the students a few moments to review the selection and write down notes. Then in groups, students should discuss how Jamie and his brother are alike and how they are different. Groups should make a list of their best ideas.

Language Function | 1 | 2 | 3 | 4

What to look for:
how well the student makes comparisons between the two characters by using details, examples, and comparatives (including phrases like *more … than*). Student should provide complete comparisons.

	Language Function Rubric
4	Student effectively performs the function.
3	Student performs the function.
2	Student does not adequately perform the function.
1	Student makes no attempt or offers a non-verbal response.

Reading and Literary Analysis

Directions: Read each question and choose the best answer.

1 Based on the meaning of the word *family*, what does the word <u>familiarity</u> mean?

   A shortage of food

   B famous for doing something

   C widely distributed throughout an area

   D knowledge or understanding of something

2 The words in the box form a word family.

> correctly, correction, corrective, correctness, correctable, corrector

Which is the root word for this word family?

   A corral

   B correct

   C correlate

   D correspond

3 Which word is **not** in the same word family as the word <u>able</u>?

   A ably

   B enable

   C disable

   D abandon

4 Based on the meaning of the root word *cred*, <u>credible</u> means

   A believed before.

   B able to be believed.

   C against being believed.

   D someone who is believed.

5 <u>Abstract</u> means

   A a feeling of regret.

   B an idea that is not concrete.

   C an ability to lead other people.

   D a response that is not appropriate.

6 An <u>acknowledgment</u> is something done to express

   A thanks.

   B surprise.

   C amazement.

   D disappointment.

7 <u>Subdued</u> means

   A quiet.

   B small.

   C careful.

   D sudden.

8 <u>Desolately</u> means

   A sadly.

   B softly.

   C slowly.

   D secretly.

UNIT 3

GO ON

Reading and Literary Analysis, *continued*

Directions: Questions 9–13 are about "Past Tense." Read the selection. Then read each question and choose the best answer.

Past Tense

A lot of my friends complain about history. I don't mean history itself; I mean having to study it. I can't think of anything better because the more I study history, the more I understand people today. Even though we humans change a lot on the surface, the deeper part of us, the part that loves and hates, hasn't changed that much in thousands of years. I know, that sounds vague and abstract, so I'll back up a few months and explain why an e-mail is like a curse tablet.

My passion is archaeology. As a kid, I was fascinated by Schliemann's discovery of Troy, I couldn't get enough of Mayan pyramids, and I dreamed about living in Machu Picchu as an Inca maiden. So when the opportunity came up to work on a volunteer dig in Israel for the summer, I had to pursue my dream.

Kia and Michael came to see me off. Kia is my best friend. We've known each other since grade school. We've both known Michael almost as long, and somewhere along the way he changed from my friend to my boyfriend. People called us the Three Musketeers because we would do almost everything as a trio. We loved spending time together, the three of us, laughing at the same jokes, enjoying the same movies and music. You couldn't ask for better friends.

A team of archaeologists work together on an archaeological dig in Israel.

The archaeology dig was fantastic. The hot, dusty land was utterly foreign, and yet it felt like an ancient home that had been waiting for me. We lived in tents, the dust got into everything, and I could never get entirely clean, but I loved every minute. I partnered up with a guy my age named Bernie. We worked side by side, using toothbrushes to wipe dirt gently from delicate objects. During the first few days, he got a nasty sunburn, so I would remind him to use his sunscreen. After I nearly passed out because of heat exhaustion, he began giving me water all the time. Pretty soon, we felt as though we'd known each other for years, almost like it felt with Michael. The only difference was that Bernie and I could rave on about cuneiform tablets for hours without running out of steam.

We loved knowing that thousands of years ago, a student had written a letter home begging his parents for money by scratching marks onto a clay tablet just as a college kid today would use e-mail or a cell phone to beg for money from home.

Cuneiform tablets illustrate early forms of writing.

We had both studied Egyptian and Mayan hieroglyphs. We could talk about the transition from pictorial representations to a sound-based alphabet. In other words, we were a matched pair of geeks, so it wasn't exactly a surprise when we began to have feelings for each other. Bernie understood that I had a boyfriend, but I went back to my tent, lay on my cot, and scolded myself for almost betraying Michael. Bernie acted like a friend, and we promised to stay in touch when the dig ended.

It was hard for me to e-mail more than once a week

Reading and Literary Analysis, *continued*

from the dig. I didn't hear from Kia or Michael often, but when I got an acknowledgment, they sounded distant. I thought it was because they missed me.

***

Kia and Michael were the first ones to welcome me when I got home. I was chattering away like a magpie when I realized how quiet they were. Then, I saw them exchanging glances, and Michael took Kia's hand. In a flash, I knew what was coming.

Michael said, "We didn't want to tell you this in e-mail. It didn't seem right to do it that way instead of face-to-face. We…Kia and I…we want to be together. But not without you. I mean, we're your friends…."

"Get out," I said. I was so furious I could hardly speak. Kia pleaded, "Sabrina, we didn't want to hide anything from you."

"*Get out!*" I screamed and they left with Kia crying. I slammed around the house feeling like the most naïve fool in the world, being loyal to Michael while he was leaving me behind here, and with my best friend.

The next few days were horrible. I did my best to evade Kia and Michael, which was hard because we tended to hang out at the same places. Bernie and I kept up our enthusiastic conversations by e-mail, but one night he wrote, "*Something seems different. Are you okay?*"

I wrote a vicious e-mail in return, pouring out my rage against Kia and Michael and finished with, "*I wish they'd drop into a black hole.*" My finger was poised over the send button when I realized that I was no different from the ancient Romans. They would inscribe curses onto lead tablets asking the gods to curse someone who had wronged them. Okay, so they

An acient Roman lead tablet with an inscribed curse.

would toss their tablets into sacred springs while I was sending my curse across an electronic network. The means were different, but the *intent* was the same. I sat back and thought about whether that was the person I wanted to be.

I knew Kia and Michael better than anyone, so I knew they would never intend to hurt me deliberately. People have been struggling with relationships for millennia. What made me any different…or any better? In a year, we would be going off in different directions to college anyway, but friendship can span a lot of distance, in both time and space. Their friendship meant more to me than a temporary bit of hurt. I erased my e-mail to Bernie and replaced it with, "*Everything's cool…more later.*" Then I sent a text message to Kia and Michael: "*Musketeers forever…let's do a movie.*"

GO ON

Reading and Literary Analysis, *continued*

9 Which sentence from the story shows that something important in the story will change?

A It was hard for me to e-mail more than once a week from the dig.

B I was chattering away like a magpie when I realized how quiet they were.

C The next few days were horrible.

D I was so furious I could hardly speak.

10 In which sentence do the author's word choices clearly reveal an informal style?

A I can't think of anything better because the more I study history, the more I understand people today.

B We worked side by side, using toothbrushes to wipe dirt gently from delicate objects.

C I slammed around the house feeling like the most naive fool in the world, being loyal to Michael while he was leaving me behnd here, and with my best friend.

D People have been struggling with relationships for millennia.

11 To <u>evade</u> means to

A insist.

B avoid.

C annoy.

D invade.

12 To do something <u>deliberately</u> means to do it

A alone.

B on time.

C for money.

D on purpose.

Directions: Read question 13. Write your answer on a separate sheet of paper.

13 Based on the text, what prediction can be made about the future relationship between Sabrina and Bernie? Explain your prediction using details from the text.

UNIT 3

Reading and Literary Analysis, *continued*

Directions: Questions 14–19 are about "The Letter." Read the selection. Then read each question and choose the best answer.

The Letter

Nikolai tossed the mail on the kitchen table and was reaching for his soccer shoes when he noticed an envelope with the university's golden seal. He stared at the large white rectangle as though it might bite his hands. Beneath his name, eager italic type proclaimed,

Nikolai Kadyrov
2502 Crocus Ct.
Portland, OR 97201

"This is the fat envelope you've been waiting for!" The fat envelope saying he'd been accepted had arrived; it was the last thing he wanted.

With a queasy sensation, he ripped the envelope open, pulled out a sheaf of papers, and began leafing through. When he discovered one titled "Financial Aid Offer," his eyes darted from side to side until they stopped at two words: "Full Scholarship." Where was he going to hide these papers so his mother wouldn't discover them? After all, he had no choice: the university was out of the question. He was going to the community college with Peter, as he had promised in sixth grade.

He had never broken a promise to Peter. They were from different families, but everyone called them the Twins because they were inseparable, always walking to school together, always sporting the same team uniforms. Peter practically kept him alive the year his father passed away and his mother started working full-time. The only thing they didn't do together was homework, since Peter did only the minimum needed to get by and expressed relief when he passed his classes. But for Nikolai, mathematical formulae came easily, and he wrote better English papers than most of the native speakers. When the counselor suggested he apply to the university he shrugged, took the examinations, and filled out the forms, thinking nothing would come of it. His mother couldn't afford university tuition, and he was only applying to get the counselor off his back. He

had already decided what community college courses he would take. But now, he thought pensively, everything felt different, because suddenly he had a choice—no, a dilemma: attend the university, or keep his promise.

When the doorbell rang, he was still lacing up his soccer shoes, so he reached over and pushed the buzzer. He was tying the last double knot when Peter burst through the apartment door, calling, "Hurry up, we're going to be late." When he reached over the table to grab an apple, the envelope caught his eye and he picked it up. Nikolai grabbed the envelope back, threw it down, and covered it with newspapers for good measure.

"Got something to hide?" laughed Peter, rummaging the college papers back out and starting to look at them. Nikolai sank down apprehensively, awaiting the worst.

"Don't worry, I'm not going," he said in what he tried to make a carefree voice, hoping to deflect whatever devastating words Peter was about to utter about broken promises.

Peter gaped in disbelief. "Not going? What are you, insane or something? Your mom's going to be dancing around the room when she sees this full scholarship."

"I'm going to the community college. I made you a promise."

Peter stared at him for a long minute before saying firmly, "Well, thanks, but no thanks. The university's the right place for you. You would go stir-crazy in the classes I'm going to take, so it's not like we'd be sitting in the same classrooms anyway, right?"

He stood up, walked to the wicker basket by the door, and pulled out the soccer ball. "This is the right thing for you to do, and me, I've got my own dreams to pursue. But I'll tell you one thing." He tossed the ball over and Nikolai raised one hand to catch it. "You forget to stay in touch, and you're in serious trouble."

Nikolai felt as light as air, like he'd be able to run a thousand miles at practice and never have to stop for breath. "Not a problem," he said with a grin, as they headed out the door. "I hear they have this little invention now called e-mail."

Reading and Literary Analysis, *continued*

14 What first tells the reader that Nikolai will face a problem in this story?

A   He stares at the envelope on the table.

B   He is not excited that the envelope is fat.

C   He is offered a full scholarship to the university.

D   He feels like he does not have a choice about school.

15 Based on Peter's response to the news about the scholarship, what can the reader infer about Peter?

A   He is inspired to become a better student.

B   He wants the best opportunities for Nikolai.

C   He wishes that he were going to the university.

D   He hopes that Nikolai will decide to stay after all.

16 What does e-mail symbolize in both "Past Tense" and "The Letter"?

A   a willingness to communicate

B   a desire to become an adult

C   the distance the characters feel

D   the difficulties of modern life

17 A <u>dilemma</u> is

A   a quality other people admire in you.

B   punishment for a crime you did not commit.

C   a situation that requires you to make a difficult choice.

D   the chance to do something over again to make it right.

18 <u>Devastating</u> means

A   doubtful.

B   confusing.

C   destructive.

D   unhappy.

Directions: Read question 19. Write your answer on a separate sheet of paper.

19 Nikolai has a particular idea about promises. Find a detail from the text that reveals his way of thinking. Then find a detail that shows how Peter corrects Nikolai's viewpoint.

UNIT 3

Reading and Literary Analysis, *continued*

Directions: Questions 20–25 are about "Tony's Choice." Read the selection. Then read each question and choose the best answer.

Tony's Choice

Jake groaned out loud when he realized the new kid was heading over to their table. The way he saw it, new kids at school were like scrawny kittens showing up and mewing on your doorstep. You had to shove them away, show a little authority. Otherwise they'd stick around forever, expecting to be part of your life.

"Someone thinks a group project means new groups," he said.

Tony and Fernando stopped talking about last night's football game and followed Jake's eyes.

"Check out the shirt," said Fernando.

"And those shoes!" snorted Jake. "Where did his mommy buy those? Yesterday's Fashions?"

The new kid was close to their table when he saw them grinning, and a half smile curved over his own face like a question mark. Just as he reached toward an empty chair, Jake put his feet up on its back rungs, his perfect new shoelaces practically tickling the kid's nose. He kicked the chair over backwards, the sound of its fall swallowed up by the noisy room.

"I'm sorry, but as you can clearly see, this table is full," he said, his smile turning hard and cold like a sword blade. "Why don't you just go on back to Yesterday's Fashions where you belong?"

Fernando doubled over in laughter as the kid walked away. "Good one, Jake," he snorted. "You saved us from certain doom!"

But Tony didn't say anything. He wasn't even smiling. He stared hard at his pencil, turning it over and over. Then he laid it down on the table, a thin yellow line between himself and the others. He looked up at Jake's broad grin.

"Let me get this straight," he said. "You're prejudiced against this kid because of his shoes?"

"Of course I am," said Jake, still laughing. "I have my pride!"

"Pride," echoed Tony. The word seemed to burrow into him. For the rest of the class, no matter how much Jake and Fernando joked around, Tony was subdued. It

started to get on Jake's nerves.

"What's with you?" he asked, trying to provoke a response, but Tony didn't answer.

Jake felt strangely relieved when the lunch bell rang. Outside the classroom, chaos reigned. Locker doors banged. People drifted in slow, swirling clumps, like icebergs, and sometimes the groups crashed into each other, knocking kids off into the swirling sea of bodies.

Backpacks and books careened around like deadly missiles. But the chaos parted magically in front of the three boys as they headed to the cafeteria. Jake felt the warm glow of contentment. This was more like it. Authority.

They were close to the choice seats in the cafeteria when Fernando caught Jake's arm. "Look, it's Mr. Stylish Shoes."

The kid was sitting alone in a deserted corner, hunched desolately over his lunch like it was the most interesting thing he'd ever seen in his life.

Jake took a step forward. "Let's have a little fun," he said.

Fernando grinned. And Tony? He was setting his jaw so firmly, it looked like it was made of granite. He turned without saying anything and started walking towards the new kid. Jake held Fernando back.

"I guess Tony finally woke up," he said. "Let's just enjoy the show. One accidental lunch-on-lap, coming up!"

He saw Tony weave through the maze of tables and come up behind the kid. Tony's mouth moved, the kid's head jerked up, and Tony reached out his hand.

"Here we go," Jake whispered, tensing with pleasure.

But something was wrong. The kid was reaching his hand out too, and shaking Tony's hand. Tony was pulling up a chair and sitting down, his shoulders friendly and casual. Jake felt his grin turning to ice.

Then it happened. Tony looked up across the sea of faces, found Jake's eyes, and held them for a long minute. Fernando was saying something, but Jake couldn't even hear. He just saw Tony swiveling his chair around to talk with the kid, leaving Jake staring at the broad, solid wall of his back.

Reading and Literary Analysis, *continued*

20 Read these sentences from the story.

> "Pride," echoed Tony. The word seemed to burrow into him.

What does Tony's short statement show about him?

A He feels fiercely loyal to Jake and the other boys.

B He is used to saying and doing whatever Jake does.

C He thinks that Jake deserves to feel a sense of pride.

D He believes Jake is showing a quality other than pride.

21 Which of these word sets from the story most help the reader to imagine the scene in which Jake, Fernando, and Tony head to the cafeteria?

A rang, doors, drifted

B relieved, outside, felt

C chaos, banged, swirling

D strangely, classroom, slow

22 Based on the last paragraph, what is most likely true about Jake?

A He will eventually realize how bad his behavior is.

B He plans to join Tony and the new kid at the table.

C He thinks that Tony is playing a practical joke on him.

D He will decide it is easier to let others be school leaders.

23 Read these sentences from "The Letter" and "Tony's Choice."

> **The Letter:** "What are you, insane or something?"
> **Tony's Choice:** "Check out the shirt," said Fernando.

The language in these sentences tells you that both characters speaking these lines

A are jealous of someone.

B are worried about someone.

C have a reason for mocking someone.

D have a reason to be angry with someone.

24 What main theme do all three stories share?

A growing up too quickly

B making difficult choices

C forgiving others for mistakes

D finding friendship in surprising places

Directions: Read question 25. Write your answers on a separate sheet of paper.

25 How does the friendship between Jake and Tony change by the end of the story? Use details from the passage to support your answer.

UNIT 3

EDGE Level C

Grammar and Writing

Directions: Read the composition. It contains errors. Then read each question and choose the best answer.

Out of Bounds

(1) My friend Robbie is an excellent musician. (2) Pick any instrument, and he seems to be good at it from the word "go." (3) My brother was envious of him. (4) To me, music is fun, but for Robbie, music is his ticket to fame and fortune—at least that is what he used to think. (5) School just seemed to be something he had to put up with in order to play music. (6) He ignored teachers, complained, and <u>says</u> that homework cut into his practice time!

(7) That's where I came in. (8) I helped him. (9) Sometimes he was so charming that I couldn't resist helping him.

(10) "I'm glad you're so smart, Grace," he said, whenever I worked with him on his homework.

(11) I tried convincing him that school was important, but he never listened.

(12) "Well, I won't get anywhere in the music business if I spend my time reading about dead people I never heard of," Robbie would say.

(13) That summed up Robbie right there. (14) <u>Him</u> gave school as little attention as possible until his dismal grades threatened his eligibility for band, and they always did.

(15) When we got to our junior year of high school, it was announced that everyone would have to pass a test to graduate. (16) Robbie didn't seem worried about it, but I was worried for him. (17) He didn't seem to get it.

(18) In our senior year, he was told by me, "You need to start studying hard."

(19) "It'll be fine," he said.

(20) He was oblivious; he cared only about band practice and auditions.

(21) One day, a few weeks before the test, he <u>will call</u> me up and started pleading his case.

(22) "Grace, I need your help. (23) I have to pass this test."

(24) "I know," I sighed.

(25) "You are the smartest person I know," he said, turning on his trademark charm.

(26) "Robbie—"

(27) "Just make sure you sit next to me and—"

(28) "No!" I blurted out. (29) "Are you crazy? (30) If we are caught, neither of <u>we</u> will graduate."

(31) "Please, just this once," he begged.

(32) "No. I'm not helping you anymore," I said.

(33) He hung up, and I knew that I wouldn't be seeing Robbie at our graduation ceremony.

GO ON

Grammar and Writing, *continued*

1 Which sentence is **not** related to the main idea in paragraph 1?

   A   sentence 1

   B   sentence 3

   C   sentence 4

   D   sentence 6

2 In sentence 6, the word <u>says</u> should be changed to

   A   say

   B   said

   C   will say

   D   No change

3 In sentence 14, the word <u>Him</u> should be changed to

   A   It

   B   He

   C   Us

   D   No change

4 Which sentence should be added after sentence 15 to support the ideas in the paragraph?

   A   I was certain the test would have algebra questions.

   B   People say I am good at taking tests.

   C   It would take three hours to finish the test.

   D   This test would decide the course of our future.

5 What change, if any, should be made to sentence 18?

   A   Change *he was told by me* to **I told him**

   B   Change *You* to **you**

   C   Change *to* to **too**

   D   No change

6 What change, if any, should be made to sentence 20?

   A   Change *was* to **is**

   B   Change the semicolon to a comma

   C   Change *he* to **He**

   D   No change

7 In sentence 21, the words <u>will call</u> should be changed to

   A   calls

   B   called

   C   calling

   D   No change

8 In sentence 30, the word <u>we</u> should be changed to

   A   us

   B   you

   C   them

   D   No change

UNIT 3

GO ON

Grammar and Writing, *continued*

Directions: Read the composition. It contains errors. Then read each question and choose the best answer.

Welcome Home

(1) Someday, when you are very old, basic things you do for yourself, like eating and getting dressed, may become difficult or impossible. (2) If that happens, whom would you most like to take care of you? (3) My guess is that you would choose your family. (4) I want to live to be 100 years old. (5) That is why I believe the elderly should be taken care of by loved ones.

(6) In many cultures around the world, the elderly live with their grown children. (7) Often, elder members of society are respected as keepers of wisdom and tradition. (8) Grandparents play an important role in raising children, because parents may work away from the home.

(9) As I see it, the elderly are viewed differently in the United States. (10) It seems to I that we see the elderly as more of a burden than an asset. (11) Even though we love and respect our parents, our solution for dealing with old and ailing people is often to put them in nursing homes or "assisted living facilities." (12) There they are cared for by professionals; however, they are surrounded by people they don't know.

(13) According to the American Association of retired persons, nearly 40 percent of Americans aged 75 and older lived alone in the year 2000. (14) In my opinion, we Americans don't bring our elderly parents into our homes because we are very uncomfortable with their loss of independence. (15) It is unpleasant to watch people—especially the people we love—decline to a state in which they are dependent on others.

(16) Our parents guide and took care of us for about twenty years. (17) Despite the mistakes we make as we grow up, and we make a lot, parents are there to help us. (18) Taking care of our parents as they near the end of their lives isn't easy, but we owe it to them after all they have done for us. (19) That's why I think we should help them when them can no longer help themselves.

GO ON

EDGE Level C

Grammar and Writing, *continued*

9 Which sentence does **not** relate to the main idea in paragraph 1?

   A sentence 1

   B sentence 3

   C sentence 4

   D sentence 5

10 In sentence 10, the word I should be changed to

   A he

   B me

   C them

   D No change

11 In sentence 11, the word love should be changed to

   A loving

   B loved

   C have loved

   D No change

12 What change, if any, should be made to sentence 12?

   A Change the semicolon to a dash

   B Change *however* to **However**

   C Change *surrounded* to **surounded**

   D No change

13 What change, if any, should be made to sentence 13?

   A Change *retired persons* to **Retired Persons**

   B Change the comma to a semicolon

   C Change *alone* to **a lone**

   D No change

14 In sentence 16, the word took should be changed to

   A take

   B will take

   C have taken

   D No change

15 Which sentence should be added after sentence 17 to support the ideas in paragraph 5?

   A We can depend on them to do what is best for us.

   B We can expect that medical care for the elderly will be costly.

   C Discussing those experiences with your parents can be educational.

   D Making mistakes is an important way for children to learn responsibility.

16 In sentence 19, the word them should be changed to

   A him

   B you

   C they

   D No change

UNIT 3

GO ON

EDGE Level C

Grammar and Writing, *continued*

Directions: Read the following writing prompt and write a composition. Write on separate sheets of paper. Use the Writer's Checklist to make sure that you do your best work.

Prompt

Your school board will be selecting one teacher from your school to be "Teacher of the Year."

Write a persuasive letter to the school board in which you convince them to vote for your favorite teacher.

Writer's Checklist

☑ Write about all parts of the prompt.

☑ Present a clear central idea, and stay focused on it.

☑ Organize your composition from its introduction to its conclusion.

☑ Use transitions to connect your thoughts for the reader.

☑ Present meaningful ideas, and support them with specific information.

☑ Use appropriate words and a variety of sentence structures.

☑ Proofread and edit your writing for grammar, usage, mechanics, and spelling.

UNIT 3

DONE!

Student Profile: Unit Tests

Directions: Use the **Answer Key** on page 147 to score the multiple-choice items. Circle the item number of each correct answer below. Calculate test scores by assigning one point for each correct answer. Use the scoring guides on page 147 to score the constructed-response items. Use the Good Writing Traits Rubric on page 122 to score the written composition. Total the scores and calculate the % score or use the conversion chart. To gauge mastery for a particular tested skill or Common Core Standard, review the Cluster Test and Unit Test results.

Reading and Literary Analysis

		ITEM ANALYSIS		TEST SCORES
Category	**Tested Skill**	**Item Numbers**	**Mastery**	**Points: Earned / Total**
Vocabulary	Word Families L.9-10.4	1 2 3 4	3 out of 4 + −	_____ / 4
	Key Vocabulary L.9-10.6	5 6 7 8 11 12 17 18	6 out of 8 + −	_____ / 8
Literary Analysis	Analyze Style RL.9-10.4	10 16 20 21 23	4 out of 5 + −	_____ / 5
Comprehension	Comprehension RL.9-10.10	9 14 15 22 24	4 out of 5 + −	_____ / 5
Constructed Response	Use Text Evidence RL.9-10.1; RL.9-10.10; W.9-10.9	Rubric Scores Item 13 _____ + Item 19 _____ + Item 25 _____ = _____		_____ / 12

Overall Score (Points Earned ÷ Total Points x 100 = %)   _____ ÷ 34 = _____%

Grammar and Writing

		ITEM ANALYSIS		TEST SCORES
Category	**Tested Skill**	**Item Numbers**	**Mastery**	**Points: Earned / Total**
Grammar	Verb Tense L.9-10.1	2 7 11 14	3 out of 4 + −	_____ / 4
	Subject and Object Pronouns L.9-10.1	3 8 10 16	3 out of 4 + −	_____ / 4
Revising and Editing	Development of Ideas W.9-10.5	1 4 9 15	3 out of 4 + −	_____ / 4
	Grammar, Mechanics, and Usage L.9-10.2	5 6 12 13	3 out of 4 + −	_____ / 4
Written Composition (Argument) W.9-10.1; W.9-10.4; W.9-10.10	Focus and Unity	Rubric Scores: _____ / 4		
	Organization	_____ / 4		
	Development of Ideas	_____ / 4 =		_____ / 20
	Voice and Style	_____ / 4		
	Written Conventions	_____ / 4		

Overall Score (Points Earned ÷ Total Points x 100 = %)   _____ ÷ 36 = _____%

UNIT 3

Project Rubric: A Reality TV Show

Score	Planning/Preparation	Content of Project	Delivery/Presentation	Collaboration
3 Great	• Reviews various reality TV shows and identifies the tasks and challenges the characters undertake as well as the personality traits needed to win. • Chooses the type of show to produce that works well with the Essential Question. • Develops contestant profiles and determines which role each person will play.	• Addresses the Essential Question. • Clearly presents the situations the characters face and the actions they take. • Is interesting and holds the audience's attention throughout the show.	• Seats the audience so they can all easily view the show. • All contestants are prepared. • The contestants speak clearly and loudly.	• Works well with others. • Assumes a clear role and related responsibilities.
2 Good	• Reviews one or two reality TV shows and identifies the tasks and challenges the characters undertake as well as the personality traits needed to win. • Chooses the type of show to produce that somewhat works with the Essential Question. • Develops most of the contestant profiles and determines some of the roles each person will play.	• Somewhat addresses the Essential Question. • The situations the characters face and the actions they take are somewhat unclear. • Somewhat interesting and holds the audience's attention for most of the show.	• Seats the audience so most of them can view the show. • Most of the contestants are prepared. • Contestant can be heard most of the time.	• Works with others but has difficulty sharing decisions and responsibilities.
1 Needs Work	• Does not review any reality TV shows. • Does not choose the type of show to produce appropriate for the Essential Question. • Does not develop contestant profiles or determine which role each person will play.	• Does not address the Essential Question. • Does not clearly present the situations the characters face and the actions they take. • Is not very interesting and does not hold the audience's attention.	• Does not consider audience's view of the show. • Contestants are not prepared. • Cannot be heard or understood well.	• Cannot work with others in most situations. • Cannot share decisions or responsibilities.

Self-Assessment

Directions: Circle the numbers that show how much you agree or disagree with each sentence. Then answer the question below. If necessary, use the back of the page.

	Not Yet	With Help	Most of the Time	Very Well
❶ When I read a story, I understand the author's style and viewpoint.	1	2	3	4
❷ When I read song lyrics, I understand rhyme.	1	2	3	4
❸ I understand the role of viewpoint in a news commentary.	1	2	3	4
❹ I know how to make inferences while reading.	1	2	3	4
❺ When I find a word I do not know, I look for word families and cognates to help me understand the meaning.	1	2	3	4
❻ I know how to write using correct verb tenses and subject and object pronouns.	1	2	3	4
❼ I know how to revise my writing for development of ideas.	1	2	3	4

❽ Think of one thing you learned really well in this unit. Tell how you will use this the next time you read or write.

_____

_____

_____

_____

_____

_____

_____

_____

_____

_____

UNIT 3

Reader Reflection

Directions: Answer questions 1–10. If necessary, use the back of the page.

"Face Facts: The Science of Facial Expressions"

1 What did you learn about cause and effect in text structure that may help you the next time you read a magazine article?

2 Explain how asking questions by self-questioning will help you the next time you read.

3 Write what you liked and did not like about "Face Facts: The Science of Facial Expressions." Include examples from the magazine article.

I liked...

I did not like...

4 Are you interested in reading more writing by Mary Duenwald? ____ Yes ____ No

5 Are you interested in reading more magazine articles by other writers? ____ Yes ____ No

"Silent Language"

6 What did you learn about problem and solution in text structure that may help you the next time you read a magazine article?

7 Explain how asking questions about bigger issues will help you the next time you read a magazine article.

8 Write what you liked and did not like about "Silent Language." Include examples from the magazine article.

I liked...

I did not like...

9 Are you interested in reading more works by Dr. Bruce Perry and/or Charlotte Latvala? ____ Yes ____ No

10 Are you interested in reading more works about body language? ____ Yes ____ No

EDGE Level C

"Face Facts" and "Silent Language"

Closed Book

Directions: Read each question and choose the best answer.

KEY VOCABULARY

1 Competent means
- Ⓐ proud.
- Ⓑ content.
- Ⓒ capable.
- Ⓓ thoughtful.

2 Emphasis means a type of
- Ⓐ talent or skill.
- Ⓑ special importance.
- Ⓒ solution to a problem.
- Ⓓ embarrassing situation.

3 To emulate famous musicians means to
- Ⓐ copy them.
- Ⓑ meet them.
- Ⓒ study them.
- Ⓓ enjoy them.

4 To enhance means to
- Ⓐ handle.
- Ⓑ endure.
- Ⓒ balance.
- Ⓓ improve.

5 To work with precision means to be very
- Ⓐ quick.
- Ⓑ strong.
- Ⓒ accurate.
- Ⓓ prepared.

6 Subtle means hard to
- Ⓐ hide.
- Ⓑ make.
- Ⓒ notice.
- Ⓓ explain.

7 To vary means to
- Ⓐ differ.
- Ⓑ hurry.
- Ⓒ travel.
- Ⓓ value.

8 To visualize something means to
- Ⓐ visit it often.
- Ⓑ receive it for free.
- Ⓒ share it with others.
- Ⓓ imagine what it looks like.

Directions: Questions 9–15 are about "Face Facts: The Science of Facial Expressions." Read each question and choose the best answer. You may look at the selection on pages 365–372 to help you answer the questions.

Open Book

LITERARY ANALYSIS

9 Which of these words signals a cause-and-effect relationship?
- Ⓐ or
- Ⓑ next
- Ⓒ meanwhile
- Ⓓ consequently

10 Ekman traveled to New Guinea because he wanted to find out
- Ⓐ what the Fore people think of other cultures.
- Ⓑ how facial expressions have changed over time.
- Ⓒ if facial expressions are the same across cultures.
- Ⓓ whether the Fore and Western cultures are similar.

GO ON

EDGE Level C

UNIT 4

"Face Facts" and "Silent Language"

 Open Book

11 Which statement from the article describes a cause-and-effect relationship?

Ⓐ Ekman may never win a gold medal.

Ⓑ Emotion usually leads to an expression.

Ⓒ The system is a few years from completion.

Ⓓ These internal responses may last for a minute or more.

12 Ekman found that facial expressions are similar around the world. What was an effect of this discovery?

Ⓐ He learned to fake expressions.

Ⓑ He decided to teach at the university.

Ⓒ He became an adviser for the federal government.

Ⓓ He realized that police officers are not good at catching liars.

COMPREHENSION

13 Read the sentence from the article.

> Chances are, you're not very good at faking a smile.

Why is this true?

Ⓐ People do not try to fake smiles often.

Ⓑ Smiling is a very complicated process.

Ⓒ No one understands how smiling occurs.

Ⓓ The muscles used for fake smiles are weak.

14 When Ekman trains people, he tries to improve their ability to

Ⓐ explain.

Ⓑ observe.

Ⓒ organize.

Ⓓ persuade.

Directions: Read question 15. Write your answer on a separate sheet of paper.

15

> No matter how skilled a person becomes at reading the clues, it's always easier to recognize when someone is lying than when he is telling the truth. And some lies are easier to catch than others. A polite lie—when a person tells her host that dinner was delicious or remarks on how much he likes a friend's new suit—is harder to spot than one that is laced with emotion. When people lie about whether they believe in the death penalty, for instance, they are not so good at hiding their true feelings. High-stakes lies, including whether one is engaged in illegal activity, for instance, are likewise difficult to cover up.

What cause-and-effect relationships are emphasized in this paragraph? Use text details to support your answer.

Directions: Questions 16–22 are about "Silent Language." Read each question and choose the best answer. You may look at the selection on pages 375–380 to help you answer the questions.

LITERARY ANALYSIS

16 A problem-and-solution article should include

Ⓐ a list of other topics related to the article.

Ⓑ an explanation of why the solution is good.

Ⓒ a discussion of why previous solutions failed.

Ⓓ an outline of the important points of the article.

 UNIT 4

"Face Facts" and "Silent Language"

Open Book

17 Which of these is an example of problem-and-solution writing?

Ⓐ a biography of a famous local musician

Ⓑ an editorial supporting a political candidate

Ⓒ a report on the outcome of an important sports event

Ⓓ an article about neighbors who clean up litter in their park

18 A friend sits with her arms crossed during a school council meeting. According to the article, what would be a good solution for her?

Ⓐ to smile while glancing around the room

Ⓑ to hold a pen to take notes with while others speak

Ⓒ to put both hands in her pockets to avoid fidgeting

Ⓓ to cross her arms and remain still throughout the meeting

COMPREHENSION

19 Read this sentence from the article.

> Some people are better at "mind reading" than others.

What do the authors mean by "mind reading"?

Ⓐ interpreting body language

Ⓑ forming pictures in your mind

Ⓒ guessing what people are thinking

Ⓓ changing how you think about things

20 The problems described in this article are all

Ⓐ rules.

Ⓑ attacks.

Ⓒ questions.

Ⓓ signals.

21 What is the author's main message to the reader?

Ⓐ People's body language will tell you every thought they have.

Ⓑ Your body language should always show that you like people.

Ⓒ Attention to body language can improve communication skills.

Ⓓ You should leave the room if you are having trouble paying attention.

Directions: Read question 22. Write your answer on a separate sheet of paper.

22

> Some people are better at "mind reading" than others. You can become better if you pay attention to body language, such as hand gestures and facial expressions. For example, when people are feeling uncomfortable, they may squirm, blush, bite their lip, pick at their fingernails, and have a hard time maintaining eye contact. When someone likes you, he or she may often look into your eyes, touch his or her hair, smile, or touch your arm when talking to you. You'll find the subtle cues a person gives off are somewhat unique—for one friend, you may find one nervous habit (fingernail biting) and with another friend a different cue (fidgety feet).

What general problem and solution does the author present in this introductory paragraph? Use text details to support your answer.

UNIT 4

DONE!

EDGE Level C

Reader Reflection

Directions: Answer questions 1–10. If necessary, use the back of the page.

"They Speak for Success"

1 What did you learn about example details that will help you the next time you read a nonfiction article?

2 You can ask questions by using question-answer relationships. Explain how this strategy will help you the next time you read.

3 Write what you liked and did not like about "They Speak for Success." Include examples from the news feature.

I liked...

I did not like...

4 Are you interested in reading more writing by Tom Seligson? _____ Yes _____ No

5 Are you interested in reading more nonfiction articles by other writers? _____ Yes _____ No

"Breaking the Ice"

6 What did you learn about humor that will help you the next time you read a humor column?

7 Explain how using a "Right There" or a "Think and Search" strategy will help you the next time you ask questions while reading.

8 Write what you liked and did not like about "Breaking the Ice." Include examples from the humor column.

I liked...

I did not like...

9 Are you interested in reading more works by Dave Barry? _____ Yes _____ No

10 Are you interested in reading more humor columns by other authors? _____ Yes _____ No

"They Speak for Success" and "Breaking the Ice"

 Closed Book

Directions: Read each question and choose the best answer.

KEY VOCABULARY

1 Abbreviated means
- Ⓐ saved.
- Ⓑ restored.
- Ⓒ improved.
- Ⓓ shortened.

2 The ambience of a restaurant means its
- Ⓐ location.
- Ⓑ price range.
- Ⓒ style of food.
- Ⓓ mood or feeling.

3 Articulate means
- Ⓐ well-known.
- Ⓑ well-spoken.
- Ⓒ well-rounded.
- Ⓓ well-adjusted.

4 Humiliation means
- Ⓐ humor.
- Ⓑ shame.
- Ⓒ persuasion.
- Ⓓ disappointment.

5 Intimidating means
- Ⓐ exciting.
- Ⓑ forgiving.
- Ⓒ surprising.
- Ⓓ frightening.

6 If you have an obligation, it means you have
- Ⓐ a duty.
- Ⓑ a regret.
- Ⓒ a question.
- Ⓓ an opportunity.

7 Stimulating means
- Ⓐ private.
- Ⓑ serious.
- Ⓒ confusing.
- Ⓓ interesting.

8 To surpass means to
- Ⓐ give up control.
- Ⓑ practice over and over.
- Ⓒ become greater or better.
- Ⓓ change in significant ways.

Directions: Questions 9–15 are about "They Speak for Success." Read each question and choose the best answer. You may look at the selection on pages 389–399 to help you answer the questions.  Open Book

LITERARY ANALYSIS

9 The students' stories are all examples of
- Ⓐ lessons learned from a speech class.
- Ⓑ how public speaking can help a career.
- Ⓒ embarrassing public speaking experiences.
- Ⓓ the importance of listening when others speak.

10 Mr. Lindsey bought Justin a suit to wear to a tournament. In the news feature, this example supports the idea that
- Ⓐ Justin was proud of his appearance.
- Ⓑ Mr. Lindsey cared about his students.
- Ⓒ Students had to dress nicely while speaking.
- Ⓓ Mr. Lindsey wasted the money from the MacArthur Fellowship.

GO ON

EDGE Level C

"They Speak for Success" and "Breaking the Ice"

 Open Book

11 Mr. Lindsey gave Steve Kuo several examples to teach him about which of these ideas?

Ⓐ the value of careful preparation

Ⓑ the need to be polite to the judges

Ⓒ the importance of not showing nervousness

Ⓓ the appropriate use of gestures when speaking

COMPREHENSION

12 The student stories are from a book called *It Doesn't Take a Genius*. This title relates to the stories because the students were

Ⓐ poor but smart.

Ⓑ just ordinary people.

Ⓒ having difficulty in school.

Ⓓ in competition with geniuses.

13 The students feel that forensics made them more

Ⓐ popular.

Ⓑ confident.

Ⓒ emotional.

Ⓓ intelligent.

14 One of the messages in this news feature is that

Ⓐ an audience is a lot like a jury.

Ⓑ good speaking skills can be learned.

Ⓒ some of the best speakers do not prepare.

Ⓓ the exact words of a speech are not important.

Directions: Read question 15. Write your answer on a separate sheet of paper.

15

> Welcome to Forensics Class at Logan High in Union City, California, twenty miles south of San Francisco. Here "forensics" does not refer to criminal science but to the word's original meaning: competitive public speaking that includes dramatic presentations, impromptu speeches, original oratory, and traditional debate. Lindsey's students are black, white, Hispanic, and Filipino; freshmen, sophomores, juniors, and seniors. Some are honors students. Some are poor or even homeless.

What is the main idea of this paragraph? Provide example details that support this idea.

Directions: Questions 16–22 are about "Breaking the Ice." Read each question and choose the best answer. You may look at the selection on pages 401–404 to help you answer the questions.

LITERARY ANALYSIS

16 What is one thing that is humorous about the author's final suggestion to call Phil Grant?

Ⓐ Phil Grant is not a real person.

Ⓑ Phil Grant is not good with girls.

Ⓒ The author would be more helpful than Phil Grant.

Ⓓ Readers cannot really call Phil Grant.

GO ON

UNIT 4

"They Speak for Success" and "Breaking the Ice"

 Open Book

17 The author calls his friend's ability to talk to girls a "mysterious superhuman power." He makes this comparison to humorously express a feeling of

Ⓐ awe.

Ⓑ relief.

Ⓒ delight.

Ⓓ satisfaction.

18 The author feared becoming a bark-eating hermit with only animal friends. This is an example of

Ⓐ odd comparisons.

Ⓑ impossible events.

Ⓒ informal language.

Ⓓ everyday situations.

COMPREHENSION

19 Which of these is true about the author of "Breaking the Ice"?

Ⓐ He gains confidence from his date with Judy.

Ⓑ He realizes that people who are funny often get dates.

Ⓒ He recommends waiting until you can drive to go on a date.

Ⓓ He seems amused that anyone would ask him for dating advice.

20 When the author was a teenager, why was asking for a date a challenge?

Ⓐ He wanted the girl to ask him first.

Ⓑ He was worried about being rejected.

Ⓒ He was afraid his mother would object.

Ⓓ He wanted to date a girl his friend liked.

21 In "Breaking the Ice," the author mainly uses humor to make fun of

Ⓐ himself.

Ⓑ Eric Knott.

Ⓒ Phil Grant.

Ⓓ teenagers.

Directions: Read question 22. Write your answer on a separate sheet of paper.

22

> Thus it was that, finally, Judy and I went on an actual date, to see a movie in White Plains, New York. If I were to sum up the romantic ambience of this date in four words, those words would be: "My mother was driving." This made for an extremely quiet drive, because my mother, realizing that her presence was hideously embarrassing, had to pretend she wasn't there. If it had been legal, I think she would have got out and sprinted alongside the car, steering through the window. Judy and I, sitting in the back seat about seventy-five feet apart, were also silent, unable to communicate without the assistance of Phil, Nancy, and Sandy.

How does the writer structure this paragraph to achieve humor? Use text details to explain your answer.

UNIT 4

DONE!

EDGE Level C

Reader Reflection

Directions: Answer questions 1–10. If necessary, use the back of the page.

"My English"	"How I Learned English"
1 What did you learn about chronological order that will help you the next time you read a nonfiction narrative?	**6** What did you learn about free verse poetry that will help you the next time you read a poem?
2 Explain how questioning the author will help you the next time you read.	**7** Explain how questioning the poet will help you the next time you read a poem.
3 Write what you liked and did not like about "My English." Include examples from this work of narrative nonfiction.	**8** Write what you liked and did not like about "How I Learned English." Include examples from the poem.

I liked...	I liked...
I did not like...	**I did not like...**

4 Are you interested in reading more writing by Julia Alvarez? _____ Yes _____ No

9 Are you interested in reading more works by Gregory Djanikian? _____ Yes _____ No

5 Are you interested in reading more nonfiction narratives by other authors? _____ Yes _____ No

10 Are you interested in reading more poetry by other authors? _____ Yes _____ No

An Excerpt from "My English" and "How I Learned English"

 **Closed Book**

Directions: Read each question and choose the best answer.

1 To accentuate something means to make it

- Ⓐ accurate.
- Ⓑ last longer.
- Ⓒ work better.
- Ⓓ more noticeable.

2 To banish means to

- Ⓐ give up.
- Ⓑ point out.
- Ⓒ send away.
- Ⓓ fall behind.

3 Countenance means

- Ⓐ a facial expression.
- Ⓑ a personal preference.
- Ⓒ an unusual characteristic.
- Ⓓ an outstanding performance.

4 If a person is discerning, it means that person

- Ⓐ learns very quickly.
- Ⓑ is willing to take risks.
- Ⓒ asks a lot of questions.
- Ⓓ makes good judgments.

5 Disrespectful means

- Ⓐ insulting.
- Ⓑ revealing.
- Ⓒ disturbing.
- Ⓓ comforting.

6 To enlist means to

- Ⓐ trust someone completely.
- Ⓑ persuade someone to help.
- Ⓒ reply to someone's question.
- Ⓓ change the way someone thinks.

7 To enumerate means to

- Ⓐ name one by one.
- Ⓑ pass back and forth.
- Ⓒ repeat over and over.
- Ⓓ switch from front to back.

8 Interminably means

- Ⓐ endlessly.
- Ⓑ comfortably.
- Ⓒ increasingly.
- Ⓓ impressively.

Directions: Items 9–15 are about the excerpt from "My English." Read each question and choose the best answer. You may look at the selection on pages 416–422 to help you answer the questions.

 **Open Book**

9 The author of "My English" uses chronological order to show the sequence of

- Ⓐ learning a new language.
- Ⓑ adjusting to a new culture.
- Ⓒ changing from a child to an adult.
- Ⓓ realizing the importance of the past.

10 Chronological order is a good way for the author to present the ideas in this narrative because she wants to

- Ⓐ describe a gradual change.
- Ⓑ teach a lesson about communication.
- Ⓒ show a cause and effect relationship.
- Ⓓ tell exactly when certain events took place.

UNIT 4

GO ON ▶

An Excerpt from "My English" and "How I Learned English" Open Book

11 Which sentence from the narrative includes a signal word that helps show the order of events?

Ⓐ A country where everyone spoke English!

Ⓑ Soon it wasn't so strange that everyone was speaking in English instead of Spanish.

Ⓒ What would it feel like to be a flower with roots in the ground?

Ⓓ Sometimes I could see wisps of gray hair that strayed from under her headdress.

12 Which of these events happens last?

Ⓐ The author moves to New York.

Ⓑ The author's mother teaches her about idioms.

Ⓒ The author uses her imagination to write stories.

Ⓓ The author has a conversation with her grandfather.

COMPREHENSION

13 Why is Sister Maria important to the author's narrative?

Ⓐ Sister Maria figures out why the author has been struggling to learn.

Ⓑ Sister Maria writes poetry that inspires the author to write her own books.

Ⓒ Sister Maria takes a special interest in the author that no one has before.

Ⓓ Sister Maria helps the author learn not just to use language, but also to love it.

14 The title, "My English," shows that the author

Ⓐ feels at home with the English language.

Ⓑ learned English with help from many people.

Ⓒ has trouble understanding people with accents.

Ⓓ is uncomfortable speaking English with her family.

Directions: Read question 15. Write your answer on a separate sheet of paper.

15

> Later, at home, Mami said that you had to take what her younger brother said "with a grain of salt." I thought she was still referring to Tío Gus's demonstration, and I tried to puzzle out what she was saying. Finally, I asked what she meant. "Taking what someone says with a grain of salt is an idiomatic expression in English," she explained. It was pure voodoo is what it was—what later I learned poetry could also do: a grain of salt could symbolize both the human brain and a condiment for human nonsense. And it could be itself, too: a grain of salt to flavor a bland plate of American food.

Describe the text structure the author uses in this paragraph. Include information provided by signal words.

Directions: Questions 16–22 are about "How I Learned English." Read each question and choose the best answer. You may look at the selection on pages 424–425 to help you answer the questions.

LITERARY ANALYSIS

16 When you read a free verse poem, you expect to see

Ⓐ rhyming words.

Ⓑ quotation marks.

Ⓒ indented paragraphs.

Ⓓ lines of different lengths.

GO ON

An Excerpt from "My English" and "How I Learned English"  Open Book

17 Free verse does **not** use

Ⓐ slang.

Ⓑ rhyme.

Ⓒ images.

Ⓓ punctuation.

18 Read these lines from the poem.

> Chuck Keller, fat even as a boy, was on first,
> His t-shirt riding up over his gut,

Why does the poet break the sentence into two lines?

Ⓐ to set the tone

Ⓑ to create suspense

Ⓒ to emphasize the image

Ⓓ to make it easier to read

19 Read these lines from the poem.

> Tipped with cirrus.
>   And there I was,
> Just off the plane and plopped in the middle

The poet separates the words "And there I was" from the other lines to emphasize the speaker's feeling of

Ⓐ anger.

Ⓑ isolation.

Ⓒ impatience.

Ⓓ embarrassment.

20 The speaker can best be described as

Ⓐ eager to fit in.

Ⓑ afraid to try new things.

Ⓒ shy about making friends.

Ⓓ homesick for his own country.

21 The boys in this poem do not all speak the same language. Which of these helps them to communicate?

Ⓐ joking

Ⓑ fighting

Ⓒ laughing

Ⓓ daydreaming

Directions: Read question 22. Write your answer on a separate sheet of paper.

22
> And everybody peeled away from me
> And dropped from laughter, and there we were,
> All of us writhing on the ground for one reason
> Or another.
>   Someone said "shin" again,
> There was a wild stamping of hands on the ground,
> A kicking of feet, and the fit
> Of laughter overtook me too,

How does the poet emphasize different ideas in the free verse structure of these lines? Refer to the text as you explain your answer.

UNIT 4

DONE!

Name _____ Date _____

Student Profile: Cluster Tests

Directions: Use the **Answer Key** and **Scoring Guides** on pages 148, 149, and 150 to score Cluster Tests 1, 2, and 3 respectively. Circle the item number of each correct answer below. Then multiply items correct by points. Include the rubric scores for the constructed-response items. Calculate the overall test score by adding to 100. To gauge mastery for a particular tested skill or Common Core Standard, review the Cluster Test and Unit Test results.

Cluster 1   Date _____

Subtest	Tested Skill	ITEM ANALYSIS		TEST SCORES
		Item Numbers	Mastery	No. Correct x Points = Score
Key Vocabulary	Key Vocabulary L.9-10.6	1 2 3 4 5 6 7 8	6 out of 8 + −	___ x 4 = ___ /32
Literary Analysis	Analyze Text Structure: Cause and Effect RI.9-10.5	9 10 11 12	3 out of 4 + −	___ x 4 = ___ /16
	Analyze Text Structure: Problem and Solution RI.9-10.5	16 17 18	2 out of 3 + −	___ x 4 = ___ /12
Comprehension	Comprehension RI.9-10.10	13 14 19 20 21	4 out of 5 + −	___ x 4 = ___ /20
Constructed Response	Use Text Evidence RI.9-10.1; RI.9-10.10; W.9-10.9	Rubric Scores Item 15 ___ + Item 22 ___ = ___		= ___ /20

Overall Score (Add Points Earned)   ___ /100

Cluster 2   Date _____

Subtest	Tested Skill	ITEM ANALYSIS		TEST SCORES
		Item Numbers	Mastery	No. Correct x Points = Score
Key Vocabulary	Key Vocabulary L.9-10.6	1 2 3 4 5 6 7 8	6 out of 8 + −	___ x 4 = ___ /32
Literary Analysis	Analyze Text Structure: Main Idea and Details RI.9-10.5	9 10 11	2 out of 3 + −	___ x 4 = ___ /12
	Analyze Humor RI.9-10.5	16 17 18	2 out of 3 + −	___ x 4 = ___ /12
Comprehension	Comprehension RI.9-10.10	12 13 14 19 20 21	5 out of 6 + −	___ x 4 = ___ /24
Constructed Response	Use Text Evidence RI.9-10.1; RI.9-10.10; W.9-10.9	Rubric Scores Item 15 ___ + Item 22 ___ = ___		= ___ /20

Overall Score (Add Points Earned)   ___ /100

Cluster 3   Date _____

Subtest	Tested Skill	ITEM ANALYSIS		TEST SCORES
		Item Numbers	Mastery	No. Correct x Points = Score
Key Vocabulary	Key Vocabulary L.9-10.6	1 2 3 4 5 6 7 8	6 out of 8 + −	___ x 4 = ___ /32
Literary Analysis	Analyze Text Structure: Chronological Order RI.9-10.5	9 10 11 12	3 out of 4 + −	___ x 4 = ___ /16
	Analyze Text Structure: Free Verse RL.9-10.5	16 17 18 19	3 out of 4 + −	___ x 4 = ___ /16
Comprehension	Comprehension RI.9-10.10	13 14 20 21	3 out of 4 + −	___ x 4 = ___ /16
Constructed Response	Use Text Evidence RL.9-10.1; RL.9-10.10; RI.9-10.1; RI.9-10.10; W.9-10.9	Rubric Scores Item 15 ___ + Item 22 ___ = ___		= ___ /20

Overall Score (Add Points Earned)   ___ /100

Language Acquisition Rubrics

Cluster 1
DEFINE AND EXPLAIN

Pair Talk ▶ page 382

Directions: Pair students. Give each student a few moments to review the selections and find a science word. Partners should then take turns telling what the word means.

Language Function | 1 | 2 | 3 | 4 |

What to look for:
how well the student defines and explains the word by using examples, details, descriptive words, and possibly visuals. For definitions, student should use sentence patterns such as *It means ...* or *A ... is a ... that ...* For explanations, students should use the phrase *for example*.

Cluster 3
USE APPROPRIATE LANGUAGE

Act It Out ▶ page 428

Directions: Give the students a few moments to review the selection. Then in small groups students should act out two scenes: one in which Julia Alvarez is talking with friends, and the other in which the students are talking to their teacher.

Language Function | 1 | 2 | 3 | 4 |

What to look for:
how well the student uses informal and formal language (both verbal and nonverbal) depending on the situation and who he/she is talking to.

Cluster 2
RECOGNIZE AND RESPOND TO HUMOR

Group Talk ▶ page 408

Directions: Give the students a few moments to review the selection and choose a passage. Then in groups, each student should share his/her passage and tell why it's funny.

Language Function | 1 | 2 | 3 | 4 |

What to look for:
how well the student recognizes humor in familiar situations, unexpected happenings, and unusual comparisons, and explains why he/she thinks it is funny. Student should respond appropriately (e.g., by laughing or smiling and using repetition in the case of unexpected events), and be sensitive to others who may not "get it" by clarifying his/her opinions.

	Language Function Rubric
4	Student effectively performs the function.
3	Student performs the function.
2	Student does not adequately perform the function.
1	Student makes no attempt or offers a non-verbal response.

UNIT 4

Reading and Literary Analysis

Directions: Read each question and choose the best answer.

1 Study the dictionary entry.

> **a·sy·lum** (e si' lem) *n.* 1. (especially in the past) a building for the housing of the mentally ill or orphaned children. 2. a safe place for criminals or those seeking to escape capture by the law. 3. shelter and protection granted to a person from a foreign country by a government in its own territory. 4. any place of safety.

Which sentence uses the word asylum as explained in definition 3?

A   The tourists wandered through the ruins of the old asylum.

B   The man accused of robbery claimed asylum inside the church.

C   The refugees were happy to receive asylum in a peaceful country.

D   The deer darted into the temporary asylum provided by the bushes.

2 Study the dictionary entry and read the sentence.

> **sed·en·tar·y** (sed'n ter'e) *adj.* 1. requiring or frequently using a sitting position. 2. characterized by lack of exercise. 3. *Zoology* a. staying in one place; not migrating b. having to do with animals that are permanently attached to something.

> Most Canada geese fly south in the winter, but the geese in Grant Park are sedentary and spend all year by the pond.

Which definition of the word sedentary is used in this sentence?

A   definition 1

B   definition 2

C   definition 3a

D   definition 3b

3 Study the dictionary entry and read the sentence.

> **shard** (shard) also sherd *n.* 1. a piece, especially a piece of broken pottery. 2. *Zoology* a. a scale. b. a shell, as of an egg or a snail. c. the hardened forewing of a beetle.

> While digging in the garbage dump of the ancient village, the student found a shard with red and black decorations painted on it.

Which definition of the word shard is used in this sentence?

A   definition 1

B   definition 2a

C   definition 2b

D   definition 2c

4 Study the dictionary entry and read the sentence.

> **chi·me·ra** or **chi·mea·ra** (ki mer'e, ki-) *n.* 1. *Mythology* (often capitalized) a monster with a lion's head, a goat's body, and a snake's tail. 2. any horrible imaginary creature. 3. a dream or anything imaginary. 4. *Biology* an organism having tissue from two or more genetically distinct sources.

> The scientist used a microscope to study a sample taken from a chimera.

Which definition of the word chimera is used in this sentence?

A   definition 1

B   definition 2

C   definition 3

D   definition 4

GO ON

UNIT 4

Reading and Literary Analysis, *continued*

Directions: Questions 5–10 are about "Netiquette." Read the selection. Then read each question and choose the best answer.

Netiquette

Stepping into a new culture means immersing yourself in languages and customs that are unfamiliar. It's wise to be aware of both the spoken and the unspoken differences beginning with your first "hello." Following the social forms of that culture, with discerning eyes and ears, communicates respect. Knowing you are being polite will help you feel confident and comfortable in any environment.

If you know to greet people with a vigorous handshake in Germany, a quiet bow in Japan, and your palms pressed together in India, then you can make a strong first impression. You're on your way to developing good connections in those countries.

In any culture, people can commit social blunders and offend someone else without meaning to. Unwittingly stepping on someone's toes can cause you to feel separated from your new group. If people perceive communication as <u>disrespectful</u>, this can escalate into an angry clash. The Internet has a community and a culture just like countries do. To prevent clashes and disruption, the Internet culture has spawned a social code called Netiquette—Network Etiquette.

Etiquette sounds like a fancy word. It evokes images of things you will probably never do, such as figuring out which fork to use at afternoon tea with the Queen of England. But actually, etiquette is simply the form of interaction required by a specific society. Etiquette means social rules of conduct that tell people what normal, respectful speech and behavior are. These codes restrict life in order to <u>enhance</u> it—at the dinner table, in the gym or the classroom, at the movie theater, and in the infinite realms of Internet communication.

The world of electronic communication, or cyberspace, has its own culture and, therefore, its own codes of behavior. Why do we need rules to tell people how to talk to each other in forums, chat rooms, and e-mail? Because being able to send instantaneous

written messages makes it too easy to say something without thinking about what you really want to communicate. Plus, you're communicating with someone that you can't see and possibly may never have met. That person can't use your body language or tone of voice for clues about your real meaning. Sometimes people almost forget they are interacting with real human beings. As a result, people may behave online in ways they never would in person.

> Netiquette helps to
> smooth over
> rough situations
> and bridge the gaps
> in our understanding with
> a few common rules.

It is sometimes said that whatever *can* be misunderstood in an e-mail message *will* be misunderstood. So, what is to be done about this dilemma of contemporary life? Netiquette helps to smooth over rough situations and bridge the gaps in our understanding with a few common rules.

Some people operate under the mistaken notion that typing in all capital letters makes them look authoritative. Do not be one of these misguided cyber souls. All caps is okay for headings or titles, but if you type whole sentences that way, you are "shouting." Speak persuasively in your e-mails, charm and entertain your reader, but please do not yell. Similarly, do not be a sender of "nasty-grams." Nasty-grams are angry e-mails sent to friends you are enraged with at the moment. Give yourself some time to cool off. When you're upset with someone, the last thing you should do is write an unpleasant e-mail message that you will later regret sending.

If you're going to forward a message, delete all the extra information and characters before you press

Reading and Literary Analysis, *continued*

"send." It's a small courtesy. The point of all forms of etiquette is that small courtesies add up. Also, please check before you start distributing information, to make sure the message isn't a hoax or an "urban legend." Check your facts before sending something on; bad information spreads like wildfire on the Internet. And here's a news flash: A lot of people don't like receiving joke lists and chain letters sent indiscriminately to fifty of your closest friends. They might never tell you directly, but they will be grateful if you respect their time and send only messages that address their specific interests.

Ask people's permission before you send attachments, such as documents, pictures, and compressed archives. A huge attachment can take a long time to download, tying up the receiver's computer. Similarly, don't send messages that are formatted in HTML, which is a computer language used to create documents; just keep to text messages.

Even if your e-mail program can generate beautifully formatted HTML, the friends you're communicating with may not have compatible programs. Also, if you use a signature file, at the end of your messages, make certain that it has no more than six lines—a small feature of elegant Netiquette.

No discussion of Netiquette is complete without ample attention paid to flaming. Flaming is when people express a strongly negative emotion online without holding back. An Internet study indicated that e-mail can evoke much stronger emotions in recipients than any other form of written communication. Don't "litter the information highway" by typing anything on your screen that you wouldn't say to someone face-to-face.

Do what is good and fair to the people who will read your online communications. Good Netiquette will soon become a habit, and you will be able to navigate in the cyberspace community with ease.

Reading and Literary Analysis, *continued*

5 In paragraph 4, the image of afternoon tea with the Queen of England is an example of which element of humor?

A odd comparisons

B impossible events

C informal language

D everyday situations

6 Read these sentences from the selection.

> Sometimes people almost forget they are interacting with real human beings. As a result, people may behave online in ways they never would in person.

Which word or phrase **best** shows that these sentences use cause-and-effect organization?

A Sometimes

B almost

C As a result

D never would

7 According to the selection, why is it important to avoid sending negative e-mail messages?

A People react strongly to messages they read online.

B People will respond with more angry messages.

C People may misunderstand the negative messages.

D People often forward messages to their friends.

8 <u>Disrespectful</u> means

A insulting.

B revealing.

C disturbing.

D comforting.

9 To <u>enhance</u> means to

A handle.

B endure.

C balance.

D improve.

Directions: Read question 10. Write your answer on a separate sheet of paper.

10 Netiquette is not terribly difficult, but being good at it does take some thought. Find two examples from the text to support this statement.

GO ON

Reading and Literary Analysis, *continued*

Directions: Questions 11–17 are about "Talking with Your Hands." Read the selection. Then read each question and choose the best answer.

Talking with Your Hands

For most people, communicating involves talking with their mouths and listening with their ears. Millions of other people communicate in a different way. They "talk" with their hands and "listen" with their eyes. This form of communication is called sign language.

People who cannot hear or speak aloud have always needed a method of communication. Over the years, several methods have been developed. In the 1500s, an Italian scientist and mathematician named Gerolamo Cardano had a son who was deaf. Cardano taught his son to understand a set of written symbols. He argued that this showed deaf people could learn even if they could not hear words. This was a great change; at the time, most scientists and educators believed that deaf people were impossible to teach. Cardano's arguments influenced another European, Juan Pablo de Bonet. In 1620, de Bonet published a book that described a manual alphabet, a system of finger shapes that represented different letters.

Cardano and de Bonet were not the only ones interested in communication for deaf people. In cities and villages where large numbers of deaf people lived, the deaf developed their own ways of talking. On Martha's Vineyard, an island off the coast of North America, many of the people were born deaf. In the 1700s, this deaf community invented a set of hand signs to communicate. Many hearing people on the island also learned to use the sign language.

Still, in many places it was hard for deaf people to communicate or get an education. In 1755, Abbé Charles Michel de L'Epée of Paris began the first free school for deaf people. Abbé de L'Epée put an <u>emphasis</u> on deaf people communicating with both others who are deaf and the hearing world. Abbé de L'Epée started with a set of signs that were already being used by a group of deaf people in Paris. Then he added his own elements to enhance the basic language and create a signed version of spoken French. While de L'Epée's school was a great advance for the deaf in France, many found his system of signs awkward and tedious.

In spite of the signing community on Martha's Vineyard, there was no school for the deaf in the United States to match de L'Epée's school in France. Thomas Hopkins Gallaudet helped to change that. Gallaudet's neighbor had a daughter who was deaf, and Gallaudet became interested in helping her communicate. In 1815, he traveled to Europe to study deaf communication. He visited the school for the deaf in Paris. Gallaudet was especially impressed by Laurent Clerc, a deaf sign language teacher at the Paris school. Gallaudet hired Clerc to come to the United States and help him open a new school.

In 1817, Gallaudet and Clerc founded the American School for the Deaf in Hartford, Connecticut. Clerc taught using de L'Epée's system of signs. Outside the classroom, he used a more casual system of signs that the local deaf community had already established. Soon, Clerc's students developed an American set of signs based in part on Clerc's Paris signs. Other schools for the deaf soon opened in the United States, mostly using these American signs.

Today, these American signs have become American Sign Language, the fourth most-spoken language in the United States. It has been called one of the most complete and expressive sign languages in the world and is a great way for <u>articulate</u> people to express <u>subtle</u> feelings.

Although American Sign Language has proven to be a great means of communication, there is also controversy about it. Many advocates for the deaf say that it is better for them to learn to speak aloud like hearing people. They point out that a person using sign language can only communicate with other sign language speakers. Others argue that most deaf people will never speak aloud well enough to be understood by the general public, so it is more important for them to use sign language and communicate with each other. They also point out that American Sign Language is an important part of deaf culture and deaf people should be proud to use it. Still others support total

GO ON ➔

Reading and Literary Analysis, *continued*

communication, which is a system that incorporates sign language, oral speech, and other methods of communication.

While the debate continues over which language people who are deaf should learn, there is no doubt that sign language is an important way of communicating.

---

11 Which detail from "Talking with Your Hands" shows it is organized in chronological order?

   A De L'Epée's system of signs is compared to the American signs.

   B Gallaudet's problem of helping his neighbor's daughter is explained.

   C Cardano's achievements are described before de L'Epée's school.

   D De Bonet's alphabet is included as an example of a sign language.

12 Why did Cardano believe that deaf people could be educated?

   A He taught his deaf son to understand written signs.

   B He had traveled to de L'Epée's school for the deaf.

   C He read de Bonet's book about the manual alphabet.

   D He was deaf himself but was able to become a scientist.

13 According to the information in the selection, which system of sign language was developed last?

   A de L'Epée's system of signs

   B American Sign Language

   C de Bonet's manual alphabet

   D Martha's Vineyard sign language

14 <u>Emphasis</u> means a type of

   A talent or skill.

   B special importance.

   C solution to a problem.

   D embarrassing situation.

15 <u>Articulate</u> means

   A well-known.

   B well-spoken.

   C well-sounded.

   D well-adjusted.

16 <u>Subtle</u> means hard to

   A hide.

   B make.

   C notice.

   D explain.

Directions: Read question 17. Write your answer on a separate sheet of paper.

17 What is the connection between Abbé Charles Michel de L'Epée and American Sign Language? Use details from the passage to support your answer.

Reading and Literary Analysis, *continued*

Directions: Questions 18–24 are about "What's So Fair About Science?" Read the selection. Then read each question and choose the best answer.

What's So Fair About Science?

You take a copy of the latest handout that your teacher is giving out and pass the stack of papers back to the next lucky recipient. You look down to see that you now have to produce a project for the next science fair. Your teacher may as well have given you an order to reach the North Pole in six weeks. You slump down in your seat, rolling your eyes. You think that you probably know more about the North Pole than doing a science project. Just remember, science is a part of life. You probably know more about it than you think. If not, you can learn a lot about it by taking part in a science fair. I can assure you that making a science project is much easier than completing an arctic expedition.

Any <u>discerning</u> polar explorer will tell you that to get to the North Pole, you do not just grab a coat and head north. There is a lot a research involved to find out everything you can about where you are going and the best way to get there. The same is true for a science project. You have two main issues to tackle. First, you have to find a question to investigate that interests you. This may seem harder than crossing sheets of floating ice. However, it will ensure that your curiosity will help you see the project through to the end. Second, you need to be certain that you understand the rules of the science fair and how your project must be presented. There are often requirements for what your project needs to include. It would be a shame to have found some really interesting answers only to find that you are disqualified because you did not cite enough references in your bibliography.

On any expedition, successful explorers do not leave the house empty handed. They gather the supplies they need to do the job beforehand. You, too, will need to select the methods you will use to investigate your question and gather the materials you will need. This is a great time to <u>enlist</u> the aid of resources such as teachers or science fair coordinators and talk to them about what you want to do and what you think you will need. They can provide suggestions and help you avoid common mistakes. You may be remembering the nightmares you used to have about your sister's first science fair project. No one ever did figure out how those ants escaped and where they went. No need to fear. You do not have to make the same mistakes she did.

At last you have <u>banished</u> all fears and are ready to brave the frozen wastes, I mean, the challenges of finding some answers to your question. Journals of many explorers tell of false starts and obstacles that they had to overcome in order to reach their destination. It is likely that you will find that things do not work exactly as you planned. The important thing is to document all you have done in a journal and be prepared to make adjustments as you go. Scientific discovery is not about finding the right answer. It is about researching a question and doing experiments to test whether a proposed answer is really true.

To accomplish a goal as lofty as reaching the point at the top of the world, you need to understand where you are going and what you need to get there. It takes careful preparation, determination, and patience to see the journey through to the end. Your task is probably much easier than you think it will be. If you give yourself the time you need, you will find that completing a science fair project is a cake walk compared to avoiding hungry polar bears and shifting ice. All you need to do is take that first step.

Reading and Literary Analysis, continued

18 If a person is <u>discerning</u>, it means that person

A learns very quickly.

B is willing to take risks.

C asks a lot of questions.

D makes good judgments.

19 To <u>enlist</u> means to

A trust someone completely.

B persuade someone to help.

C reply to someone's questions.

D change the way someone thinks.

20 To <u>banish</u> means to

A give up.

B point out.

C send away.

D fall behind.

21 How is this selection organized?

A Ideas are discussed in the order of their importance.

B A problem is described and solutions are proposed.

C Events are described in the order in which they occur.

D The relationship between causes and effects is explained.

22 Which sentence from the selection is an example of exaggeration?

A You look down to see that you now have to produce a project for the next science fair.

B This may seem harder than crossing sheets of floating ice.

C They can provide suggestions and help you avoid common mistakes.

D Your task is probably much easier than you think it will be.

23 Which sentence from the selection signals a flashback?

A Your teacher may as well have given you an order to reach the North Pole in six weeks.

B Any discerning polar explorer will tell you that to get to the North Pole, you do not just grab a coat and head north.

C On any expedition, successful explorers do not leave the house empty handed.

D You may be remembering the nightmares you used to have about your sister's first science fair project.

24 The flashback in this selection helps the readers understand the

A reasons they may fear science projects.

B experiences they have had working on science projects.

C opinion they have about creating successful projects.

D methods they use to find resources for completing projects.

Directions: Read question 25. Write your answer on a separate sheet of paper.

25 The author's argument in this passage is based on a comparison between a student and a polar explorer. Assess whether this is a valid comparison. Provide details from the text to support your ideas.

UNIT 4

DONE!

Grammar and Writing

Directions: Read the composition. It contains errors. Then read each question and choose the best answer.

Robert Capa, Photojournalist

(1) Communication is most effective when <u>he</u> delivers a meaningful message with an emotional impact. **(2)** Photojournalist Robert Capa was a master communicator. **(3)** He told the story of war through the universal language of pictures—providing some of the most intense and personal photographs of war ever made.[1]

(4) Hungarian-born Capa became politically active at a young age. **(5)** He was drawn to adventure, especially when people were fighting for a cause. **(6)** Several years into his professional career, he accepted an important assignment—the Spanish Civil War—taking photographs that captured both violent and sensitive moments. **(7)** The British magazine *picture post* called him the greatest war photographer in the world—and he was only 25![2]

(8) Capa often said, "If your pictures aren't good enough, you aren't close enough."[3] **(9)** And so he put himself in the middle of the action. **(10)** One of <u>its</u> bravest moments was going ashore with the first wave of soldiers during the D-Day invasion of World War II. **(11)** As the bullets tore holes in the water around <u>him</u>, he kept repeating something he had learned during the Spanish Civil War. **(12)** "Es una cosa muy seria." **(13)** (This is very serious business.)[4] **(14)** He shot four rolls of 35mm film during those fearful moments, but a darkroom technician, trying to rush the processing of the precious film, ruined all but 11 frames. **(15)** Those 11 images are some of the most dramatic war images of all time.

(16) Capa rarely photographed the dead, but many of his photographs were at the edge of death—images of people who moments later were killed or images of survivors mourning the death of someone close to them. **(17)** His last photograph was haunting in a different way. **(18)** Taken in 1954, it showed soldiers scanning a field for land mines in Indochina. **(19)** Moments later, Capa stepped on a mine and was killed, camera in hand. **(20)** He was only 40, but he had lived <u>their</u> life exactly as he had wanted. **(21)** He had been a participant, not just an observer.[5] **(22)** Through his photographs, he left a legacy that provides an intimate view of the emotion and impact of war.

Footnotes:

1. Capa, Cornell, and Richard Whalen, eds. Robert Capa, Photographs. New York: Alfred A. Knopf, Inc., 1985.

2. *Ibid.*

3. Robert Capa, Photographs. New York: Aperture, 1996.

4. Kershaw, Alex. Blood and Champagne: The Life and Times of Robert Capa. New York: Da Capo Press, 2004.

5. Capa, Cornell, and Richard Whalen, eds. Robert Capa, Photographs. New York: Alfred A. Knopf, Inc., 1985.

Grammar and Writing, *continued*

1 In sentence 1, the word <u>he</u> should be changed to

A   it

B   him

C   they

D   No change

2 Which transition should be added to the beginning of sentence 2 to show a connection to the previous sentence?

A   All in all

B   In other words

C   As a consequence

D   By this definition

3 What change, if any, should be made to sentence 7?

A   Change *magazine* to **magizine**

B   Put a comma after *magazine*

C   Change *picture post* to *Picture Post*

D   No change

4 In sentence 10, the word <u>its</u> should be changed to

A   their

B   your

C   Capa's

D   No change

5 In sentence 11, the word <u>him</u> should be changed to

A   it

B   us

C   them

D   No change

6 What change, if any, should be made to sentence 18?

A   Remove the comma after 1954

B   Change *scanning* to **scaning**

C   Change *Indochina* to **indochina**

D   No change

7 In sentence 20, the word <u>their</u> should be changed to

A   its

B   his

C   our

D   No change

8 Which sentence is an example of a good transition?

A   sentence 1

B   sentence 9

C   sentence 21

D   sentence 22

UNIT 4

Grammar and Writing, *continued*

Directions: Read the composition. It contains errors. Then read each question and choose the best answer.

Be Careful with Customs

(1) The world is full of adventures just waiting to happen, and traveling to different countries and cultures opens the doors of exploration for <u>her</u>. **(2)** But you have to be careful. **(3)** Just one wrong head turn or one small gesture can get you into trouble. **(4)** Actions and customs that are common and acceptable in the United States can be misunderstood and even insulting in other countries.

(5) You might get a rude look when you give a thumbs-up sign in Iran or an OK sign in Brazil, or if you turn your peace/victory sign the wrong way in England. **(6)** Whistling indoors in Russia is impolite. **(7)** And, if you forget to take off your shoes when entering a Japanese household, <u>he is</u> a great insult.

(8) The customs around eating are also varied. **(9)** In most countries, it is impolite to start eating before everyone is served. **(10)** In Japan, it is an insult to the person cooking if you don't start eating right away while the food is at its best. **(11)** In some countries, it is rude to eat everything on your plate. **(12)** In France, you are expected to soak up the last bits of food and sauce with a piece of bread—a tribute to <u>his</u> fine cuisine.

(13) Some rules relate to the hands and feet. **(14)** In many countries, it's rude to talk with your hands in your pockets, to put your hands on your hips (a sign of aggression), or to point or beckon with one finger. **(15)** There are all kinds of rules related to how you speak and what you wear. **(16)** It's bad manners to cross your legs in an Arab country, because showing the soles of your feet is an insult. **(17)** In Thailand and India, you should be sure your feet are not pointing toward someone or something. **(18)** And, in many countries, wearing street shoes in the house is forbidden.

(19) As a visitor to a country, whether for business or pleasure, the important customs are worth learning so that you better understand the culture. **(20)** The choice is <u>theirs</u>. **(21)** It's best to be a welcome guest and a good ambassador.

Grammar and Writing, *continued*

9 In sentence 1, the word <u>her</u> should be changed to

A me

B you

C him

D No change

10 What change, if any, should be made to sentence 4?

A Change *acceptable* to **acceptible**

B Change *United States* to **united states**

C Put parentheses around the phrase *and even insulting*

D No change

11 In sentence 7, the words <u>he is</u> should be changed to

A it is

B you are

C they are

D No change

12 In sentence 12, the word <u>his</u> should be changed to

A her

B our

C its

D No change

13 Which transition should be added to the beginning of sentence 17 to show a connection to the previous sentence?

A Similarly

B Therefore

C Otherwise

D Meanwhile

14 What change, if any, should be made to sentence 19?

A Change *pleasure* to **plesure**

B Remove the commas around *whether for business or pleasure*

C Change *the important customs are worth learning* to **you should learn the important customs**

D No change

15 In sentence 20, the word <u>theirs</u> should be changed to

A his

B mine

C yours

D No change

16 Which sentence disrupts the flow of ideas in paragraph 4?

A sentence 14

B sentence 15

C sentence 16

D sentence 18

GO ON ▶

EDGE Level C

UNIT 4

Grammar and Writing, *continued*

Directions: Read the following writing prompt, and write a composition. Write on separate sheets of paper. Use the Writer's Checklist to make sure that you do your best work.

Prompt

You have read in the selection "My English" about how Julia Alvarez made the English language, including idioms, her own.

Write a report about idioms. Use the three sources provided on the following pages, the literature in the unit, and your own knowledge of idioms. Include one or more citations in your report, as well as one graphic aid (such as a table, diagram, or chart).

Writer's Checklist

☑ Write about all parts of the prompt.

☑ Present a clear central idea, and stay focused on it.

☑ Organize your composition from its introduction to its conclusion.

☑ Use transitions to connect your thoughts for the reader.

☑ Present meaningful ideas, and support them with specific information.

☑ Use appropriate words and a variety of sentence structures.

☑ Proofread and edit your writing for grammar, usage, mechanics, and spelling.

UNIT 4

Grammar and Writing, *continued*

Source 1:

Wikipedia, the free encyclopedia

Idiom

An **Idiom** is an expression (i.e., term or phrase) whose meaning cannot be deduced from the literal definitions and the arrangement of its parts, but refers instead to a figurative meaning that is known only through conventional use. In linguistics, idioms are widely assumed to be figures of speech that contradict the principle of compositionality; however, some debate has recently arisen on this subject.

In the English expression *to kick the bucket*, a listener knowing only the meaning of *kick* and *bucket* would be unable to deduce the expression's actual meaning, which is *to die*. Although it can refer literally to the act of striking a specific bucket with a foot, native speakers rarely use it that way. It cannot be directly translated to other languages — for example, the same expression in Polish is *to kick the calendar*, with the calendar being as detached from its usual meaning as the bucket in the English phrase is.

Idioms, hence, tend to confuse those not already familiar with them; students of a new language must learn its idiomatic expressions the way they learn its other vocabulary. In fact, many natural language words have *idiomatic origins,* but they have been sufficiently assimilated so that their figurative senses have been lost.

Idioms and Culture

Idioms are, in essence, often colloquial metaphors—terms which require some foundational knowledge, information, or experience, to use only within a culture where parties have common reference—and as such are not considered an official part of the language, but rather a part of the culture. As cultures are typically localized, idioms are often not useful for communication outside of local context. However, some idioms are more universally used than others, and they can be easily translated, or their metaphorical meaning can be more easily deduced.

The most common idioms can have deep roots, traceable across many languages. *To have blood on one's hands* is a familiar example, whose meaning is relatively obvious, although the context within English literature (see Macbeth and Pontius Pilate) may not be. Many have translations in other languages and tend to become international.

GO ON

Name _____ Date _____

Grammar and Writing, *continued*

Source 2:

Table of Idioms	
Dictionary of English Idioms and Idiomatic Expressions	
All over the map	Something that does not relate to the main topic, but addresses multiple unrelated topics.
Babe in the woods	A naive, defenseless young person.
Catch as catch can	To try to get something any way you can.
Dime a dozen	Something that is common, possibly too common.
Eat humble pie	To apologize and show a lot of remorse for something.
Face the music	To accept the negative consequences for something you have done wrong.
Gild the lily	To decorate something that is already ornate.
Half-baked	An idea or scheme that has not been thought through or planned very well.
In a pickle	To be in some trouble or mess.
Jack-of-all-trades	Someone who can do many different jobs.

GO ON

EDGE Level C

UNIT 4

Grammar and Writing, *continued*

Source 3:

Idioms
The New Dictionary of Cultural Literacy

It isn't always the nonnative speaker's accent (which may be perfect) that enables people to recognize instantly an outsider who is learning their language—it's the odd mistakes that no native speaker would make. The idiomatic use of words such as *to, for,* and *with* varies from language to language. Just as each person has a unique, characteristic signature, each language has unique idioms. Thus, each language contains expressions that make no sense when translated literally into another tongue. The humorist Art Buchwald wrote a famous column, often reprinted, in which he translated some of our Thanksgiving (Mercidonnant) terms into literal French, with comic results. If a German or Spaniard or Italian literally translated *birthday suit* and *get down to brass tacks*, the terms would make no sense, or the wrong sense. Even a native speaker of English who is not used to hearing literate idioms such as *fits and starts*, *cock-and-bull story*, *hue and cry*, and *touch and go* will not be able to make sense of them. Our purpose in defining these idioms is to *let the cat out of the bag* for those who haven't heard them often enough to catch their meanings.

Other idioms are really allusions or foreign-language terms that make no sense unless you know what the allusions or terms mean. *Carry coals to Newcastle* translates adequately into any language, but it makes no sense to a person who doesn't know that Newcastle is a coal-mining city. Knowing the *literal* meaning of idioms won't enable you to understand them unless you also know what they allude to. Such ignorance is an *Achilles' heel* and an *albatross around one's neck*. Moreover, just knowing a *baker's dozen* of them is not enough; you have to know them *en masse*. Educators who complain about the illiteracy of the young but pay no attention to teaching idioms are just weeping *crocodile tears*. We have therefore decided to *cut the Gordian knot* by systematically defining some of the most widely used idioms in American literate culture. —E.D.H.

DONE!

EDGE Level C

Student Profile: Unit Tests

Directions: Use the **Answer Key** on page 151 to score the multiple-choice items. Circle the item number of each correct answer below. Calculate test scores by assigning one point for each correct answer. Use the scoring guides on page 151 to score the constructed-response items. Use the Good Writing Traits Rubric on page 122 to score the written composition. Total the scores and calculate the % score or use the conversion chart. To gauge mastery for a particular tested skill or Common Core Standard, review the Cluster Test and Unit Test results.

Reading and Literary Analysis

Category	Tested Skill	ITEM ANALYSIS		TEST SCORES
		Item Numbers	Mastery	Points: Earned / Total
Vocabulary	Use a Dictionary L.9-10.4	1 2 3 4	3 out of 4 + −	_____ / 4
	Key Vocabulary L.9-10.6	8 9 14 15 16 18 19 20	6 out of 8 + −	_____ / 8
Literary Analysis	Analyze Text Structures RI.9-10.5	5 6 11 13 21 22 23 24	6 out of 8 + −	_____ / 8
Comprehension	Comprehension RI.9-10.10	7 12	1 out of 2 + −	_____ / 2
Constructed Response	Use Text Evidence RI.9-10.1; RI.9-10.10; W.9-10.9	Rubric Scores Item 10 _____ + Item 17 _____ + Item 25 _____ = _____		_____ / 12

Overall Score (Points Earned ÷ Total Points x 100 = %)　　_____ ÷ 34 = _____%

Grammar and Writing

Category	Tested Skill	ITEM ANALYSIS		TEST SCORES
		Item Numbers	Mastery	Points: Earned / Total
Grammar	Pronouns L.9-10.1	1 5 9 11	3 out of 4 + −	_____ / 4
	Possessive Words L.9-10.1	4 7 12 15	3 out of 4 + −	_____ / 4
Revising and Editing	Organization W.9-10.5	2 8 13 16	3 out of 4 + −	_____ / 4
	Grammar, Mechanics, and Usage L.9-10.2	3 6 10 14	3 out of 4 + −	_____ / 4
Written Composition (Informative/ Explanatory) W.9-10.2; W.9-10.4; W.9-10.7; W.9-10.8; W.9-10.10	Focus and Unity	Rubric Scores: _____ / 4		
	Organization	_____ / 4		
	Development of Ideas	_____ / 4	=	_____ / 20
	Voice and Style	_____ / 4		
	Written Conventions	_____ / 4		

Overall Score (Points Earned ÷ Total Points x 100 = %)　　_____ ÷ 40 = _____%

EDGE Level C

UNIT 4

Project Rubric: A Multimedia Presentation

Score	Planning/Preparation	Content of Project	Delivery/Presentation	Collaboration
3 Great	• Locates a wide variety of media to evaluate for use in the presentation. • Experiments with different ways of combining media.	• Clearly and thoroughly addresses the Essential Question. • Contains a clear main idea. • Incorporates a wide variety of media that support the main idea.	• Is streamlined, well-organized, and easy to follow. • Uses proper equipment to display media.	• Works well with others. • Assumes a clear role and related responsibilities.
2 Good	• Locates an adequate amount of media to evaluate for use in the presentation. • Tries one way of combining media.	• Adequately addresses the Essential Question. • Contains a somewhat clear main idea. • Incorporates several different types of media that somewhat support the main idea.	• Is mostly organized, though there are some lapses and pauses in the flow. • Uses proper equipment for the most part to display media.	• Works with others most of the time. • Sometimes has difficulty sharing decisions and responsibilities.
1 Needs Work	• Locates only a few types of media to evaluate for use in the presentation. • Does not try to combine media.	• Minimally or barely addresses the Essential Question. • Does not contain a clear main idea. • Incorporates only one or two forms of media that do not support the main idea.	• Is disorganized, chaotic, and hard to follow. • Does not use proper equipment to display media.	• Cannot work with others in most situations. • Cannot share decisions or responsibilities.

Name _____ Date _____

Self-Assessment

Directions: Circle the numbers that show how much you agree or disagree with each sentence. Then answer the question below. If necessary, use the back of the page.

	Not Yet	With Help	Most of the Time	Very Well
1 When I read nonfiction, I understand how to analyze cause-and-effect and problem-and-solution text structures.	1	2	3	4
2 When I read, I understand the role of main ideas and details and of chronological order.	1	2	3	4
3 I understand the features of a humor column and a free verse poem.	1	2	3	4
4 I know how to self-question, use question-answer relationships, and question the author.	1	2	3	4
5 When I find a word I do not know, I can use various strategies to help me understand the meaning.	1	2	3	4
6 I know how to use possessive forms and pronouns in prepositional phrases, and can make my pronouns agree.	1	2	3	4
7 I know how to organize my writing for a research report.	1	2	3	4

8 Think of one thing you learned really well in this unit. Tell how you will use this the next time you read or write.

_____

_____

_____

_____

_____

_____

_____

_____

_____

UNIT 4

Reader Reflection

Directions: Answer questions 1–10. If necessary, use the back of the page.

"Say It with Flowers"

1 What did you learn about plot structure and plot devices that will help you the next time you read a short story?

2 Explain how making connections will help you the next time you read a short story.

3 Write what you liked and did not like about "Say It With Flowers." Include examples from the short story.

I liked...

I did not like...

4 Are you interested in reading more writing by Toshio Mori? ____ Yes ____ No

5 Are you interested in reading more short stories about people's values? ____ Yes ____ No

"The Journey"

6 What did you learn about metaphor and extended metaphor that will help you the next time you read a poem?

7 Explain how making personal connections will help you the next time you read a poem.

8 Write what you liked and did not like about "The Journey." Include examples from the poem.

I liked...

I did not like...

9 Are you interested in reading more works by Mary Oliver? ____ Yes ____ No

10 Are you interested in reading more poetry about making decisions? ____ Yes ____ No

 EDGE Level C

"Say It with Flowers" and "The Journey"

Closed Book

Directions: Read each question and choose the best answer.

KEY VOCABULARY

1 To <u>disarm</u> people means to
- Ⓐ win their trust.
- Ⓑ ask their opinions.
- Ⓒ shake their hands.
- Ⓓ earn their gratitude.

2 An <u>ensuing</u> event
- Ⓐ saves time.
- Ⓑ follows later.
- Ⓒ requires planning.
- Ⓓ provides entertainment.

3 When things <u>harmonize</u>, it means they
- Ⓐ provide focus.
- Ⓑ fit together well.
- Ⓒ look like each other.
- Ⓓ increase awareness.

4 If a person is <u>inquisitive</u>, it means the person is
- Ⓐ curious.
- Ⓑ attractive.
- Ⓒ generous.
- Ⓓ intelligent.

5 To have <u>integrity</u> means to value
- Ⓐ ability.
- Ⓑ money.
- Ⓒ bravery.
- Ⓓ honesty.

6 To be <u>irritating</u> means to be
- Ⓐ sad.
- Ⓑ foolish.
- Ⓒ annoying.
- Ⓓ confusing.

7 To feel <u>melancholy</u> means to feel
- Ⓐ lazy.
- Ⓑ angry.
- Ⓒ lonely.
- Ⓓ gloomy.

8 A <u>transaction</u> happens when a shopper
- Ⓐ enters a store.
- Ⓑ buys something.
- Ⓒ compares prices.
- Ⓓ looks for bargains.

Directions: Questions 9–15 are about "Say It with Flowers." Read each question and choose the best answer. You may look at the selection on pages 461–472 to help you answer the questions.

Open Book

LITERARY ANALYSIS

9 Which of these lines relates to the exposition of the story?
- Ⓐ Mr. Sasaki rolled out several bills from his pocketbook.
- Ⓑ In a couple of weeks, Teruo was just as good a clerk as we had had in a long time.
- Ⓒ Sometimes, looking embarrassedly at us, he would take the customers to the fresh flowers in the rear and complete the sale.
- Ⓓ While Teruo was selling the fresh flowers in the back to a customer, Mr. Sasaki came in quietly and watched the transaction.

10 Which of these is a complication in the story?
- Ⓐ Teruo walks out of the shop whistling.
- Ⓑ Tommy teaches Teruo about the florist game.
- Ⓒ A customer asks Teruo if the flowers will keep.
- Ⓓ Mr. Sasaki leaves Tommy in charge of the shop.

GO ON

EDGE Level C

UNIT 5

"Say It with Flowers" and "The Journey"

Open Book

11 Which of these statements relates to the resolution of the story?

Ⓐ 'That's a hard thing to say when you know it isn't true.'

Ⓑ He walked out of the shop with his shoulders straight, head high, and whistling.

Ⓒ This time he not only went back to the rear for the fresh ones but added three or four extras.

Ⓓ 'You're a good boy, and I know you need a job, but you've got to be a good clerk here or you're going out.'

COMPREHENSION

12 Which statement best shows that Teruo has made a decision about his problem?

Ⓐ All day Teruo looked sick.

Ⓑ He was curious almost to a fault and a glutton for work.

Ⓒ He was unusually high-spirited, and I couldn't account for it.

Ⓓ When the boss was out to lunch, Teruo went on a mad spree.

13 Why does Mr. Sasaki ask his clerks to sell old flowers?

Ⓐ He wants to see if they can follow orders.

Ⓑ He is a businessman who needs to make money.

Ⓒ He believes there is no difference between old and new flowers.

Ⓓ He cannot get to the wholesale market often enough to buy fresh flowers.

14 What does Teruo discover about himself?

Ⓐ He values honesty more than money.

Ⓑ He wants to avoid conflict with people.

Ⓒ He wants to become a successful florist.

Ⓓ He values customers more than the other clerks.

Directions: Read question 15. Write your answer on a separate sheet of paper.

15

"I wish I could sell like you," Teruo said. "Whenever they ask me, 'Is this fresh? How long will it keep?' I lose all sense about selling the stuff and begin to think of the difference between the fresh and the old stuff. Then the trouble begins."

"Remember, the boss has to run the shop so he can keep it going," Tommy told him. "When he returns next week, you better not let him see you touch the fresh flowers in the rear."

Think about the events of the story's plot. What does this passage show about the story's conflict? Refer to the text as you explain your answer.

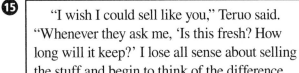

EDGE Level C

"Say It with Flowers" and "The Journey"

Open Book

Directions: Questions 16–22 are about "The Journey." Read each question and choose the best answer. You may look at the selection on pages 474–475 to help you answer the questions.

LITERARY ANALYSIS

16 What is the extended metaphor in this poem?

Ⓐ Voices are compared to a trembling house.

Ⓑ Many old voices are compared to a single new one.

Ⓒ A journey is compared to making and carrying out a decision.

Ⓓ A journey is compared to a road full of broken branches and stones.

17 In this poem, "the voices" are a metaphor for

Ⓐ people who cling.

Ⓑ people who leave.

Ⓒ fear of the unknown.

Ⓓ the sound of the wind.

18 In a metaphor, a writer

Ⓐ gives human traits to something that is not human.

Ⓑ gives hints about what will happen later in a story.

Ⓒ establishes a rhythm by choosing certain words.

Ⓓ compares two unlike things to express an idea.

COMPREHENSION

19 In this poem, the speaker is talking to a person. The person decides to

Ⓐ live alone in the woods.

Ⓑ pay attention to personal needs.

Ⓒ listen to the advice of the voices.

Ⓓ sacrifice happiness to help others.

20 It is most likely that the person the poem is about has been

Ⓐ taking care of others.

Ⓑ studying to be a doctor.

Ⓒ planning to buy a new house.

Ⓓ spending a lot of time in the woods.

21 Which word best describes the person at the end of the poem?

Ⓐ afraid

Ⓑ amused

Ⓒ confident

Ⓓ confused

Directions: Read question 22. Write your answer on a separate sheet of paper.

22

> It was already late
> enough, and a wild night,
> and the road full of fallen
> branches and stones.

What is the meaning of the metaphor "the road full of fallen/branches and stones"? How does this meaning relate to the main idea of "The Journey"?

DONE!

EDGE Level C

UNIT 5

Reader Reflection

Directions: Answer questions 1–9. If necessary, use the back of the page.

"Just Lather, That's All"

1 What did you learn about the plot device of suspense that will help you the next time you read a short story?

2 Explain how making connections using a Double-Entry Journal will help you the next time you read a short story.

3 Write what you liked and did not like about "Just Lather, That's All." Include examples from the short story.

I liked...

I did not like...

4 Are you interested in reading more writing by Hernando Téllez? _____ Yes _____ No

5 Are you interested in reading more short stories with suspense by other authors? _____ Yes _____ No

"The Woman Who Was Death"

6 What did you learn about myths that will help you the next time you read a myth?

7 Explain how making connections using self-stick notes will help you the next time you read a poem.

8 Write what you liked and did not like about "The Woman Who Was Death." Include examples from the myth.

I liked...

I did not like...

9 Are you interested in reading more myths? _____ Yes _____ No

EDGE Level C

UNIT 5

"Just Lather, That's All" and "The Woman Who Was Death" 📕 Closed Book

Directions: Read each question and choose the best answer.

KEY VOCABULARY

1 If something is your <u>destiny</u>, it is

Ⓐ meant to happen.

Ⓑ an important goal.

Ⓒ desired very much.

Ⓓ an unfortunate accident.

2 Something <u>indelible</u> cannot be

Ⓐ enclosed.

Ⓑ erased.

Ⓒ excused.

Ⓓ exchanged.

3 <u>Indifference</u> means to show a lack of

Ⓐ concern.

Ⓑ direction.

Ⓒ experience.

Ⓓ intelligence.

4 If a person is <u>inflexible</u>, it means that person is

Ⓐ rigid.

Ⓑ unfair.

Ⓒ foolish.

Ⓓ elderly.

5 When something is <u>poised</u>, it is

Ⓐ about to end.

Ⓑ over very quickly.

Ⓒ ready and waiting.

Ⓓ moving into position.

6 If a project takes <u>priority</u>, it means the project is

Ⓐ most important.

Ⓑ very complicated.

Ⓒ carefully planned.

Ⓓ expertly managed.

7 A <u>regime</u> is a system of

Ⓐ education.

Ⓑ government.

Ⓒ measurement.

Ⓓ transportation.

8 To have <u>virtue</u> means to have

Ⓐ peace.

Ⓑ benefits.

Ⓒ reasons.

Ⓓ experience.

Directions: Questions 9–15 are about "Just Lather, That's All." Read each question and choose the best answer. You may look at the selection on pages 485–493 to help you answer the questions.

**Open Book**

LITERARY ANALYSIS

9 At the beginning of the story, what two objects does the author use to create suspense?

Ⓐ the razor and the gun holster

Ⓑ the wall hook and the military cap

Ⓒ the soap and the brush

Ⓓ the bullet-studded belt and the barber chair

10 How does the author use the details of the shaving to create suspense?

Ⓐ They reveal that the barber is skilled.

Ⓑ They help the reader to care about Torres.

Ⓒ They focus the reader's attention on the shaving process.

Ⓓ They show how easy it would be for the barber to kill Torres.

GO ON

"Just Lather, That's All" and "The Woman Who Was Death" Open Book

11 The ending of the story is ironic because it is

Ⓐ logical.

Ⓑ exciting.

Ⓒ frightening.

Ⓓ unexpected.

COMPREHENSION

12 What is the main reason Torres comes to the barber shop?

Ⓐ to kill the barber

Ⓑ to test the barber

Ⓒ to persuade the barber to change sides

Ⓓ to get secret information from the barber

13 What is the main question the barber has to answer for himself?

Ⓐ Where can I go if I kill Torres?

Ⓑ Should I kill Torres or let him live?

Ⓒ How can I explain it if I let Torres live?

Ⓓ Does Torres know that I am a revolutionary?

14 Which line from the story reveals the barber's moment of truth?

Ⓐ You are an executioner, and I am only a barber.

Ⓑ And with an enemy under my roof, I felt responsible.

Ⓒ I'm sure that one solid stroke, one deep incision, would prevent any pain.

Ⓓ A good barber like me takes pride in never allowing this to happen to a client.

Directions: Read question 15. Write your answer on a separate sheet of paper.

15

> I'm sure that one solid stroke, one deep incision, would prevent any pain. He wouldn't suffer. But what would I do with the body? Where would I hide it? I would have to flee, leave all I have behind, and seek shelter far, far away. But they would follow until they caught me.

In this passage, the author expresses what the narrator is thinking. Explain how the author uses the narrator's thoughts to help create suspense. Cite text evidence in your answer.

GO ON

"Just Lather, That's All" and "The Woman Who Was Death" Open Book

Directions: Questions 16–22 are about "The Woman Who Was Death." Read each question and choose the best answer. You may look at the selection on pages 495–498 to help you answer the questions.

LITERARY ANALYSIS

16 This story is a myth because it explains

Ⓐ reincarnation.

Ⓑ Indian culture.

Ⓒ a natural event.

Ⓓ the creation of the world.

17 In this myth, what is personified?

Ⓐ death

Ⓑ illness

Ⓒ famine

Ⓓ emptiness

18 Read this sentence from the myth.

> And the earth itself groaned beneath the weight upon it.

Which word personifies the earth?

Ⓐ itself

Ⓑ weight

Ⓒ beneath

Ⓓ groaned

19 Which of these is **not** true about myths?

Ⓐ They often involve life lessons.

Ⓑ They are typically linked to the beliefs of a culture.

Ⓒ They usually have ordinary human beings as the main characters.

Ⓓ They have usually been passed down orally from one generation to the next.

COMPREHENSION

20 The woman in this myth makes several discoveries. What is her most important discovery?

Ⓐ her name

Ⓑ her creator

Ⓒ her cruelty

Ⓓ her destiny

21 Why does the woman flee from Lord Brahma?

Ⓐ She is afraid that he will hurt her.

Ⓑ She is overwhelmed by his cruelty.

Ⓒ She is horrified to learn about her task.

Ⓓ She is in despair about the emptiness in her life.

Directions: Read question 22. Write your answer on a separate sheet of paper.

22

> "Hush, daughter. Listen. Death shall not be evil, or cruel, or without virtue. Without death, there can be no peace, no rest for the suffering, the aged. Without death, there can be no rebirth. Daughter, death shall not be the destroyer of the world, but its protector."

Think about these words from Lord Brahma. In what sense do they express cultural beliefs, values, and experiences? Refer to the text as you explain your answer.

DONE!

Reader Reflection

Directions: Answer questions 1–10. If necessary, use the back of the page.

"Be-ers and Doers"

1 What did you learn about foreshadowing that will help you the next time you read a short story?

2 You can make connections by tracking details with a chart. Explain how this strategy will help you the next time you read.

3 Write what you liked and did not like about "Be-ers and Doers." Include examples from the short story.

I liked...
I did not like...

4 Are you interested in reading more writing by Budge Wilson? _____ Yes _____ No

5 Are you interested in reading more about individuals' turning points? _____ Yes _____ No

"My Moment of Truth"

6 What did you learn about author's purpose that will help you the next time you read a magazine article?

7 You can also make connections by comparing your connections to a partner's. Explain how this strategy will help you the next time you read.

8 Write what you liked and did not like about "My Moment of Truth." Include examples from the magazine article.

I liked...
I did not like...

9 Are you interested in reading more magazine articles? _____ Yes _____ No

10 Are you interested in reading more about moments of truth? _____ Yes _____ No

UNIT 5

"Be-ers and Doers" and "My Moment of Truth"

 Closed Book

Directions: Read each question and choose the best answer.

1 To <u>accelerate</u> is to increase
- Ⓐ skill.
- Ⓑ speed.
- Ⓒ safety.
- Ⓓ strength.

2 <u>Commentary</u> is a series of
- Ⓐ revisions.
- Ⓑ requirements.
- Ⓒ achievements.
- Ⓓ interpretations.

3 If a person is a <u>conformist</u>, it means that person
- Ⓐ helps other people.
- Ⓑ is very comfortable.
- Ⓒ thinks of new ideas.
- Ⓓ does what other people do.

4 Things that are <u>contrary</u> are
- Ⓐ familiar.
- Ⓑ constant.
- Ⓒ opposite.
- Ⓓ dependent.

5 <u>Malleable</u> means easy to
- Ⓐ mail.
- Ⓑ bend.
- Ⓒ store.
- Ⓓ paint.

6 A <u>revelation</u> is
- Ⓐ a long journey.
- Ⓑ a bad decision.
- Ⓒ a difficult choice.
- Ⓓ a sudden insight.

7 To <u>saturate</u> means to
- Ⓐ seal.
- Ⓑ save.
- Ⓒ soak.
- Ⓓ strike.

8 <u>Temporary</u> means that something
- Ⓐ happens often.
- Ⓑ lasts a short time.
- Ⓒ causes confusion.
- Ⓓ requires a lot of thought.

Directions: Questions 9–15 are about "Be-ers and Doers." Read each question and choose the best answer. You may look at the selection on pages 507–521 to help you answer the questions.  **Open Book**

9 One of the reasons an author uses foreshadowing is to
- Ⓐ create suspense.
- Ⓑ support the theme.
- Ⓒ describe characters.
- Ⓓ establish the setting.

10 The author stresses the differences between the father and the mother in order to foreshadow
- Ⓐ a mood.
- Ⓑ a conflict.
- Ⓒ the theme.
- Ⓓ the resolution.

GO ON ➡

"Be-ers and Doers" and "My Moment of Truth"

 Open Book

11 Which line foreshadows what Albert will be like as an adult?

Ⓐ 'Can't see no sense in working hard at something I'll never use.'

Ⓑ I could see that she'd made up her mind that Albert was going to be a perfect son.

Ⓒ 'You pull up your socks by Easter or you're going to be in deep trouble.'

Ⓓ While most of us stood there in immovable fear, Albert had already grabbed Jennifer, carriage and all, and rushed out to the barn with her.

COMPREHENSION

12 What is Albert's "moment of truth" in this story?

Ⓐ when he leaves home

Ⓑ when he shuts his eyes and faints

Ⓒ when he says, "Call the fire department."

Ⓓ when he says, "I ain't gonna be what you want."

13 Which of these is true about the mother and father?

Ⓐ The mother is timid; the father is forceful.

Ⓑ The mother follows orders; the father is bossy.

Ⓒ The mother has an even temper; the father gets angry easily.

Ⓓ The mother is constantly busy; the father takes time to enjoy nature.

14 What is the theme of the story?

Ⓐ People have to be themselves.

Ⓑ Doing is more important than being.

Ⓒ There is only one way to be successful.

Ⓓ There are only two kinds of people in the world.

Directions: Read question 15. Write your answer on a separate sheet of paper.

15

> . . . I could see that she'd made up her mind that Albert was going to be a perfect son. That meant, among other things, that he was going to be a fast-moving doer. And even when he was three or four, it wasn't hard for me to know that this wasn't going to be easy. Because Albert was a be-er. *Born* that way.

Think about the plot of this story. What later event or events are foreshadowed by the narrator's words about her mother at this point? Use text evidence to support your answer.

GO ON

"Be-ers and Doers" and "My Moment of Truth"

 Open Book

Directions: Questions 16–22 are about "My Moment of Truth." Read each question and choose the best answer. You may look at the selection on pages 525–528 to help you answer the questions.

LITERARY ANALYSIS

16 The authors most likely wrote "My Moment of Truth" in order to

Ⓐ entertain readers with amusing stories.

Ⓑ persuade readers to change their lives.

Ⓒ inspire readers with personal experiences.

Ⓓ inform readers about gymnastics and jazz.

17 In the part of the article about Wynton Marsalis, the author inspires the reader by

Ⓐ reflecting upon his musical contributions.

Ⓑ describing a shift in his plans as a musician.

Ⓒ persuading the reader to listen carefully to jazz.

Ⓓ presenting an entertaining story about a jazz band.

18 The most likely reason the authors included two stories in their article was to show that moments of truth

Ⓐ can happen only to famous people.

Ⓑ take different forms for different people.

Ⓒ occur for women more often than for men.

Ⓓ are often related to professional challenges.

COMPREHENSION

19 Marsalis's moment of truth occurred when he

Ⓐ met John Coltrane.

Ⓑ played in a funk band.

Ⓒ received a Pulitzer Prize for Music.

Ⓓ listened to a record until he could appreciate it.

20 Marsalis's turning point led to a change in

Ⓐ his ability to play the trumpet.

Ⓑ his enjoyment of classical music.

Ⓒ the course of his musical development.

Ⓓ the way he felt about his father's friends.

21 Dawes and Marsalis have an important similarity. They both

Ⓐ listened to their inner voices.

Ⓑ retired while they were young.

Ⓒ followed their family traditions.

Ⓓ resented choices made by others.

Directions: Read question 22. Write your answer on a separate sheet of paper.

22

> Dominique Dawes's young life has been a series of dazzling, dramatic highlights. She began taking gymnastics at age six and was competing by age ten. Just five years later, she burst onto the international scene in 1992, becoming the first African American gymnast to ever qualify and compete in the Olympic Games in Barcelona.

What is the author's purpose for this paragraph? How does the paragraph contribute to the purpose of the article as a whole? Refer to text details in your answer.

DONE!

EDGE Level C

UNIT 5

Student Profile: Cluster Tests

Directions: Use the **Answer Key** and **Scoring Guides** on pages 152, 153, and 154 to score Cluster Tests 1, 2, and 3 respectively. Circle the item number of each correct answer below. Then multiply items correct by points. Include the rubric scores for the constructed-response items. Calculate the overall test score by adding to 100. To gauge mastery for a particular tested skill or Common Core Standard, review the Cluster Test and Unit Test results.

Cluster 1   Date _____

Subtest	Tested Skill	ITEM ANALYSIS		TEST SCORES
		Item Numbers	Mastery	No. Correct x Points = Score
Key Vocabulary	Key Vocabulary L.9-10.6	1 2 3 4 5 6 7 8	6 out of 8 + −	_____ x 4 = _____ /32
Literary Analysis	Analyze Structure: Plot RL.9-10.5	9 10 11	2 out of 3 + −	_____ x 4 = _____ /12
	Analyze Language: Metaphor and Extended Metaphor RL.9-10.4	16 17 18	2 out of 3 + −	_____ x 4 = _____ /12
Comprehension	Comprehension RL.9-10.10	12 13 14 19 20 21	5 out of 6 + −	_____ x 4 = _____ /24
Constructed Response	Use Text Evidence RL.9-10.1; RL.9-10.10; W.9-10.9	Rubric Scores Item 15 _____ + Item 22 _____ = _____		= _____ /20

Overall Score (Add Points Earned)   _____ /100

Cluster 2   Date _____

Subtest	Tested Skill	ITEM ANALYSIS		TEST SCORES
		Item Numbers	Mastery	No. Correct x Points = Score
Key Vocabulary	Key Vocabulary L.9-10.6	1 2 3 4 5 6 7 8	6 out of 8 + −	_____ x 4 = _____ /32
Literary Analysis	Analyze Structure: Suspense RL.9-10.5	9 10 11	2 out of 3 + −	_____ x 4 = _____ /12
	Analyze World Literature RL.9-10.6	16 17 18 19	3 out of 4 + −	_____ x 4 = _____ /16
Comprehension	Comprehension RL.9-10.10	12 13 14 20 21	4 out of 5 + −	_____ x 4 = _____ /20
Constructed Response	Use Text Evidence RI.9-10.1; RI.9-10.10; W.9-10.9	Rubric Scores Item 15 _____ + Item 22 _____ = _____		= _____ /20

Overall Score (Add Points Earned)   _____ /100

Cluster 3   Date _____

Subtest	Tested Skill	ITEM ANALYSIS		TEST SCORES
		Item Numbers	Mastery	No. Correct x Points = Score
Key Vocabulary	Key Vocabulary L.9-10.6	1 2 3 4 5 6 7 8	6 out of 8 + −	_____ x 4 = _____ /32
Literary Analysis	Analyze Structure: Foreshadowing RL.9-10.5	9 10 11	2 out of 3 + −	_____ x 4 = _____ /12
	Determine Author's Purpose RI.9-10.6	16 17 18	2 out of 3 + −	_____ x 4 = _____ /12
Comprehension	Comprehension RL.9-10.10; RI.9-10.10	12 13 14 19 20 21	5 out of 6 + −	_____ x 4 = _____ /24
Constructed Response	Use Text Evidence RL.9-10.1; RL.9-10.10; RI.9-10.1; RI.9-10.10; W.9-10.9	Rubric Scores Item 15 _____ + Item 22 _____ = _____		= _____ /20

Overall Score (Add Points Earned)   _____ /100

       EDGE Level C

Language Acquisition Rubrics

Cluster 1
EVALUATE

Group Talk ▶ page 478

Directions: Group students. Give them a few moments to review the selection. Groups should then evaluate the behavior of the characters.

Language Function | 1 | 2 | 3 | 4

What to look for:
how well the student evaluates by expressing judgment and opinions with phrases such as *I think, I feel, I believe,* and *In my opinion.* Student should support his/her thoughts with examples and explain why he/she agrees or disagrees.

Cluster 2
CLARIFY

Pair Talk ▶ page 500

Directions: Pair students. Give them a few moments to review the selection and consider the task. Each student should state a viewpoint and be given an opportunity to clarify according to his/her partner's questions.

Language Function | 1 | 2 | 3 | 4

What to look for:
how well the student clarifies his/her viewpoint by restating or defining confusing words, or using comparisons, examples, or synonyms. Student should also be able to ask for clarification with questions such as *What do you mean by … ?* or *What does it mean … ?*

Cluster 3
VERIFY INFORMATION

Pair Talk ▶ page 530

Directions: Pair students. Give them a few moments to review the selection. Partners should take turns naming instructions that Albert gives in the selection. Instructions can be true or false and each partner needs to confirm the information his/her partner gives.

Language Function | 1 | 2 | 3 | 4

What to look for:
how well the student gives correct and incorrect statements from the selection and how well he or she verifies the information. Student should use phrases such as *Is it true that … ?* and *Could you verify/confirm that … ?*

	Language Function Rubric
4	Student effectively performs the function.
3	Student performs the function.
2	Student does not adequately perform the function.
1	Student makes no attempt or offers a non-verbal response.

UNIT 5

Reading and Literary Analysis

Directions: Read each question and choose the best answer.

Use the thesaurus entry to answer questions 1 and 2.

> **elaborate** *The queen wore an elaborate gown for the event: adj.* having great detail; detailed, complicated, rich, fancy.

1 Which word **best** completes the chart?

word	definition	synonym	antonym
elaborate	having great detail	fancy	

A costly

B simple

C natural

D beautiful

2 Polite is to rude as elaborate is to _____.

A old

B rich

C long

D plain

Use the thesaurus entry to answer questions 3 and 4.

> **intense** *The heat in Phoenix, Arizona, can be intense: adj.* of an extreme kind or filled with great emotion; strong, powerful, forceful, deep, extreme.

3 Which word **best** completes the chart?

word	definition	synonym	antonym
intense	of an extreme kind		reasonable

A weak

B kind

C calm

D powerful

4 Intense is to extreme as satisfied is to _____.

A content

B excited

C demanding

D disappointed

GO ON

Reading and Literary Analysis, *continued*

Directions: Questions 5–12 are about "Good Sense." Read the selection. Then read each question and choose the best answer.

Good Sense

Luke adjusted his backpack with a sigh as he turned the corner in the musty stairwell. It had been another exhausting day at work, and he was more than ready to make himself a hot meal and relax. He swung open the thick metal door that led into his hallway, and immediately he sensed that something was terribly wrong.

Sometimes Luke suspected that he had a sixth sense. He noticed things that other people didn't recognize, and his feelings about situations usually turned out to be accurate. Perhaps this was because of his inquisitive mind, which was always hungry for more information about the universe and the people around him. He had been baffling his mom with difficult questions since the day he could first form words.

Right at this moment Luke had a powerful sense of dread that he just couldn't shake. His eyes scanned the hall frantically as he moved forward with wary, noiseless steps, but nothing appeared out of the ordinary until he reached his apartment door. The door stood ajar, and it was covered with smashed eggs that dripped down to the worn carpet below. Beyond the open door, the room seemed deathly silent.

The ensuing moments passed in a blur. Luke hastily pushed the door open and entered the darkened room with heart pounding and backpack in hand, ready to swing at any movement. But there was no movement, only the shock of the disaster that assaulted his eyes. Lamps had been smashed, furniture overturned, and pictures torn off the walls. Several drawers and cabinets hung open, with their contents scattered. And most distressing of all, the shoebox in the closet that had contained a couple of months' worth of savings was completely empty. Luke felt sick to his stomach.

He quickly checked the rest of the apartment to be certain it was vacant, and then he dialed 911. After the police arrived and took his statement, Luke cleared off a single chair and sat alone in the darkness. He had a strong suspicion about who had done this. Several days earlier some kids from a neighborhood gang had sprayed graffiti in the hallway outside his apartment. Burglary and destruction of personal property were exactly the kinds of things a gang leader would require as initiation for potential gang members.

Luke understood the circumstances these kids faced. He had grown up in this neighborhood, where kids were considered extremely lucky to have one decent parent. The majority of the time those parents had to work two jobs and were rarely home, leaving their kids with generous amounts of free time. Often when people are bored or desperate, they make some seriously foolish decisions.

Of course he understood these things, but he was still furious. He had chosen the right path, the path of integrity, with his life. And he had worked far too hard to have some punks break in and steal his hard-earned money.

Over the next few hours, Luke tackled the chaos in the apartment. He swept up the broken glass and righted the furniture. When he opened the door to leave for work the next morning, he realized he had forgotten all about the smashed eggs on it, which by this time had dried into a sticky, smelly pattern. Oh well, he thought grimly, that task would just have to wait until after work.

That evening Luke returned to his apartment, and he was startled to find that his apartment door and the floor and walls around it had been scrubbed spotless. As he unlocked the door, he sensed a movement in the shadows of the hallway. Luke's hands formed fists, and he spun around to find a boy standing quietly, holding a soapy bucket.

"I know you—you're Gina's brother! What are you doing here?" Luke snarled, taking a menacing step forward.

The boy stepped back quickly, sloshing water on himself.

"Please, Luke, just listen! You know what a person has to do for initiation. Up until last night, all I ever wanted was to be in a gang and I finally had the opportunity.

GO ON

EDGE Level C

UNIT 5

Reading and Literary Analysis, *continued*

But hitting your place was just wrong. I'm so sorry. Here—" The boy fumbled nervously in his pocket and pulled out a wad of dollar bills, which he thrust clumsily at Luke.

"I know it's not all the money you lost, but it was my share. Please take it back. I'll do whatever I can to make this up to you." The boy took a step forward, and Luke could see the fear burning in his eyes, but he saw something else, too. He glared at the boy for a long moment, but the boy stood his ground.

All of Luke's anger was rushing forward in his brain, but he stood motionless. His mind flashed through images of his destroyed apartment and the empty shoebox, and back to the boy again. Suddenly he saw himself at fifteen years old, gazing at his mother with that same lost, fearful, defiant expression. That day…he remembered that terrible, amazing day so well. That was the day he made the decision to follow the right path with his life, no matter what difficulties that resolution would bring. And that choice, he knew, had been made because of his mother's forgiveness. Luke felt that familiar sixth sense forcing itself into his consciousness.

Luke exhaled slowly and felt his hands unclench. He gently reached out and took the crumpled bills from the boy's shaking hand. "Come on, son. I still haven't finished cleaning up the place. I'm sure I can find something for you to do!"

Reading and Literary Analysis, *continued*

5 Which detail from the first paragraph **best** helps to build suspense?

A   Luke sighs as he turns the corner.

B   Luke has found the day exhausting.

C   Luke is ready to relax and have dinner.

D   Luke senses something odd in the hallway.

6 What causes Luke to forgive the boy who breaks into his home?

A   He knows who the boy's sister is.

B   He sees the lost look on the boy's face.

C   He remembers a day from his own past.

D   He realizes that nothing valuable is missing.

7 Which of these is a metaphor that is used throughout the story?

A   clenching fists

B   cleaning up messes

C   choosing the right path

D   finding an empty shoebox

8 The plot events in the story ultimately show that Luke and the boy both

A   belong to a gang.

B   want to do what is right.

C   have a difficult family life.

D   want to please their mothers.

9 If a person is <u>inquisitive</u>, it means the person is

A   curious.

B   attractive.

C   generous.

D   intelligent.

10 An <u>ensuing</u> event

A   saves time.

B   follows later.

C   requires planning.

D   provides entertainment.

11 To have <u>integrity</u> means to value

A   ability.

B   money.

C   bravery.

D   honesty.

Directions: Read question 12. Write your answer on a separate sheet of paper.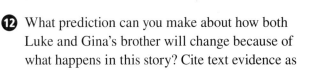

12 What prediction can you make about how both Luke and Gina's brother will change because of what happens in this story? Cite text evidence as you explain your prediction.

GO ON

EDGE Level C

UNIT 5

Reading and Literary Analysis, *continued*

Directions: Questions 13–19 are about "Waking Truth." Read the selection. Then read each question and choose the best answer.

Waking Truth

I am in that comfortable, murky world between sleep and waking—drifting dreamily—when suddenly I am interrupted by intense light glaring redly through my eyelids. It compels my eyes to open, exposing blurry figures that shift purposefully above me.

"She's conscious," a doctor's voice murmurs calmly. "Her vitals are strong."

I blink several times, and the blurry figures morph into official-looking individuals dressed in white. An IV hangs beside me, and there is an exceptionally uncomfortable tube down my throat. I'm not in any specific pain; I'm just confused.

The principal issue plaguing me is determining why I have been hospitalized. My last recollection is of training for an upcoming cross-country meet. I am the fastest distance runner in my class.

A burst of color catches my eye, and I cautiously tilt my head to observe dozens of purple flowers lining the windowsill. They appear <u>poised</u> and crisp, as though they may march obediently across the barren floor at my command. This thought makes me smile slightly, and I will them to move, but they defy me, naturally.

A commotion at the door startles me. I see an elderly woman arguing vigorously with a nurse.

"If you don't lemme see her raht this second, ah am gonna speak to your supervisor, and ah swear you don't want that!"

The nurse shrugs resignedly, and the woman pushes triumphantly past. She marches toward my bed and halts abruptly when she realizes I am staring at her.

"Well, honey, you are awake! Ah am so glad!" But she doesn't appear glad at all, wearing a shuddering lower lip and tearing eyes.

While puzzling in my still-hazy brain about why this stranger is weeping over me, I suddenly realize that I cannot feel my legs. I reach down and pinch my thighs, but I feel absolutely nothing. I pinch again, as fiercely as I can. Perhaps I will leave an <u>indelible</u> mark on my leg, creating another issue for the nurses to

resolve. It will be the least of my concerns, it appears, because as I attempt to lift my legs, nothing happens.

A wordless cry escapes from my lips, and the woman's eyes overflow. "Ah am so sorry, honey; Ah am so sorry! You jes ran like a rabbit out in front of my car!"

A thousand pinpoints explode inside my eyes, and I slam them shut, hoping frantically that when I open them again, by some miraculous twist, this will all have been a dream. I've seen shows about people who are paralyzed, spending their entire lives in wheelchairs. That cannot possibly be me—I don't even remember anything happening!

> A thousand pinpoints explode
> inside my eyes and I slam them shut,
> hoping frantically that when I
> open them again, by some miraculous twist,
> this will all have been a dream.

The woman—she did this. She hit me, and now I am frozen in place. My legs betray their <u>indifference</u> to my commands and lie there like dead wood under the sheet. I will never run again, and it is all due to her incompetent, irresponsible driving.

I open my eyes furiously, but she has momentarily disappeared, and there is a purple flower draped across my sheet. I strain to reach it so I can toss it on the floor. What is it with this misguided southern tradition that thinks flowers can make everything better?

I cannot reach the flower, and just like the ones on the windowsill, I cannot will it to move, so I squeeze my eyes again to shut it out.

My mind flashes suddenly…I am running through the neighborhood, attempting a personal best. The light is red, but no cars are visible, so I go for it. In a split second, my eye catches movement, and I realize my mistake, but it is too late.

My mistake…

It was not the driver's fault; it was mine. In my foolish ambition, I had paralyzed myself. If only I could go back. What is it worth to beat your time but lose your legs?

GO ON

Reading and Literary Analysis, *continued*

Burning tears pressure my closed lids, and I feel a withered hand on mine, uncertain, trembling. In my fog, I want nothing more than to lash out and rip her hand away. But one truth conclusively pierces the swirling cloud, and I cannot ignore it. I lift my other hand and gently place it on top of hers.

⓭ Read the sentence from the story.

> My last recollection is of training for an upcoming cross-country meet.

The foreshadowing in this sentence helps readers form an idea about

A how the narrator was injured.

B where the narrator is waking up.

C how skilled a runner the narrator is.

D whether the narrator is telling the truth.

⓮ Which phrase is a signal that the author is taking the story back in time?

A A wordless cry escapes from my lips…

B I open my eyes furiously…

C My mind flashes suddenly…

D I lift my other hand…

⓯ The words "murky," "hazy," and "fog" are part of the extended metaphor that describes the narrator's

A pain.

B words.

C eyesight.

D thoughts.

⓰ When something is <u>poised</u>, it is

A about to end.

B standing very still.

C ready and waiting.

D moving into position.

⓱ Which idea from the story is an example of irony?

A The runner runs a red light and is hit by a car.

B The runner wills her legs to move but they are still.

C The runner runs her fastest but loses the use of her legs.

D The runner opens her eyes and sees a purple flower.

⓲ Which character from the story speaks in a unique dialect?

A the nurse

B the driver

C the doctor

D the narrator

⓳ Something <u>indelible</u> cannot be

A enclosed.

B erased.

C excused.

D exchanged.

Directions: Read question 20. Write your answer on a separate sheet of paper.

⓴ How does the narrator's thinking change as this story unfolds? Use details from the passage to explain how her thinking changes.

GO ON

UNIT 5

Reading and Literary Analysis, *continued*

Directions: Questions 21–25 are about "The First Sit-Ins." Read the selection. Then read each question and choose the best answer.

The First Sit-Ins

On February 1, 1960, Ezell Blair, David Richmond, Joseph McNeil, and Franklin McCain entered a Woolworth's department store in Greensboro, North Carolina, and sat down at the lunch counter. Something that would be unthinkable today was commonplace then: the lunch counter was for Caucasians only. The four college students were African Americans. When they asked for service, the waitress shook her head. She couldn't serve African Americans because that was contrary to the rules. They were not welcome.

However, the four college students didn't move; they stayed in their seats and waited. Soon a manager came over, but he was <u>inflexible</u>. The four African Americans would not be served, and they were asked to leave. The students, however, didn't budge. Eventually, out of desperation, the manager closed the lunch counter and store early, thinking it was the only way to get rid of them. He did not succeed, however.

The next day the students were back—with friends. Again they sat down and asked for service, and once again they were refused, but they were determined to provoke change. They sat in the seats at the counter and waited. Their actions prevented others from buying lunch.

In the ensuing days and weeks, more and more students joined the sit-in. They were always quiet and respectful; in fact, many brought their textbooks to study. Sometimes they discussed Martin Luther King Jr.'s ideas of peaceful protest. They created rules for sit-ins, such as wearing coats and ties and not holding conversations. They remained respectful by sitting facing forward on the lunch counter stools.

Month after month the sit-in continued. Newspapers around the country heard about the sit-in and followed the progress. For the manager, what had been <u>irritating</u> at first, quickly became a financial disaster because without the lunch counter, and with the tension the sit-ins brought, the store was losing thousands of dollars.

Meanwhile, young African Americans were also holding sit-ins at other lunch counters in Greensboro. The idea spread as people in other cities and states began using the same technique to show support for the students. What started out small and local had become a movement, a movement toward change!

McNeil and McCain are shown here with Billy Smith and Clarence Henderson (seated left to right). All were early followers of Dr. Martin Luther King.

Near the end of July 1960, Ezell Blair, David Richmond, Joseph McNeil, and Franklin McCain once again entered the Woolworth's in Greensboro, and again, they asked for service. This time, the waiter took their orders. The sit-in was successful, and the store had changed its rules. The lunch counter was now open to all.

GO ON

EDGE Level C

Reading and Literary Analysis, continued

21 The purpose of this selection is to

A to inform readers about the protests in Greensboro.

B to persuade readers to change their society.

C to entertain readers with stories about life in the South.

D to reflect upon the nature of equality so that readers could do the same.

22 The factual tone of "The First Sit-Ins" is intended to make the information in the article

A exciting.

B personal.

C objective.

D persuasive.

23 If a person is inflexible, it means that person is

A rigid.

B unfair.

C foolish.

D elderly.

24 To be irritating means to be

A sad.

B foolish.

C annoying.

D confusing.

Directions: Read question 25. Write your answer on a separate sheet of paper.

25 Martin Luther King Jr. believed in peaceful protest. How does the text support his viewpoint?

DONE!

UNIT 5

Grammar and Writing

Directions: Read the composition. It contains errors. Then read each question and choose the best answer.

Why Vote?

(1) I've always been a big believer in the power of voting. (2) I truly believe it is the duty of every citizen to vote, and I try to inspire others to vote, too.

(3) I had a plan to get my friend Tamika involved in politics, taking an interest in important issues, and to vote. (4) I knew it would be hard to convince her. (5) She sticks to ideas stubbornly than anyone else I know. (6) That was how she became a varsity volleyball player. (7) The day she turned eighteen, I gave her a birthday card and presented her with a voter registration form.

(8) "What is this?" she asked, looking skeptic at the form.

(9) "It's so you can register to vote," I responded.

(10) "C'mon, Mitch. (11) You know I don't care about that stuff," she said, shoving the form aside.

(12) "But you're eighteen now. (13) Don't you want your voice to be heard?"

(14) "Who is going to listen?" she retorted.

(15) "The politcians, of course," I explained.

(16) Tamika shook her head.

(17) "They don't listen to people like us. (18) We're kids. (19) They're all the same—they tell biggest lies than the last one so they can get re-elected," she said matter-of-factly.

(20) "There's no need to be so miserable," I assured her.

(21) "I'm just a glass-half-empty kind of girl."

(22) "I understand why you're frustrated. (23) There are politicians who are dishonest. (24) That's exactly why you should vote. (25) If you don't vote, there will be no one to replace them, and nothing will change," I argued.

(26) She considered my point for a moment. (27) Then she said, "Still, my vote alone isn't going to change anything."

(28) I had heard this before, and I was ready.

(29) "You're not alone, though. (30) Lots of people out there have the same views as you. (31) It's a little bit like playing on a team. (32) You play together to win."

(33) I could see that she was considering my case carefully. (34) Finally, she said, "I'll think it over."

(35) "Oh, one last reason," I added. (36) "you get extra credit for Mr. Andersen's class."

(37) "Now there's a cause I can believe in," she said. (38) "Do you have a pen?"

(39) We laughed, and then we sat down to fill out the registration form.

GO ON

UNIT 5

Grammar and Writing, *continued*

1 Which sentence should be added after sentence 2 to support the ideas in the first paragraph?

A I think citizens have a lot of responsibilities.

B I am looking forward to the presidential election.

C I believe that every one of us can make a difference.

D I like to talk with the people who work at the polls.

2 What change, if any, should be made to sentence 3?

A Change *politics* to **Politics**

B Change *taking* to **to take**

C Change *issues* to **issue's**

D No change

3 In sentence 5, the word <u>stubbornly</u> should be changed to

A more stubbornly

B more stubborner

C most stubbornest

D No change

4 In sentence 8, the word <u>skeptic</u> should be changed to

A skeptical

B skepticism

C skeptically

D No change

5 In sentence 19, the word <u>biggest</u> should be changed to

A big

B bigger

C most biggest

D No change

6 In sentence 20, the word <u>miserable</u> should be changed to

A enraged

B desperate

C distrustful

D No change

7 What change, if any, should be made to sentence 36?

A Change *you* to **You**

B Change *for* to **four**

C Change *Andersen's* to **Andersens**

D No change

8 Which idea is **not** explained in the composition?

A why it would be hard to convince her to vote

B how the narrator planned to get Tamika to vote

C why Tamika received a form in her birthday card

D how being stubborn helped her be a volleyball player

GO ON ▶

UNIT 5

Grammar and Writing, *continued*

Directions: Read the composition. It contains errors. Then read each question and choose the best answer.

What Goes Around

(1) In our modern world, we take it for granted that the earth revolves around the sun, is round, and turning on an axis. (2) However, had you lived 500 years ago, you probably would have believed that the sun revolved around the earth. (3) Not only that, but you would have regarded anyone who thought otherwise as crazy. (4) It took the work of a man named Galileo to revolutionize the way people viewed the universe.

(5) The concept that the sun is the center of our universe and that the planets revolve around it is called heliocentrism. (6) Conversely, the belief that the sun and other planets revolve around the earth is called geocentrism. (7) At the beginning of the 1600s, geocentrism was still the best view of the universe and the view sanctioned by the Catholic Church. (8) Galileo used a new invention, the telescope, to observe the stars and planets—something no one had done before.

(9) Unfortunately for Galileo, the stronger opponent of heliocentrism was the Catholic Church. (10) During Galileo's lifetime, the Roman Catholic Church was a powerful political force. (11) Many within the church worried that heliocentrism contradicted the Bible's portrayal of the universe.

(12) In 1616, Galileo was ordered by the church to stop promoting heliocentrism in his writing. (13) For many years, he did just that. (14) Ultimately, Galileo did return to writing about heliocentrism and published a book about it in 1632. (15) In the church's view, this book advocated heliocentrism. (16) As a result, the Catholic Church put him under house arrest for the rest of his life and forbade him from publishing any more books.

(17) Though Galileo was free not to share his work with the public, he continued his work until the end of his life. (18) "All truths are easy to understand once they are discovered; the point is to discover them", he once said. (19) With his observations and scientific experiments, Galileo was able to lend dramatic support to heliocentrism. (20) Though others before him had suggested that the earth orbits the sun, Galileo proved it more successfully than any other person of his day.

Grammar and Writing, continued

9 What change, if any, should be made to sentence 1?

A Change *world,* to **world—**

B Change *turning* to **turns**

C Change *axis* to **axes**

D No change

10 In sentence 7, the word best should be changed to

A regular

B average

C accepted

D No change

11 Which sentence below should be added after sentence 7 to help develop the ideas in the paragraph?

A Galileo was born in Pisa, Italy, in 1564.

B However, Galileo Galilei was about to challenge that.

C During this time, Italy experienced great cultural development.

D The Catholic Church is headed by the Pope, who lives in Vatican City.

12 In sentence 9, the word stronger should be changed to

A strong

B strongest

C more stronger

D No change

13 In sentence 17, the words was free not to share his work should be changed to

A was not free to share his work

B was free to share not his work

C was free to not share his work

D No change

14 What change, if any, should be made to sentence 18?

A Change *easy to* to **easy too**

B Change *the* to **The**

C Change *them", he* to **them," he**

D No change

15 In sentence 20, the words more successfully should be changed to

A most success

B most successful

C more successfuler

D No change

16 Which idea is **not** explained in the composition?

A why Galileo was placed under house arrest

B why the Catholic Church was a powerful political force

C why Galileo was ordered to stop promoting heliocentrism

D why the Catholic Church was an opponent of heliocentrism

GO ON

UNIT 5

Grammar and Writing, *continued*

Directions: Read the following writing prompt, and write a composition. Write on separate sheets of paper. Use the Writer's Checklist to make sure that you do your best work.

Prompt

A moment of truth occurs in many of the selections in this unit.

Think about a selection you read in this unit or something else you have read in which the author describes a moment of truth.

Write a composition in which you reflect on how the moment of truth changed the author or a character in his or her work.

Writer's Checklist

☑ Write about all parts of the prompt.

☑ Present a clear central idea, and stay focused on it.

☑ Organize your composition from its introduction to its conclusion.

☑ Use transitions to connect your thoughts for the reader.

☑ Present meaningful ideas, and support them with specific information.

☑ Use appropriate words and a variety of sentence structures.

☑ Proofread and edit your writing for grammar, usage, mechanics, and spelling.

DONE!

EDGE Level C

Name _____ Date _____

Student Profile: Unit Tests

Directions: Use the **Answer Key** on page 155 to score the multiple-choice items. Circle the item number of each correct answer below. Calculate test scores by assigning one point for each correct answer. Use the scoring guides on page 155 to score the constructed-response items. Use the Good Writing Traits Rubric on page 122 to score the written composition. Total the scores and calculate the % score or use the conversion chart. To gauge mastery for a particular tested skill or Common Core Standard, review the Cluster Test and Unit Test results.

Reading and Literary Analysis

		ITEM ANALYSIS		TEST SCORES
Category	**Tested Skill**	**Item Numbers**	**Mastery**	**Points: Earned / Total**
Vocabulary	Word Relationships L.9-10.5	1 2 3 4	3 out of 4 + −	_____ / 4
	Key Vocabulary L.9-10.6	9 10 11 16 19 23 24	6 out of 7 + −	_____ / 7
Literary Analysis	Analyze Structure RL.9-10.5	5 6 8 13 14	4 out of 5 + −	_____ / 5
	Analyze Language RL.9-10.4	7 15 17 18	3 out of 4 + −	_____ / 4
	Determine Author's Purpose RI.9-10.6	21 22	1 out of 2 + −	_____ / 2
Constructed Response	Use Text Evidence RL.9-10.1; RL.9-10.10; W.9-10.9	Rubric Scores Item 12 _____ + Item 20 _____ + Item 25 _____ = _____		_____ / 12

Overall Score (Points Earned ÷ Total Points x 100 = %)   _____ ÷ 34 = _____%

Grammar and Writing

		ITEM ANALYSIS		TEST SCORES
Category	**Tested Skill**	**Item Numbers**	**Mastery**	**Points: Earned / Total**
Grammar	Adverbs L.9-10.1	3 4 13 15	3 out of 4 + −	_____ / 4
	Adjectives L.9-10.1	5 6 10 12	3 out of 4 + −	_____ / 4
Revising and Editing	Development of Ideas W.9-10.5	1 8 11 16	3 out of 4 + −	_____ / 4
	Grammar, Mechanics, and Usage L.9-10.2	2 7 9 14	3 out of 4 + −	_____ / 4
Written Composition (Informative/ Explanatory) W.9-10.2; W.9-10.4; W.9-10.10	Focus and Unity	Rubric Scores: _____ / 4		_____ / 20
	Organization	_____ / 4		
	Development of Ideas	_____ / 4 =		
	Voice and Style	_____ / 4		
	Written Conventions	_____ / 4		

Overall Score (Points Earned ÷ Total Points x 100 = %)   _____ ÷ 36 = _____%

Project Rubric: A Skit

Score	Planning/Preparation	Content of Project	Delivery/Presentation	Collaboration
3 Great	• Reviews a wide variety of short play scripts to understand the form. • Chooses a subject for the skit that directly relates to the Essential Question.	• Clearly addresses the Essential Question. • Contains a fully developed plot, setting, and characters. • Contains believable dialogue that moves the action forward. • Is interesting and innovative.	• Costumes and props are relevant and well-planned. • Actors have had extensive practice and know their lines. • The presentation flows smoothly with no major glitches.	• Works well with others. • Assumes a clear role and related responsibilities.
2 Good	• Reviews a few short play scripts to understand the form. • Chooses a subject for the skit that somewhat relates to the Essential Question.	• Somewhat addresses the Essential Question. • Contains a somewhat developed plot, setting, and characters. • Contains somewhat believable dialogue that somewhat helps to move the action forward. • Is somewhat interesting and innovative.	• Costumes and props are somewhat relevant and well-planned. • Actors have had ample practice and know most of their lines. • The presentation flows relatively smoothly with only one major glitch.	• Works with others most of the time. • Sometimes has difficulty sharing decisions and responsibilities.
1 Needs Work	• Reviews one or no short play scripts to understand the form. • Chooses a subject for the skit that does not relate to the Essential Question.	• Does not address the Essential Question. • Does not contain a developed plot, setting, or characters. • Contains dialogue that is not believable and that does not help to move the action forward. • Is not interesting or innovative.	• Costumes and props are nonexistent or irrelevant and not well-planned. • Actors have had little or no practice and do not know their lines. • The presentation does not flow smoothly and has many major glitches.	• Cannot work with others in most situations. • Cannot share decisions or responsibilities.

Self-Assessment

Directions: Circle the numbers that show how much you agree or disagree with each sentence. Then answer the question below. If necessary, use the back of the page.

	Not Yet	With Help	Most of the Time	Very Well
1 When I read a story, I understand plot structure, suspense, and foreshadowing.	1	2	3	4
2 When I read a poem, I understand metaphors and extended metaphors.	1	2	3	4
3 I understand the features of a myth and the author's purpose in a magazine article.	1	2	3	4
4 I know how to make connections while reading.	1	2	3	4
5 When I find a word I do not know, I look for word connections and relationships to help me understand the meaning.	1	2	3	4
6 I know how to elaborate using adjectives and adverbs.	1	2	3	4
7 I know how to develop my ideas in a literary research report.	1	2	3	4

8 Think of one thing you learned really well in this unit. Tell how you will use this the next time you read or write.

_____

_____

_____

_____

_____

_____

_____

_____

_____

Reader Reflection

Directions: Answer questions 1–10. If necessary, use the back of the page.

"Too Young to Drive?"

1 What did you learn about analyzing arguments that will help you the next time you read an editorial?

2 You can synthesize by drawing conclusions. Explain how this strategy will help you the next time you read.

3 Write what you liked and did not like about "Too Young to Drive?" Include examples from the editorial.

I liked...
I did not like...

4 Are you interested in reading more writing by Fred Boyles and/or Maureen Downey?
_____ Yes _____ No

5 Are you interested in reading more editorials by other writers? _____ Yes _____ No

"Rules of the Road"

6 What did you learn about analyzing the development of ideas that will help you the next time you read a how-to article?

7 You can also synthesize by combining how-to instructions and by evaluating the information for a complete picture. Explain how this strategy will help you the next time you read.

8 Write what you liked and did not like about "Rules of the Road." Include examples from the how-to article.

I liked...
I did not like...

9 Are you interested in reading more writing by Lynn Lucia? _____ Yes _____ No

10 Are you interested in reading more how-to articles? _____ Yes _____ No

EDGE Level C

"Too Young to Drive?" and "Rules of the Road"

 Closed Book

Directions: Read each question and choose the best answer.

KEY VOCABULARY

1 Consistently means

  Ⓐ equally.

  Ⓑ partially.

  Ⓒ carefully.

  Ⓓ suddenly.

2 Excessive means

  Ⓐ exciting.

  Ⓑ extreme.

  Ⓒ excellent.

  Ⓓ expensive.

3 Intrusion means

  Ⓐ immature behavior.

  Ⓑ intended consequences.

  Ⓒ unwelcome interference.

  Ⓓ uncomfortable surroundings.

4 A precaution is

  Ⓐ a fear of the unknown.

  Ⓑ an activity that is dangerous.

  Ⓒ a preview of what is to come.

  Ⓓ an action to protect against harm.

5 Proficiency means

  Ⓐ usefulness.

  Ⓑ skillfulness.

  Ⓒ carelessness.

  Ⓓ helplessness.

6 To restrict means to

  Ⓐ hurt.

  Ⓑ limit.

  Ⓒ reply.

  Ⓓ force.

7 To transform means to

  Ⓐ trade for something better.

  Ⓑ change into something else.

  Ⓒ inform somebody of the rules.

  Ⓓ replace something that is broken.

8 To violate a rule means to

  Ⓐ state it.

  Ⓑ value it.

  Ⓒ follow it.

  Ⓓ break it.

GO ON

"Too Young to Drive?" and "Rules of the Road"

 Open Book

Directions: Questions 9–15 are about "Too Young to Drive?" Read each question and choose the best answer. You may look at the selection on pages 563–569 to help you answer the questions.

LITERARY ANALYSIS

9 What evidence does Bayles use to support his argument about driver's education?

Ⓐ news stories

Ⓑ legislative bills

Ⓒ a survey taken by driving instructors

Ⓓ a poll conducted by college students

10 Which sentence from the editorial signals that it is persuasive?

Ⓐ Parents often overestimate their children's proficiency behind the wheel.

Ⓑ Despite the advances in both car and road safety, teen deaths remain fairly constant.

Ⓒ Teen drivers should not be allowed to carry nonfamily members in the car during their first year.

Ⓓ Police blamed a recent crash that killed a high school senior on excessive speed and erratic driving.

11 Which statement takes the **pro** side of the argument to raise the driving age?

Ⓐ Teen driving curfews should be lowered to 9 p.m.

Ⓑ Teenagers mature more quickly after the age of 17.

Ⓒ Driving instructors should be better prepared to teach.

Ⓓ Better road conditions will reduce the number of accidents.

COMPREHENSION

12 Both authors argue that teen drivers

Ⓐ should not be allowed to drive.

Ⓑ should be supervised by their parents.

Ⓒ should be given more difficult driving tests.

Ⓓ should not be allowed to transport family members.

13 The two authors **disagree** that the solution to the problem is

Ⓐ safer road conditions.

Ⓑ an ealier teen curfew.

Ⓒ a higher driving age.

Ⓓ stronger state laws.

14 Bayles believes that

Ⓐ driving schools should be run by the parents of teenagers.

Ⓑ parents should take responsibility for their teenage drivers.

Ⓒ legislators should decide who has the right to drive and when.

Ⓓ teenagers should be able to decide when they are ready to drive.

Directions: Read question 15. Write your answer on a separate sheet of paper.

15

> Fixing driver's ed and cracking down on the testing system are essential steps forward, but other efforts are required. The Legislature should act on proposals that require more supervised experience behind the wheel.
>
> National data suggest that teens become safer drivers if their first year behind the wheel is limited and supervised. There is no evidence, however, that having teens cool their heels until they are 17 will magically make them better, more mature drivers.

What argument, or claim, does the writer make in this passage? What evidence is given to support that argument?

GO ON ▶

"Too Young to Drive?" and "Rules of the Road"

Open Book

Directions: Questions 16–22 are about "Rules of the Road." Read each question and choose the best answer. You may look at the selection on pages 571–575 to help you answer the questions.

UNIT 6

LITERARY ANALYSIS

16 Under which subhead can you find information about flashing lights on a bus?

- Ⓐ Go slow near schools.
- Ⓑ Cut down on distractions.
- Ⓒ Be cautious in bad weather.
- Ⓓ Don't assume what other drivers will do.

17 Which of these would be a suitable subhead for "Rules of the Road"?

- Ⓐ Avoid obstacles in the road.
- Ⓑ A police officer tells his story.
- Ⓒ The first five years of driving.
- Ⓓ Vehicles that help save lives.

18 Which sentence could be added under the subhead "Don't rely only on mirrors when changing lanes"?

- Ⓐ You might not see a car next to you.
- Ⓑ You might not see a car backing up.
- Ⓒ You might not see a person crossing the street.
- Ⓓ You might not have enough space to stop quickly.

19 The ideas developed in this article are meant to help readers learn how to

- Ⓐ avoid breaking laws.
- Ⓑ study for a driving test.
- Ⓒ learn to maintain a car.
- Ⓓ be responsible drivers.

COMPREHENSION

20 What would probably happen if all drivers followed the advice in this article?

- Ⓐ Fewer traffic accidents would occur.
- Ⓑ City driving conditions would improve.
- Ⓒ Bad weather would be easier to drive in.
- Ⓓ Speed limits would be broken less often.

21 According to the article, driving with an experienced driver in the car can help you to

- Ⓐ judge the safety of a left turn in traffic.
- Ⓑ watch for pedestrians at intersections.
- Ⓒ watch for other cars while changing lanes.
- Ⓓ judge the space behind you while backing up.

Directions: Read question 22. Write your answer on a separate sheet of paper.

22

> **Be cautious in bad weather.** Rain, snow, and ice make streets harder to drive on, so when roads are wet, slow down. A good rule is to double the space between you and the vehicle in front of you. This will give you more space to stop if you have to hit the brakes. Turn your headlights on anytime you need to turn your windshield wipers on. This will help you see other cars and other cars see you. Some states require that all vehicles turn on their lights during bad weather.

What does the writer do to develop the idea stated in the subhead? Cite text evidence to support your answer.

DONE!

EDGE Level C

Reader Reflection

Directions: Answer questions 1–10. If necessary, use the back of the page.

"Piracy Bites!"

1 What did you learn about evaluating arguments that will help you the next time you read persuasive nonfiction?

2 You can synthesize by comparing evidence across texts. Explain how this strategy will help you the next time you read.

3 Write what you liked and did not like about "Piracy Bites!" Include examples from these pieces of persuasive nonfiction.

I liked...

I did not like...

4 Are you interested in reading more persuasive nonfiction? _____ Yes _____ No

5 Are you interested in reading more about piracy? _____ Yes _____ No

"Doonesbury on Downloading"

6 What did you learn about analyzing central ideas that will help you the next time you read an editorial cartoon?

7 You can also synthesize by using a chart to compare. Explain how this strategy will help you the next time you read.

8 Write what you liked and did not like about "Doonesbury on Downloading." Include examples from the editorial cartoon.

I liked...

I did not like...

9 Are you interested in reading more cartoons by Garry Trudeau? _____ Yes _____ No

10 Are you interested in reading more editorial cartoons? _____ Yes _____ No

"Piracy Bites!" and "Doonesbury on Downloading"

Closed Book

Directions: Read each question and choose the best answer.

KEY VOCABULARY

1 To access means to
- Ⓐ steal.
- Ⓑ respect.
- Ⓒ gain entry to.
- Ⓓ create as a group.

2 Counterfeit means
- Ⓐ new.
- Ⓑ fake.
- Ⓒ stolen.
- Ⓓ counted.

3 To facilitate means to
- Ⓐ react in a positive way.
- Ⓑ handle in a mature way.
- Ⓒ face the truth about something.
- Ⓓ help make something happen.

4 Fundamental means
- Ⓐ basic.
- Ⓑ frantic.
- Ⓒ special.
- Ⓓ thoughtful.

5 To have an impact means to
- Ⓐ answer.
- Ⓑ imitate.
- Ⓒ influence.
- Ⓓ understand.

6 Merit means
- Ⓐ risk.
- Ⓑ hope.
- Ⓒ value.
- Ⓓ support.

7 Repercussion means
- Ⓐ a related event.
- Ⓑ a negative effect.
- Ⓒ an angry discussion.
- Ⓓ a loud, banging noise.

8 To verify something means to
- Ⓐ defy it.
- Ⓑ check it.
- Ⓒ display it.
- Ⓓ identify it.

UNIT 6.

GO ON

"Piracy Bites!" and "Doonesbury on Downloading"

UNIT 6

Directions: Questions 9–15 are about "Piracy Bites!" Read each question and choose the best answer. You may look at the selection on pages 584–592 to help you answer the questions.

LITERARY ANALYSIS

9 Both authors compare

Ⓐ the Internet to a shopping mall.

Ⓑ intellectual property to cargo from a ship.

Ⓒ the value of intellectual property to the earnings of a day of work.

Ⓓ copyrighted materials on the Internet to the items for sale in a store.

10 What evidence does Smith use to show that piracy threatens national security?

Ⓐ international news stories

Ⓑ examples of criminal trafficking

Ⓒ information about annual profits

Ⓓ the number of CDs stolen each year

11 Which sentence from "Piracy Bites!" appeals to the reader's sense of right and wrong?

Ⓐ Colleges and universities are prime locations for illegal downloads.

Ⓑ If Congress needs to help facilitate the necessary discussions, we will be more than happy to do so.

Ⓒ Intellectual property represents the largest single sector of the American economy, employing 4.3 million Americans.

Ⓓ News stories reveal that terrorist organizations receive hundreds of millions of dollars through pirate organizations.

12 Which statement supports the argument that intellectual theft is a widespread problem?

Ⓐ Piracy affects small businesses the most.

Ⓑ The impact of intellectual property thieves is huge.

Ⓒ Forty percent of university students have pirated software.

Ⓓ Terrorist organizations need a lot of money to fund their activities.

COMPREHENSION

13 How does Smith believe intellectual property rights should be protected?

Ⓐ with stronger laws

Ⓑ with industry self-regulation

Ⓒ with better labels and packaging

Ⓓ with a focus on consumer responsibilities

14 Who does Towns believe most needs protection from the effects of piracy?

Ⓐ content companies

Ⓑ local business owners

Ⓒ computer manufacturers

Ⓓ low-income communities

Directions: Read question 15. Write your answer on a separate sheet of paper.

15 Under current law, we can prosecute someone for trafficking in fake labels for a computer program, but we cannot prosecute for faking the hologram that the software maker uses to verify that the software is genuine. We criminalize trafficking in counterfeit documentation and packaging of software programs, but not music and other products.

What point does Rep. Smith make in this paragraph? How well does it help Smith persuade readers to agree with his overall argument against piracy? Refer to text details in your answer.

GO ON

"Piracy Bites!" and "Doonesbury on Downloading"

 Open Book

Directions: Questions 16–22 are about "Doonesbury on Downloading." Read each question and choose the best answer. You may look at the selection on pages 595–599 to help you answer the questions.

LITERARY ANALYSIS

16 Garry Trudeau created this editorial cartoon in order to

Ⓐ convince readers that piracy is not really stealing.

Ⓑ explain how much life has changed since the 1960s.

Ⓒ show how parents should discuss issues with their children.

Ⓓ reveal different attitudes toward intellectual property theft.

17 In one panel, the cartoonist did not use speech balloons because he wanted to

Ⓐ change the topic.

Ⓑ show agreement.

Ⓒ make the readers think.

Ⓓ show the characters pausing.

18 What evidence does the cartoonist use to support the father's argument about piracy?

Ⓐ People pay for movies.

Ⓑ Piracy is okay because it is so common.

Ⓒ People in his generation had to pay for music.

Ⓓ Piracy does not include sharing computer files.

19 In which of these sentences of dialogue does Trudeau use humor to focus on his central idea?

Ⓐ "That's a looter's logic, Alex."

Ⓑ "You throw my gift back in my face?"

Ⓒ "All of which you thoughtfully pirated for me?"

Ⓓ "And you can't deny entertainment has value."

COMPREHENSION

20 Why does the daughter ask her father for advice about drugs?

Ⓐ She wants to learn about drugs.

Ⓑ She wants to change the subject.

Ⓒ She does not think her father is a good parent.

Ⓓ She does not want to discuss her problems with her father.

21 The daughter believes that her father

Ⓐ is angry about greedy musicians.

Ⓑ knows more about drugs than piracy.

Ⓒ does not understand her point of view.

Ⓓ blames young people for corporate problems.

Directions: Read the first four panels of "Doonesbury on Downloading" on page 596. Then read question 22. Write your answer on a separate sheet of paper.

22 How do the four opening cartoon panels begin to point to the central idea of the editorial cartoon?

DONE!

EDGE Level C

Reader Reflection

Directions: Answer questions 1–10. If necessary, use the back of the page.

"Long Walk to Freedom"

1 What did you learn about word choice that will help you the next time you read arguments?

2 Explain how forming generalizations will help you the next time you read an autobiography.

3 Write what you liked and did not like about "Long Walk to Freedom." Include examples from the autobiography.

I liked...
I did not like...

4 Are you interested in reading more writing by Nelson Mandela? _____ Yes _____ No

5 Are you interested in reading more autobiographies by other authors? _____ Yes _____ No

"We Hold These Truths"

6 What did you learn about relating arguments that will help you the next time you read declarations?

7 Explain how forming generalizations will help you the next time you read related selections.

8 Write what you liked and did not like about "We Hold These Truths." Include examples from the declarations.

I liked...
I did not like...

9 Are you interested in reading more declarations or arguments? _____ Yes _____ No

10 Are you interested in reading more about the Declaration of Independence and the Declaration of Sentiments? _____ Yes _____ No

"Long Walk to Freedom" and "We Hold These Truths"

 Closed Book

Directions: Read each question and choose the best answer.

KEY VOCABULARY

1 Apathetic means
- Ⓐ pitiful.
- Ⓑ annoying.
- Ⓒ indifferent.
- Ⓓ sympathetic.

2 A distinction is a
- Ⓐ problem.
- Ⓑ difference.
- Ⓒ correction.
- Ⓓ discussion.

3 Emancipation means the act of
- Ⓐ hiring.
- Ⓑ freeing.
- Ⓒ agreeing.
- Ⓓ deciding.

4 Exploitation means the act of
- Ⓐ exposing people's weaknesses.
- Ⓑ using people selfishly for personal gain.
- Ⓒ excusing people when they make mistakes.
- Ⓓ seeing the world through the eyes of other people.

5 To have an inclination for something means to
- Ⓐ like it.
- Ⓑ try it.
- Ⓒ buy it.
- Ⓓ avoid it.

6 To liberate means to
- Ⓐ locate.
- Ⓑ fight for.
- Ⓒ set free.
- Ⓓ celebrate.

7 To be motivated means to be
- Ⓐ stubborn.
- Ⓑ prepared.
- Ⓒ ambitious.
- Ⓓ determined.

8 Oppression means the act of
- Ⓐ confessing to a crime.
- Ⓑ overcoming a difficult situation.
- Ⓒ choosing to disagree with a government.
- Ⓓ preventing people from having equal rights.

Directions: Questions 9–15 are about "Long Walk to Freedom." Read each question and choose the best answer. You may look at the selection on pages 609–620 to help you answer the questions.

 Open Book

LITERARY ANALYSIS

9 Read this sentence from "Long Walk to Freedom."

> Finally, the white rulers determined that all nonwhites should be allowed the right to vote.

Which type of word choice does this sentence contain?
- Ⓐ repetition
- Ⓑ a comparison
- Ⓒ a signal word
- Ⓓ emotion-filled words

10 Read this sentence from the autobiography.

> That day had come about through the unimaginable sacrifices of thousands of my people...

Mandela uses the word "unimaginable" to
- Ⓐ encourage South Africans to make more sacrifices.
- Ⓑ show readers the importance of South African history.
- Ⓒ emphasize the need for South Africans to take action.
- Ⓓ help readers understand the suffering of South Africans.

 GO ON

75k

EDGE Level C

"Long Walk to Freedom" and "We Hold These Truths"

 Open Book

11 Read this sentence from the selection.

> But I have discovered the secret that after climbing a great hill, one only finds that there are many more hills to climb.

Mandela's decision to talk about "hills" helps the reader understand that

- Ⓐ Africans lost much of their land to European countries.
- Ⓑ being elected president of South Africa was a great honor.
- Ⓒ some black Africans hid in the hills to avoid being arrested.
- Ⓓ to achieve human rights requires a long, continuous struggle.

12 Read these sentences from the selection.

> Time and again, I have seen men and women risk and give their lives for an idea. I have seen men stand up to attacks and torture without breaking, showing a strength and resiliency that defies the imagination.

Mandela repeats "I have seen" in these sentences to emphasize that

- Ⓐ people should honor bravery.
- Ⓑ many South Africans have acted bravely.
- Ⓒ he has suffered more than anyone else has.
- Ⓓ the people of South Africa have many ideals.

COMPREHENSION

13 Why did Mandela suffer so much?

- Ⓐ He fought for the right to vote.
- Ⓑ He struggled to meet family obligations.
- Ⓒ He struggled for the rights of all people.
- Ⓓ He fought to understand the meaning of courage.

14 Even while he was in jail, Mandela remained hopeful because he

- Ⓐ believed in the goodness of people.
- Ⓑ knew that things would change someday.
- Ⓒ knew that the world would help fight injustice.
- Ⓓ believed he would soon be elected president.

Directions: Read question 15. Write your answer on a separate sheet of paper.

15

> That day had come about through the unimaginable sacrifices of thousands of my people, people whose suffering and courage can never be counted or repaid. I felt that day, as I have on so many other days, that I was simply the sum of all those African patriots who had gone before me. That long and noble line ended and now began again with me. I was pained that I was not able to thank them and that they were not able to see what their sacrifices had wrought.

What type or types of word choice—emotion-filled words, repetition of words, or signal words—does this paragraph illustrate? What is the purpose of the choice or choices? Give examples from the text.

 GO ON

EDGE Level C

"Long Walk to Freedom" and "We Hold These Truths"

Open Book

Directions: Questions 16–22 are about "We Hold These Truths." Read each question and choose the best answer. You may look at the selection on pages 623–625 to help you answer the questions.

LITERARY ANALYSIS

16 Unlike the Declaration of Independence, the Declaration of Sentiments is based on a desire for which of the following?

Ⓐ free trade

Ⓑ gender equality

Ⓒ self-government

Ⓓ a new Constitution

17 In both declarations, the writers argue that

Ⓐ the rule of Great Britain has been oppressive.

Ⓑ all governments, over time, become tyrannical.

Ⓒ the people they represent have waited patiently for change.

Ⓓ they are fighting for the self-esteem of the people they represent.

18 In their arguments, the writers of both declarations agree that the existing government

Ⓐ has gotten its power from the people whom it governs.

Ⓑ has denied the right of trial by jury to some of the people.

Ⓒ has done away with the laws that the people have written.

Ⓓ has forced some of the people to live without an education.

19 Which declaration argues that the world must witness the writers' complaints?

Ⓐ both

Ⓑ neither

Ⓒ the Declaration of Sentiments

Ⓓ the Declaration of Independence

COMPREHENSION

20 The Declaration of Independence blames the writers' unhappiness on which of the following?

Ⓐ the tyrannical British Parliament

Ⓑ the various colonial governments

Ⓒ the British armies stationed in the colonies

Ⓓ the current king of Great Britain (George III)

21 According to the Declaration of Sentiments, the denial of equal rights to women

Ⓐ has happened throughout human history.

Ⓑ is based on a misunderstanding of God's will.

Ⓒ cannot change unless American men support the idea.

Ⓓ makes women want to leave their husbands and families.

Directions: Read question 22. Write your answer on a separate sheet of paper.

22

> (*from* the Declaration of Independence)
> We, therefore . . . solemnly publish and declare, That these United Colonies are, and of Right ought to be Free and Independent States . . .
>
> (*from* the Declaration of Sentiments)
> Now, . . . because women do feel themselves aggrieved, oppressed, and fraudulently deprived of their most sacred rights, we insist that they have immediate admission to all the rights and privileges which belong to them as citizens of the United States. . . .

Compare these statements from the two declarations. How is the purpose of the statements the same? How do the statements differ? Refer to both texts in your answer.

DONE!

Student Profile: Cluster Tests

Directions: Use the **Answer Key** and **Scoring Guides** on pages 156, 157, and 158 to score Cluster Tests 1, 2, and 3 respectively. Circle the item number of each correct answer below. Then multiply items correct by points. Include the rubric scores for the constructed-response items. Calculate the overall test score by adding to 100. To gauge mastery for a particular tested skill or Common Core Standard, review the Cluster Test and Unit Test results.

Cluster 1   Date _____

Subtest	Tested Skill	ITEM ANALYSIS		TEST SCORES
		Item Numbers	Mastery	No. Correct x Points = Score
Key Vocabulary	Key Vocabulary L.9-10.6	1 2 3 4 5 6 7 8	6 out of 8 + −	_____ x 4 = _____ /32
Literary Analysis	Evaluate Argument RI.9-10.8	9 10 11	2 out of 3 + −	_____ x 4 = _____ /12
	Analyze Development of Ideas RI.9-10.3	16 17 18 19	3 out of 4 + −	_____ x 4 = _____ /16
Comprehension	Comprehension RI.9-10.10	12 13 14 20 21	4 out of 5 + −	_____ x 4 = _____ /20
Constructed Response	Use Text Evidence RI.9-10.1; RI.9-10.10; W.9-10.9	Rubric Scores Item 15 _____ + Item 22 _____ = _____		= _____ /20

Overall Score (Add Points Earned) | _____ /100 |

Cluster 2   Date _____

Subtest	Tested Skill	ITEM ANALYSIS		TEST SCORES
		Item Numbers	Mastery	No. Correct x Points = Score
Key Vocabulary	Key Vocabulary L.9-10.6	1 2 3 4 5 6 7 8	6 out of 8 + −	_____ x 4 = _____ /32
Literary Analysis	Evaluate Arguments RI.9-10.8	9 10 11 12	3 out of 4 + −	_____ x 4 = _____ /16
	Analyze Central Idea RL.9-10.2	16 17 18 19	3 out of 4 + −	_____ x 4 = _____ /16
Comprehension	Comprehension RI.9-10.10	13 14 20 21	3 out of 4 + −	_____ x 4 = _____ /16
Constructed Response	Use Text Evidence RL.9-10.1; RL.9-10.10; RI.9-10.1; RI.9-10.10; W.9-10.9	Rubric Scores Item 15 _____ + Item 22 _____ = _____		= _____ /20

Overall Score (Add Points Earned) | _____ /100 |

Cluster 3   Date _____

Subtest	Tested Skill	ITEM ANALYSIS		TEST SCORES
		Item Numbers	Mastery	No. Correct x Points = Score
Key Vocabulary	Key Vocabulary L.9-10.6	1 2 3 4 5 6 7 8	6 out of 8 + −	_____ x 4 = _____ /32
Literary Analysis	Analyze Viewpoint: Word Choice RI.9-10.4; RI.9-10.6	9 10 11 12	3 out of 4 + −	_____ x 4 = _____ /16
	Relate Arguments RI.9-10.9	16 17 18 19	3 out of 4 + −	_____ x 4 = _____ /16
Comprehension	Comprehension RI.9-10.10	13 14 20 21	3 out of 4 + −	_____ x 4 = _____ /16
Constructed Response	Use Text Evidence RI.9-10.1; RI.9-10.10; W.9-10.9	Rubric Scores Item 15 _____ + Item 22 _____ = _____		= _____ /20

Overall Score (Add Points Earned) | _____ /100 |

Language Acquisition Rubrics

Cluster 1
EXPRESS AND SUPPORT OPINIONS
Group Talk ▶ page 578

Directions: Group students. Give them a few moments to review the selections and take notes. Students should then share their opinions with the group about teen drivers.

Language Function	1	2	3	4

What to look for:
how well the student expresses his/her opinion with words such as *I think, I believe, I feel,* and *In my opinion.* Student should use a confident tone and support his/her opinion with specific examples, facts, and evidence.

Cluster 3
PERSUADE
Pair Talk ▶ page 628

Directions: Pair students. Give them a few moments to consider the task. Then partners should take turns persuading each other to agree with their opinions about an injustice.

Language Function	1	2	3	4

What to look for:
how well the student persuades his/her partner using persuasive and emotional words such as *We must, It is unfair,* and *We have to.* Student should provide facts, use a strong tone, and employ techniques such as overgeneralizations, testimonials, and urgency.

Cluster 2
PERSUADE
Group Talk ▶ page 602

Directions: Give the students a few moments to consider the task and write notes if desired. Then in small groups students should state their position on music piracy and convince the others to agree.

Language Function	1	2	3	4

What to look for:
how well the student convinces others to agree with his/her position using persuasive words such as *I think, I don't agree, We must, Why don't we, You might want to, should,* and *should not, etc.* Student should support his/her position with strong, convincing reasons.

	Language Function Rubric
4	Student effectively performs the function.
3	Student performs the function.
2	Student does not adequately perform the function.
1	Student makes no attempt or offers a non-verbal response.

Reading and Literary Analysis

UNIT 6

Directions: Read each question and choose the best answer.

1 Which word has a similar meaning to the underlined word but has a **positive** connotation?

Her skinny legs were like a blur as she raced to the finish line.

A   bony

B   gaunt

C   slender

D   scrawny

2 Which word has a similar meaning to the underlined word but has a **negative** connotation?

Mr. Adams is thrifty in terms of spending.

A   cheap

B   efficient

C   careful

D   economical

3 Which word has a similar meaning to the underlined word but has a **neutral** connotation?

My mother nagged me about my homework.

A   scolded

B   bothered

C   reminded

D   pestered

4 Which word has the **most positive** connotation?

A   fine

B   good

C   decent

D   wonderful

GO ON

Reading and Literary Analysis, continued

Directions: Questions 5–10 are about "The William Winter Institute for Racial Reconciliation."
Read the selection. Then read each question and choose the best answer.

The William Winter Institute for Racial Reconciliation

Mississippi is the historic site of some of the most deeply held racist beliefs and cruel acts of racial violence since our nation was born. Its people have done hard work to change this. They have dug deep into the dark places of their southern homeland to make a new Mississippi. They have stories to tell, a depth of understanding about racism, and some real solutions to share.

The changes Mississippians have made over the last four decades with regard to race relations are amazing. They show the rest of us what is possible. It makes sense for us to learn from those who have worked the hardest for emancipation, and it's the right thing to do for the sake of continued progress in race relations. It's time for all the big northern and mid-western cities in the United States to seek help from the William Winter Institute for Racial Reconciliation at the University of Mississippi.

The Institute was founded in 1999 and named for William Winter, the governor of Mississippi from 1980-1984. He was best known for educational reforms that gave everyone the same rights to public education, regardless of their race or class.

The Institute's document on core values declares: "America has been, is now, and increasingly will be a multi-racial nation. But racism has diminished every aspect of our society. We have no choice but to speak the truth about race and racism, and seek equality, justice, and reconciliation."

Cultural and political changes in Mississippi really began in the 1970s. Some of those changes have to do with what the Institute describes as "systemic racism." This kind of racism is found in places like universities, corporations, and the government. It may have been around so long that people don't even recognize it anymore. Recognizing it is always the first step in reconciliation, or defeating differences.

An example of systemic racism is the Mississippi State Sovereignty Commission, which was dissolved in 1977. The commission worked secretly to prevent African Americans from registering to vote.

As a first step in fighting racism, people must begin to heal the pain of the past. One way to do this is to tell the truth about past injustices. Mississippi provides public access to the Mississippi Department of Archives and History, a research library with information about the past. Documents, such as those from the State Sovereignty Commission, are available for people to view. Once we acknowledge the sins of the past, we can become motivated to change the future.

William Winter in his home in Jackson, Mississippi, 2006.

The Institute defines the second step in reconciliation as giving power to local communities. One way they do this is by getting historically divided groups to talk to each other and tell the truth about healing past wrongs. The Core Values document notes that this is a difficult process. People feel pain and anger at the way that they and their ancestors have been treated. In these talks, people don't try to mask, or cover up, their feelings. They respect emotions and guide individuals in public ceremonies that honor such feelings. This leads to healing in the whole community.

The many local community programs that the Winter Institute helps lead include The First Amendment School

GO ON ➡

Reading and Literary Analysis, *continued*

Project at Lanier, an all-African American, inner-city high school. It encourages freedom of speech through activities such as creating a school newspaper and constitution. This helps students learn the importance of being informed and active citizens. Another example is the Sunflower County Freedom Project. This unusual program teaches young people in the mostly African American Delta region to become good leaders. They use the historical example of leadership in the 1960s as inspiration.

The third step in the process is called "restorative justice." The goal of restorative justice is to correct wrongs that have been done to people. An example of this is how Mississippi's legal system has sought prosecutions for civil rights crimes committed decades ago. Many of these crimes have been made the subject of popular movies. One is *Mississippi Burning,* a film about how the Ku Klux Klan killed civil rights workers Andrew Goodman, James Cheney, and Michael Schwerner in 1964. *Ghosts of Mississippi* is about the slaying of NAACP leader Medgar Evers. Both crimes remained unsolved; both cases were reopened as part of Mississippi's effort to come to terms with its past and embrace a new identity.

These three steps are a start, but the Institute is working to extend its reach even further. In March 2006, it held a conference called Southern Exposure: A Regional Summit on Racial Violence and Reconciliation. Participants came from Alabama, Georgia, Florida, Mississippi, Texas, North Carolina, South Carolina, Washington, D.C.—even Massachusetts and Minnesota.

How does the Institute see its future? The Core Values document says: "Although grounded in Mississippi and the South and the unique challenges confronting reconciliation between blacks and whites, the Institute recognizes that the need for reconciliation extends to all races and aspires to be a resource for the nation and the world in matters of race and racism."

The William Winter Institute for Racial Reconciliation is ready to help the nation and the world to face their racial conflicts, and to transform them into unity.

Let's listen to them. We can learn what they have struggled so hard to understand. Maybe we can benefit from some of the wisdom and peace they've worked so hard for.

Reading and Literary Analysis, *continued*

5 Which words in the first paragraph reveal the author's bias?

A site, acts, stories

B cruel, violence, dark

C deeply, hard, share

D historic, beliefs, real

6 What signal word in the last paragraph shows a call to action?

A We

B Let's

C peace

D they've

7 The main purpose of this selection is to persuade the reader that

A racism still exists in surprising ways today.

B young people can be taught to be good leaders.

C healing occurs when past injustices become public.

D the services of the Institute can be a tool against racism.

8 <u>Emancipation</u> means the act of

A hiring.

B freeing.

C agreeing.

D deciding.

9 To <u>transform</u> means to

A trade for something better.

B change into something else.

C inform somebody of the rules.

D replace something that is broken.

Directions: Read question 10. Write your answer on a separate sheet of paper.

10 Racism is a problem that cannot be solved overnight. Use text evidence to explain how this selection makes that idea clear.

GO ON

EDGE Level C

Reading and Literary Analysis, *continued*

Directions: Questions 11–17 are about "Get Help—It's Your Right." Read the selection. Then read each question and choose the best answer.

Get Help—It's Your Right

For the victim of a crime, it can be a long, strange road back to normal life. People who have experienced any kind of criminal attack or <u>intrusion</u> know the feelings of deep loneliness, rage, and even shame that can haunt them for years. The desire can be strong to shrink back from the world. But I urge you, and anyone you know who has or will be struck by crime, not to do that. What feels like a very private, individual issue is actually a matter of public rights. If you are the victim of a crime, don't be afraid to ask for the help available to you.

> If you are the victim of a crime, don't be afraid to ask for the help available to you.

I understand the emotional <u>impact</u> of a criminal attack because I've been there twice in my lifetime, in two very different ways.

The first time, I was on my way home from a dance class on an early spring evening in Boston; the sun had fallen below the city buildings, and sky was growing dark. I left the subway and walked down the empty sidewalk toward my apartment, my bag of dancing clothes and shoes slung over my shoulder. Suddenly, I felt two large hands clap hard onto both of my shoulders. I spun around and found myself face-to-face with a young man I had never seen before.

He hesitated just long enough for the thought to occur in my mind: Is this the end of my life? Then, he grabbed my dance bag and ran down the sidewalk, around the corner, and out of sight. I stood frozen in shock and rage. I could have, and should have, gone to the police to report the crime and to have my story heard. But I never told anyone, because I was so overcome with guilt and shame. I found out much later that this is a classic response to the trauma of attack. I was not alone in this feeling, but I felt alone. It was a decade before I could walk down a street and not experience intense panic at the sound of footsteps behind me.

Many years after I regained my safe footing on city streets, crime found me again. This time, it was an identity theft. Out of nowhere, I began receiving painful, accusing letters from businesses and collection agencies, implying that I was a criminal and telling me I'd better pay up or accept the consequences.

Here's what had happened: a stranger had written checks issued to me in error by a credit card company. I had recently closed the account, so there were no credit funds to cover the checks. But it was a terrible experience to receive all these accusing and threatening letters—and to realize my identity had been stolen.

I felt that same shame as I considered reporting this crime to the police. But this time I did it. I was even able to sit down and talk to someone about what happened and how it made me feel. I couldn't believe the support and understanding I received, and how quickly I was able to move through both the maze of paperwork and the process of feeling better—and eventually safer.

Our country has always guaranteed legal rights for those accused of crimes, and we have a system that is supposed to treat criminals decently, no matter what they have done. Around 1980, government organizations began to focus on recognizing and serving the rights of *victims* of crimes.

Crime victims have legal public rights that include "protection, dignity, and the right to be heard," according to the Office for Victims of Crimes, created by the United States Department of Justice in 1983. NOVA, the National Organization for Victim Assistance, helps 60,000 crime victims every year with programs and services to move them through the recovery process and back into open-hearted lives.

If a crime is ever committed against you, don't pull back into fear and isolation. Come out and <u>access</u> the help you need—you'll be amazed at the support and kindness you will receive.

> If a crime is ever committed against you, don't pull back into fear and isolation. Come out and access the help you need…

GO ON

Reading and Literary Analysis, *continued*

UNIT 6

11 The author of the selection would like the reader to draw the conclusion that

A if you are the victim of a crime, you just need time and you will feel better.

B if you are the victim of a crime, you have the right to pursue criminal charges.

C you need to be extra careful to ensure you do not become a victim of a crime.

D you should not be afraid of seeking emotional help if you are the victim of a crime.

12 Both "The William Winter Institute" and "Get Help—It's Your Right" speak directly to the reader. What effect does this have?

A It helps to prove that the information is true.

B It allows the author to show a sense of humor.

C It makes the argument of the author more clear.

D It increases the emotional effect of the argument.

13 Both "The William Winter Institute" and "Get Help—It's Your Right" focus on an appeal to

A justice.

B loyalty.

C honesty.

D forgiveness.

14 Intrusion means

A immature behavior.

B intended consequences.

C unwelcome interference.

D uncomfortable surroundings.

15 To have an impact means to

A answer.

B imitate.

C influence.

D understand.

16 To access means to

A steal.

B respect.

C gain entry to.

D create as a group.

Directions: Read question 17. Write your answer on a separate sheet of paper.

17 Explain how being the victim of a crime affects the emotions of the victim. Cite details from the passage to support your answer.

GO ON ▶

Reading and Literary Analysis, *continued*

Directions: Questions 18–25 are about "An Awkward Silence." Read the selection. Then read each question and choose the best answer.

An Awkward Silence

I got a job teaching English a few years ago, and as part of my job, I was to teach students to write arguments. Like many English classes, we spent some time looking at current events in order to select topics to write about. At the time, the United States was going to war with Iraq, and it was already at war in Afghanistan. Not all citizens agreed on what the United States should do, so I expected some heated discussions in class. How wrong I was.

When I asked for my students' opinions, I received little or no response, although this wasn't a surprise at first. Teenagers don't always offer their opinions right away; in fact, sometimes it's like pulling teeth to get them to talk in class; however, as I continued to try to facilitate discussion, I found deeper reasons for their lack of passion.

"I don't watch the news. It's just the same stuff over and over anyway. Honestly, I don't have time for it. I just started a new job," said one student.

Another chimed in, "Yeah, I feel like it'd be a full-time job just to try to keep track of all of the information about the war. How can I have an opinion if I'm so uninformed? I know the media twists information all the time so people will believe their side of the story. That's why I just don't trust any of it."

I was both pleased and dismayed by their thinking. I was pleased because they were thinking. There was good reason for them to be overwhelmed by information. I thought of all the junk mail and junk e-mail I get. I never read it. Instead, I simply turn myself off to it, and that's exactly what my students were doing to information presented by the news media.

I was dismayed when I thought of the repercussion of an uninformed society. The population of teenagers in America is bigger than it has ever been. Wouldn't choosing to remain uninformed only make it easier for people with evil intentions to do whatever they want? Instead of trying to convince people, policy makers

will just act according to their whims. However, I considered that policy makers are elected officials. But how will they get elected in the future if society doesn't know who they are or what their job is?

"How will you vote in the next election if you don't keep up with the news? Some of you are old enough to vote right now, and within a few years you'll all be able to vote," I said.

"Oh, I don't vote," said an eighteen-year-old student. "What if I choose the wrong person? I let the people who care do that."

"It's not like the vote counts anyway," said another.

"You need a master's degree in political science to figure any of it out," said another.

It was my turn to be silent. I asked myself, What kind of impact will such lack of concern have on our society? What will happen to our right to vote if we choose not to exercise it? What kind of people will come to power? I'm afraid I don't want to find out.

GO ON

Reading and Literary Analysis, continued

18 What evidence does the author of the selection mainly rely on for his argument?

 A facts

 B statistics

 C expert opinions

 D personal experiences

19 What do the students' statements in the selection have in common?

 A They show anger about the war.

 B They reflect a feeling of powerlessness.

 C They prove that the media twists information.

 D They use facts to explain why voters are confused.

20 What main conclusion would the author of "An Awkward Silence" like the reader to draw?

 A The news media can be an enormously powerful political weapon.

 B Young people need to be more active in and informed about current events.

 C Media bias makes current events too difficult for young people to understand.

 D It is the responsibility of policy makers to ensure that they are being clear and honest.

21 The arguments in "Get Help—It's Your Right" and "An Awkward Silence" would both be most strengthened by

 A current statistics.

 B personal stories.

 C shocking graphics.

 D historical comparisons.

22 What does "The William Winter Institute" include that "An Awkward Silence" would benefit from?

 A personal opinions

 B quotations from real people

 C stories to support the main idea

 D information from published sources

23 To <u>facilitate</u> means to

 A react in a positive way.

 B handle in a mature way.

 C face the truth about something.

 D help make something happen.

24 <u>Repercussion</u> means

 A a related event.

 B a negative effect.

 C an angry discussion.

 D a loud banging noise.

Directions: Read question 25. Write your answer on a separate sheet of paper.

25 The author is concerned that these teens' attitudes may be widespread. What does the author predict about the future if these attitudes do not change? Cite text details in your answer.

DONE!

Grammar and Writing

Directions: Read the composition. It contains errors. Then read each question and choose the best answer.

Smoking, Secondhand

(1) The smoke comes toward me like a floating monster, and I start to cough. (2) I am reminded how I hate having the smell of cigarette smoke on my clothes and the taste of smoke in my mouth from people smoking close to me. (3) Smoking has been proven to be dangerous. (4) So I made a conscious choice not to smoke. (5) And yet, when inconsiderate smokers are around, it's as if I'm smoking…their smoke. (6) Secondhand smoke puts everyone at risk, and nonsmokers need protection.

(7) The facts about the dangers of smoking and secondhand smoke are alarming. (8) Each year, more than 390,000 Americans die from the effects of smoking. (9) <u>There are more than 60 chemicals in cigarette smoke although they are carcinogenic</u>, and smoking has been directly linked as a cause of cancer. (10) The United States Surgeon General reported that, "Secondhand smoke is a serious health hazard that can lead to disease and premature death in children and nonsmoking adults." (11) According to the report exposure to smoke at home or work increases a nonsmoker's risk of developing heart disease by 25 to 30 percent and lung cancer by 20 to 30 percent.

(12) Some smokers might say they have the freedom to do what they <u>want and smoking,</u> especially in their own home, is their right. (13) But I believe they shouldn't be able to do what they want when the smoke they leave in the air is harmful to others.

(14) State and city governments are beginning to recognize that the only way to protect everyone from these health risks is to enact comprehensive clean-air laws that prohibit smoking in all indoor, public places and workplaces. (15) Smoking in private spaces is a more difficult issue. (16) The fact remains that smokers should be aware of the dangers that secondhand smoke presents, especially for the developing bodies of infants and children.

(17) I ask all public health advocates to study the research on secondhand smoke, to consider the effects of cigarette smoke on children and adult nonsmokers, <u>and supporting clean-air laws.</u> (18) And smokers, give us nonsmokers a break. (19) You can choose to smoke, but be considerate—let us choose not to.

Grammar and Writing, *continued*

1 Which sentence states the main idea of the composition?

A sentence 1

B sentence 3

C sentence 5

D sentence 6

2 Sentence 3 should be changed to

A Smoking prove to be dangerous.

B To smoke has been proven to be dangerous.

C Smoking have been proven to be dangerous.

D No change

3 What change, if any, should be made to sentence 8?

A Remove *than 390,000*

B Change *Americans* to **americans**

C Change *effects* to **affects**

D No change

4 In sentence 9, the underlined part should be changed to

A There are more than 60 chemicals in cigarette smoke that are carcinogenic

B There are more than 60 chemicals in cigarette smoke and they are carcinogenic

C There are more than 60 chemicals in cigarette smoke because they are carcinogenic

D No change

5 What change, if any, should be made to sentence 11?

A Change *report* to **Report**

B Put a comma after *report*

C Change *developing* to **developeing**

D No change

6 In sentence 12, the words want and smoking should be changed to

A want, smoking

B want and, smoking

C want, and smoking

D No change

7 Which sentence presents a counter-argument to the main argument of the essay?

A sentence 7

B sentence 12

C sentence 14

D sentence 16

8 In sentence 17, the underlined part should be changed to

A support clean-air laws.

B and support clean-air laws.

C and to support clean-air laws.

D No change

UNIT 6

GO ON

Grammar and Writing, *continued*

Directions: Read the composition. It contains errors. Then read each question and choose the best answer.

Trucking in Afghanistan

(1) The sun was blazing, and the desert sand was starting to sizzle when the truck pulled up to take us across the north of Afghanistan. (2) It was the monday mail truck, and we had been waiting days for the ride. (3) The truck left the village.

(4) We were adventurers all right. (5) Not many Americans in the '70s had taken this route and certainly not many women. (6) In order <u>breathing</u> as much fresh air as we could during the 10-hour trip, we sat on the open-air seats near the back of the truck. (7) (Little did we know that we would soon be covered with the fine desert dust that churned up from the truck wheels just below us.) (8) Alice and I climbed aboard.

(9) At the next stop, with their chickens, goats, and sacks of grain about 20 Afghanis climbed aboard too. (10) Three were women. (11) Their colorful veils covered their whole bodies except for a little net rectangle in front of their eyes—so that they could see out, but no one could see in. (12) I smiled at them as the truck took us off through the desert, but of course, I couldn't see if they were smiling back.

(13) We bumped along in the heat for hours, amazed that the driver could find a path through the sand. (14) Alice's hat looked good. (15) The women were quiet. (16) The chickens squawked. (17) <u>Closing my eyes</u>, I dreamed of cool forests and rushing water.

(18) Suddenly one of the women started beating on the cab of the truck. (19) The truck stopped. (20) The woman got out. (21) She brought a baby out from under her veil. (22) She had alerted the driver because the baby had become ill. (23) I couldn't believe it! (24) For hours, she had been sitting quietly with her baby in her arms, through the bumps and the heat and dust. (25) I knew at that moment that she was a model of strength. (26) Although I never saw her face, she has inspired me to this day.

GO ON

Grammar and Writing, *continued*

9 What change, if any, should be made to sentence 2?

   A Change *monday* to **Monday**

   B Change *mail* to **male**

   C Put quotes around *monday mail truck*

   D No change

10 In sentence 6, the word breathing should be changed to

   A breathe

   B breathed

   C to breathe

   D No change

11 What change, if any, should be made to sentence 9?

   A Put a comma after *grain*

   B Change *Afghanis* to **afghanis**

   C Change *aboard* to **abord**

   D No change

12 Which sentence does **not** follow the logical order of events?

   A sentence 3

   B sentence 8

   C sentence 9

   D sentence 12

13 In sentence 17, the words Closing my eyes should be changed to

   A Close my eyes

   B Closed my eyes

   C To close my eyes

   D No change

14 Which detail is **not** relevant and should be removed from paragraph 4?

   A sentence 13

   B sentence 14

   C sentence 15

   D sentence 17

15 Which of these is the **best** way to combine sentences 20 and 21?

   A The woman got out, but she brought a baby out from under her veil.

   B The woman got out, and she brought a baby out from under her veil.

   C The woman got out because she brought a baby out from under her veil.

   D The woman got out although she brought a baby out from under her veil.

16 Sentence 22 should be changed to

   A She had alerted the driver and the baby had become ill.

   B She had alerted the driver, but the baby had become ill.

   C Because she had alerted the driver, the baby had become ill.

   D No change

Grammar and Writing, *continued*

UNIT 6

Directions: Read the following writing prompt, and write a composition. Use the Writer's Checklist to make sure that you do your best work.

Prompt

Some people believe that students should be required to pass an exit exam in order to graduate from high school. Others do not, believing that such exams do not provide an accurate measure of a student's knowledge and skills.

Write a composition in which you argue for or against requiring students to pass a high school exit exam. Use the fact sheet below to support your position.

Fact Sheet About High School Exit Exams

The primary purpose of high school exit exams is to significantly improve student achievement in public high schools and to ensure that students who graduate from public high schools can demonstrate grade-level competency in reading, writing, and mathematics.

Proponents of testing argue that exit exams lead to achievement and other gains:

- Students know what is expected and that the test really counts, so they work harder.
- Schools identify and can address student weaknesses early.

Students who do not pass a part of the exam may retake that part of the exam.

With adequate supports and the right policy context, exit exams probably have some positive effects on student motivation and achievement and on curriculum and instruction, at least for some groups of students.

Critics say the tests sometimes are too hard, lead teachers to teach to the test, take time away from instruction, and are expensive.

Education researchers say they fear that high-stakes tests intimidate students and lead to higher dropout rates, especially among low-income, minority, or disabled students.

There is some evidence of negative effects of these exams, such as encouraging some students to pursue a GED instead of a diploma.

Writer's Checklist

- ☑ Write about all parts of the prompt.
- ☑ Present a clear central idea, and stay focused on it.
- ☑ Organize your composition from its introduction to its conclusion.
- ☑ Use transitions to connect your thoughts for the reader.
- ☑ Present meaningful ideas, and support them with specific information.
- ☑ Use appropriate words and a variety of sentence structures.
- ☑ Proofread and edit your writing for grammar, usage, mechanics, and spelling.

DONE!

EDGE Level C

Student Profile: Unit Tests

Directions: Use the **Answer Key** on page 159 to score the multiple-choice items. Circle the item number of each correct answer below. Calculate test scores by assigning one point for each correct answer. Use the scoring guides on page 159 to score the constructed-response items. Use the Good Writing Traits Rubric on page 122 to score the written composition. Total the scores and calculate the % score or use the conversion chart. To gauge mastery for a particular tested skill or Common Core Standard, review the Cluster Test and Unit Test results.

Reading and Literary Analysis

Category	Tested Skill	ITEM ANALYSIS		TEST SCORES
		Item Numbers	Mastery	Points: Earned / Total
Vocabulary	Word Relationships L.9-10.5	1 2 3 4	3 out of 4 + −	_____ / 4
	Key Vocabulary L.9-10.6	8 9 14 15 16 23 24	6 out of 7 + −	_____ / 7
Literary Analysis	Analyze Viewpoint RI.9-10.6	5 6 7 13	3 out of 4 + −	_____ / 4
	Evaluate Arguments RI.9-10.8	12 18 21 22	3 out of 4 + −	_____ / 4
	Comprehension RI.9-10.10	11 19 20	2 out of 3 + −	_____ / 3
Constructed Response	Use Text Evidence RI.9-10.1; RI.9-10.10; W.9-10.9	Rubric Scores Item 10 _____ + Item 17 _____ + Item 25 _____ = _____		_____ / 12

Overall Score (Points Earned ÷ Total Points x 100 = %)　　_____ ÷ 34 = _____ %

Grammar and Writing

Category	Tested Skill	ITEM ANALYSIS		TEST SCORES
		Item Numbers	Mastery	Points: Earned / Total
Grammar	Infinitives and Gerunds L.9-10.1	2 8 10 13	3 out of 4 + −	_____ / 4
	Sentences L.9-10.1	4 6 15 16	3 out of 4 + −	_____ / 4
Revising and Editing	Focus and Unity W.9-10.5	1 7 12 14	3 out of 4 + −	_____ / 4
	Grammar, Mechanics, and Usage L.9-10.2	3 5 9 11	3 out of 4 + −	_____ / 4
Written Composition (Argument) W.9-10.1; W.9-10.4; W.9-10.10	Focus and Unity	Rubric Scores: _____ / 4		
	Organization	_____ / 4		
	Development of Ideas	_____ / 4	=	_____ / 20
	Voice and Style	_____ / 4		
	Written Conventions	_____ / 4		

Overall Score (Points Earned ÷ Total Points x 100 = %)　　_____ ÷ 40 = _____ %

Project Rubric: A Political Campaign

Score	Planning/Preparation	Content of Project	Delivery/Presentation	Collaboration
3 Great	• Reviews a variety of different political ads, speeches, and other campaign materials. • Chooses platform issues that are relevant to the Essential Question.	• Incorporates strong persuasive techniques to promote issues. • Appeals to the campaign's primary audience. • Clearly addresses the Essential Question.	• Incorporates a variety of campaign materials, such as speeches, bumper stickers, posters, buttons, etc. • Contains no errors in grammar, usage, mechanics, and spelling.	• Works well with others. • Assumes a clear role and related responsibilities.
2 Good	• Reviews a few political ads and speeches. • Chooses platform issues that have some relevance to the Essential Question.	• Incorporates mostly strong persuasive techniques to promote issues. • Somewhat appeals to the campaign's primary audience. • Somewhat addresses the Essential Question.	• Incorporates a few different kinds of campaign materials. • Contains a few errors in grammar, usage, mechanics, and spelling.	• Works with others most of the time. • Sometimes has difficulty sharing decisions and responsibilities.
1 Needs Work	• Does not review different political ads, speeches, or other campaign materials. • Chooses platform issues that have no relevance to the Essential Question.	• Incorporates faulty persuasive techniques, if any, to promote issues. • Does not appeal to the campaign's primary audience. • Does not address the Essential Question.	• Incorporates only one type of campaign material. • Contains many errors in grammar, usage, mechanics, and spelling.	• Cannot work with others in most situations. • Cannot share decisions or responsibilities.

EDGE Level C

Self-Assessment

Directions: Circle the numbers that show how much you agree or disagree with each sentence. Then answer the question below. If necessary, use the back of the page.

	Not Yet	With Help	Most of the Time	Very Well
1 When I read an argument, I know how to analyze and evaluate central ideas, the development of ideas (including word choices), and elements of persuasion.	1	2	3	4
2 I understand the features of a how-to article, an editorial cartoon, an autobiography, and historical declarations.	1	2	3	4
3 I know how to relate arguments about similar topics.	1	2	3	4
4 I know how to synthesize information by drawing conclusions, comparing evidence, and forming generalizations.	1	2	3	4
5 I know how to build my word knowledge by using a dictionary or thesaurus and by identifying connotations.	1	2	3	4
6 I know how to use gerunds and infinitives, vary sentences, and write compound and complex sentences.	1	2	3	4
7 I know how to make my writing focused and unified in a persuasive essay.	1	2	3	4

8 Think of one thing you learned really well in this unit. Tell how you will use this the next time you read or write.

_____

_____

_____

_____

_____

_____

_____

_____

UNIT 6

Reader Reflection

Directions: Answer questions 1–10. If necessary, use the back of the page.

"The Jewels of the Shrine"

1 What did you learn about analyzing a writer's choice of dramatic elements that will help you the next time you read a play?

2 You can visualize by mentally re-creating scenes. Explain how this strategy will help you the next time you read.

3 Write what you liked and did not like about "The Jewels of the Shrine." Include examples from the play.

I liked...

I did not like...

4 Are you interested in reading more writing by James Ene Henshaw? _____ Yes _____ No

5 Are you interested in reading more plays by other playwrights? _____ Yes _____ No

"Remembered"

6 What did you learn about analyzing word choices that will help you the next time you read a poem?

7 You can also visualize by recording information about images and your reaction to them in a chart. Explain how this strategy will help you the next time you read.

8 Write what you liked and did not like about "Remembered." Include examples from the poem.

I liked...

I did not like...

9 Are you interested in reading more writing by Naomi Shihab Nye? _____ Yes _____ No

10 Are you interested in reading more poems by other poets? _____ Yes _____ No

"The Jewels of the Shrine" and "Remembered"

 Closed Book

Directions: Read each question and choose the best answer.

KEY VOCABULARY

1 To <u>compensate</u> workers means to
- Ⓐ fire them.
- Ⓑ pay them.
- Ⓒ hire them.
- Ⓓ train them.

2 <u>Destitute</u> means
- Ⓐ fearless.
- Ⓑ left behind.
- Ⓒ undesirable.
- Ⓓ without money.

3 To behave <u>impudently</u> means to behave
- Ⓐ dishonestly.
- Ⓑ ineffectively.
- Ⓒ impressively.
- Ⓓ disrespectfully.

4 To <u>infuriate</u> means to
- Ⓐ debate.
- Ⓑ imitate.
- Ⓒ enrage.
- Ⓓ criticize.

5 A <u>prophecy</u> is a
- Ⓐ protest.
- Ⓑ problem.
- Ⓒ prediction.
- Ⓓ preference.

6 <u>Respectably</u> means
- Ⓐ eagerly.
- Ⓑ properly.
- Ⓒ certainly.
- Ⓓ peacefully.

7 <u>Traditional</u> means according to
- Ⓐ age.
- Ⓑ ability.
- Ⓒ chance.
- Ⓓ custom.

8 An example of something <u>traditional</u> is
- Ⓐ to train hard for a sports event, such as a marathon.
- Ⓑ to use your grandmother's recipes for a holiday dinner.
- Ⓒ to try a variety of options to see which one you like best.
- Ⓓ to travel around the world, learning about different cultures.

GO ON

UNIT 7

"The Jewels of the Shrine" and "Remembered"

Open Book

Directions: Questions 9–15 are about "The Jewels of the Shrine." Read each question and choose the best answer. You may look at the selection on pages 663–710 to help you answer the questions.

LITERARY ANALYSIS

9 Why is "The Jewels of the Shrine" separated into two acts?

  Ⓐ to change the setting

  Ⓑ to show the passage of time

  Ⓒ to introduce a new character

  Ⓓ to show how the grandsons changed

10 What setting did the writer choose for Scene II?

  Ⓐ the farm

  Ⓑ the market in the city

  Ⓒ inside Okorie's house

  Ⓓ in the garden behind Okorie's house

11 Which element of a script does a writer use to give instructions to the actors?

  Ⓐ the setting

  Ⓑ the dialogue

  Ⓒ the stage directions

  Ⓓ the cast of characters

12 The stage directions at the end of Scene I tell the reader that

  Ⓐ a voice laughs at Arob, Ojima, and Bassi.

  Ⓑ Arob, Ojima, and Okorie all go outside to dig.

  Ⓒ Arob and Ojima have given Okorie a good burial.

  Ⓓ Arob and Ojima have sold most of their possessions.

COMPREHENSION

13 What does the play show about traditional culture in Okorie's village?

  Ⓐ People honored the elderly.

  Ⓑ Strangers were never trusted.

  Ⓒ Old people did all of the farming.

  Ⓓ Valuable property was buried to keep it safe.

14 What role does the Stranger play in Okorie's life?

  Ⓐ He is Okorie's best friend.

  Ⓑ He writes Okorie's will for him.

  Ⓒ He teaches Okorie how to read and write.

  Ⓓ He helps Okorie teach the grandsons a lesson.

Directions: Read question 15. Write your answer on a separate sheet of paper.

15

> Among the beads which my father got from the early white men were real jewels . . . In a big ceremony the jewels were placed on our shrine. But it was not for long. Some said they were stolen. But the stranger who came here knew where they were. He said that they were buried somewhere near the big oak tree on our farm. I must go out and dig for them. They can be sold for fifty pounds these days.

What is Okorie's purpose in saying this to his grandsons? How well is that purpose fulfilled? Refer to text details in your answer.

Directions: Questions 16–22 are about "Remembered." Read each question and choose the best answer. You may look at the selection on pages 671–673 to help you answer the questions.

LITERARY ANALYSIS

16 Which of these lines from the poem is an example of literal imagery?

  Ⓐ He scrawled the episodes out in elaborate longhand

  Ⓑ Sleeping in that house was like falling down a deep well,

  Ⓒ He gave these things unexpectedly. You went to see him

  Ⓓ how to be dark and the forest remembered how to be mysterious

UNIT 7

GO ON

"The Jewels of the Shrine" and "Remembered"

17 The word choices in the third stanza (lines 18-24) create a feeling of

- Ⓐ security.
- Ⓑ excitement.
- Ⓒ anticipation.
- Ⓓ disappointment.

18 Read this line from the poem.

> Some days his brain could travel backwards easier
> than it could sit in a chair, right there.

What does the speaker mean by this?

- Ⓐ The man was very restless.
- Ⓑ The man often forgot where he was.
- Ⓒ The man could not remember much about the past.
- Ⓓ The man's focus was more on the past than the present.

19 Which of these lines from the poem is an example of figurative imagery?

- Ⓐ At night we propped our feet by the fireplace
- Ⓑ Walking with him across the acres of piney forest,
- Ⓒ and in bed, the quilts remembered how to tuck up under our chins.
- Ⓓ In the mornings we'd stagger away from an unforgettable breakfast

COMPREHENSION

20 Which sentence below describes the speaker's feelings about the man?

- Ⓐ She is tired of his stories.
- Ⓑ She is loving and respectful.
- Ⓒ She thinks he is too forgetful.
- Ⓓ She thinks he should remember others.

21 What does the reader learn about the man from the poem?

- Ⓐ He is too old to do anything but tell stories.
- Ⓑ He wants his life and experiences to be valued.
- Ⓒ His memory is fading, so he writes things down.
- Ⓓ He likes people to leave him alone with his memories.

Directions: Read question 22. Write your answer on a separate sheet of paper.

22

> . . . But the need for remembrance silenced me,
> a ringing rising up out of the soil's centuries, the ones
> who plowed this land, whose names we do not know.

What new information does the speaker reveal at the end of "Remembered"? How does it relate to the overall theme of the poem? Cite text evidence in your analysis.

DONE!

Reader Reflection

Directions: Answer questions 1–10. If necessary, use the back of the page.

"Romeo and Juliet"

1 What did you learn about blank verse that will help you the next time you read a play by William Shakespeare?

2 You can visualize by creating a mental picture or a drawing. Explain how this strategy will help you the next time you read.

3 Write what you liked and did not like about "Romeo and Juliet." Include examples from the play.

I liked...

I did not like...

4 Are you interested in reading more writing by William Shakespeare? _____ Yes _____ No

5 Are you interested in reading more plays by other authors? _____ Yes _____ No

"West Side Story"

6 What did you learn about relating a story to its source that will help you the next time you read a play or other story?

7 You can also visualize comparisons the writer is making. Explain how this strategy will help you the next time you read.

8 Write what you liked and did not like about "West Side Story." Include examples from the screenplay.

I liked...

I did not like...

9 Are you interested in reading more writing by Ernest Lehman? _____ Yes _____ No

10 Are you interested in reading more screenplays by other authors? _____ Yes _____ No

EDGE Level C

"Romeo and Juliet" and "West Side Story"

Closed Book

Directions: Read each question and choose the best answer.

KEY VOCABULARY

1 Attitude means
- Ⓐ ability.
- Ⓑ outlook.
- Ⓒ method.
- Ⓓ personality.

2 Dense means
- Ⓐ tall.
- Ⓑ bare.
- Ⓒ thick.
- Ⓓ pretty.

3 Envious means
- Ⓐ furious.
- Ⓑ jealous.
- Ⓒ suspicious.
- Ⓓ dangerous.

4 Feud means a long-standing
- Ⓐ quarrel.
- Ⓑ question.
- Ⓒ appointment.
- Ⓓ arrangement.

5 Fractured means
- Ⓐ frozen.
- Ⓑ broken.
- Ⓒ captured.
- Ⓓ distracted.

6 Mature means
- Ⓐ mated for life.
- Ⓑ taken by force.
- Ⓒ fully developed.
- Ⓓ completely over.

7 Perfection means without
- Ⓐ fault.
- Ⓑ hope.
- Ⓒ reason.
- Ⓓ purpose.

8 A resolution is
- Ⓐ a polite request.
- Ⓑ a strong decision.
- Ⓒ an immediate reply.
- Ⓓ an unsolved mystery.

Directions: Questions 9–15 are about "Romeo and Juliet." Read each question and choose the Open Book
best answer. You may look at the selection on pages 705–715 to help you answer the questions.

LITERARY ANALYSIS

9 "Romeo and Juliet" is an example of
- Ⓐ free verse.
- Ⓑ modern verse.
- Ⓒ rhymed verse.
- Ⓓ blank verse.

10 Meter refers to
- Ⓐ a type of rhyme scheme.
- Ⓑ the number of acts in a play.
- Ⓒ the kind of imagery used in plays.
- Ⓓ the rhythm of stressed and unstressed beats.

11 Which of these lines is written in iambic pentameter?
- Ⓐ It's just your name that's my enemy, not you.
- Ⓑ See how she leans her cheek upon her hand.
- Ⓒ Who is that hiding in the darkness, spying on me?
- Ⓓ I wouldn't want them to catch you here for anything in the world.

GO ON

"Romeo and Juliet" and "West Side Story"

 Open Book

12 Which of these lines uses imagery?

Ⓐ O, that she knew she were!

Ⓑ I am too bold. 'Tis not to me she speaks.

Ⓒ How cam'st thou hither, tell me, and wherefore?

Ⓓ I have night's black cloak to hide me from their eyes.

COMPREHENSION

13 Why is Juliet upset about her love for Romeo?

Ⓐ Their families are enemies.

Ⓑ She thinks he is from a poor family.

Ⓒ She is worried that he will die in a fight.

Ⓓ They have not known each other long enough.

14 Why does Romeo reveal his presence to Juliet?

Ⓐ He told her he would meet her.

Ⓑ He thinks she has seen him hiding.

Ⓒ He hears her talking fondly about him.

Ⓓ He is worried her relatives might see him.

Directions: Read question 15. Write your answer on a separate sheet of paper.

15

> **ROMEO.** Alack, there lies more peril in thine eye
> Than twenty of their swords. Look thou but sweet,
> And I am proof against their enmity.

What does Romeo mean? In what way are his words similar to poetry? In what way are they similar to natural speech? Refer to text details in your answer.

GO ON

UNIT 7

"Romeo and Juliet" and "West Side Story"

Open Book

Directions: Questions 16–22 are about "West Side Story." Read each question and choose the best answer. You may look at the selections on pages 717–719 to help you answer the questions.

LITERARY ANALYSIS

16 "West Side Story" draws upon "Romeo and Juliet," but it changes

Ⓐ the end of the story.

Ⓑ the setting of the story.

Ⓒ the ages of the main characters.

Ⓓ the main characters' attitudes toward each other.

17 Which of the following is true about the young lovers in both stories?

Ⓐ They express their feelings by singing.

Ⓑ They are members of the same ethnic group.

Ⓒ They come from groups that hate each other.

Ⓓ They say that they are willing to die for the sake of love.

18 Which character in "West Side Story" is based upon a member of the Montague family in "Romeo and Juliet"?

Ⓐ Tony

Ⓑ Papa

Ⓒ Maria

Ⓓ Bernardo

19 One theme in "West Side Story" that finds its source in "Romeo and Juliet" is that

Ⓐ love is stronger than fear.

Ⓑ it is wrong to keep love a secret.

Ⓒ it takes time for true love to develop.

Ⓓ women feel love more deeply than men do.

COMPREHENSION

20 What does Tony mean when he tells Maria that he is not "one of them"?

Ⓐ He is not someone who is afraid of love.

Ⓑ He wants Maria to treat him as if he were Latino.

Ⓒ He is willing to give up his family if he can be with her.

Ⓓ He is not like the young men who hate Bernardo's gang.

21 What is the main idea of the song that Tony and Maria sing in this scene?

Ⓐ I will never leave you.

Ⓑ From now on, all that I care about is you.

Ⓒ Love helps ordinary people do amazing things.

Ⓓ Tonight is the most wonderful night of my life.

Directions: Read question 22. Write your answer on a separate sheet of paper.

22

> **TONY.** [*calling*] Maria . . .
> [*She appears on the fire escape, moves forward, sees Tony.*]
> **MARIA.** Quiet! If Bernardo—
> **TONY.** Come down.
> **MARIA.** [*turning*] My father and mother will wake up—
> **TONY.** Just for a minute.
> **MARIA.** [*smiles*] A minute is not enough.
> **TONY.** [*smiles*] For an hour, then.
> **MARIA.** I cannot.
> **TONY.** Forever.

In what sense does this scene draw from "Romeo and Juliet"? How is it different? Refer to both texts in your answer.

DONE!

UNIT 7

Reader Reflection

Directions: Answer questions 1–10. If necessary, use the back of the page.

"Poems for the Earth"

1 What did you learn about ways of representing a subject through words and through artwork that will help you the next time you read an illustrated poem?

2 You can visualize images in writing that appeal to any or all of the five senses. Explain how this strategy will help you the next time you read.

3 Write what you liked and did not like about "Poems for the Earth." Include examples from the poems.

I liked...
I did not like...

4 Are you interested in reading more poems by these poets? _____ Yes _____ No

5 Are you interested in reading more poetry by other authors? _____ Yes _____ No

"I Was Born Today"/"Touching the Earth"

6 What did you learn about analyzing structure and style that will help you the next time you read a poem?

7 You can use a response chart to help visualize sensory images. Explain how this strategy will help you the next time you read.

8 Write what you liked and did not like about "I Was Born Today"/"Touching the Earth." Include examples from the poems.

I liked...
I did not like...

9 Are you interested in reading more poems by Amado Nervo? _____ Yes _____ No

10 Are you interested in reading more essays by bell hooks? _____ Yes _____ No

"Poems for the Earth" and "Born Today" / "Touching Earth" Closed Book

Directions: Read each question and choose the best answer.

KEY VOCABULARY

1 Commercial means having to do with
Ⓐ living and dying.
Ⓑ giving and taking.
Ⓒ coming and going.
Ⓓ buying and selling.

2 To endure means to
Ⓐ ignore.
Ⓑ enable.
Ⓒ survive.
Ⓓ struggle.

3 The essence of something means its
Ⓐ value when sold.
Ⓑ source of energy.
Ⓒ most important quality.
Ⓓ connection to the earth.

4 Industrial means having to do with
Ⓐ traveling.
Ⓑ recycling.
Ⓒ advertising.
Ⓓ manufacturing.

5 To perish means to
Ⓐ die.
Ⓑ hide.
Ⓒ steal.
Ⓓ punish.

6 To have resolve means to have
Ⓐ doubt.
Ⓑ difficulty.
Ⓒ resources.
Ⓓ determination.

7 To suffice means to
Ⓐ slice.
Ⓑ suffer.
Ⓒ satisfy.
Ⓓ submit.

8 Tremulous means
Ⓐ timid.
Ⓑ sleepy.
Ⓒ jealous.
Ⓓ relieved.

GO ON

"Poems for the Earth" and "Born Today" / "Touching Earth"

Directions: Questions 9–15 are about "Poems for the Earth." Read each question and choose the best answer. You may look at the selections on pages 728–736 to help you answer the questions.

LITERARY ANALYSIS

9 What aspect of the poem "Mi Madre" does the painting *Orange Light on the Four Peaks* illustrate?

Ⓐ the desert setting

Ⓑ the many different kinds of cacti

Ⓒ the appearance of sudden storms

Ⓓ the three herbs that the poet mentions

10 The poem "Hard Questions" and the painting *Down Eighteenth Street* both attempt to represent

Ⓐ the abundance of life in swamps and forests.

Ⓑ a wild human heart that refuses to become "civilized."

Ⓒ people's habit of destroying nature for the sake of "progress."

Ⓓ the possibility that children appreciate nature more than their parents do.

11 The painting *Forest* shows only a few trees—no people. What explanation for the absence of people does the poem "There Will Come Soft Rains" suggest?

Ⓐ The forest is on another planet.

Ⓑ A terrible war has killed everyone.

Ⓒ The scene existed before humans existed.

Ⓓ Humanity has been wiped out by a plague.

12 What idea in the poem "Fire and Ice" does the painting *Snow Storm* capture?

Ⓐ the power of hate

Ⓑ the power of desire

Ⓒ the speaker's wish to live forever

Ⓓ the speaker's fear about the end of the world

COMPREHENSION

13 The authors of "Mi Madre" and "Hard Questions" are similar because they both

Ⓐ write about the desert.

Ⓑ believe that humans are destructive.

Ⓒ suggest that humans need the earth.

Ⓓ describe ways humans can learn from the earth.

14 What idea is in both "Fire and Ice" and "There Will Come Soft Rains"?

Ⓐ the end of civilization

Ⓑ the indifference of nature

Ⓒ the destructiveness of fire

Ⓓ the effect of climate change

Directions: Read question 15. Write your answer on a separate sheet of paper.

15

> She: the desert
> She: strong mother.

What does Pat Mora mean by calling the desert "strong mother"? What do you think the other poets in the "Poems for the Earth" group would call "strong"? Refer to at least one detail from each poem.

"Poems for the Earth" and "Born Today" / "Touching Earth"

 Open Book

Directions: Questions 16–22 are about "I Was Born Today" and "Touching the Earth." Read each question and choose the best answer. You may look at the selections on pages 739–741 to help you answer the questions.

LITERARY ANALYSIS

16 Which of these is **not** an element of a writer's style?

Ⓐ form

Ⓑ topic

Ⓒ word choice

Ⓓ organization

17 Why does the poet use dialogue in "I Was Born Today"?

Ⓐ to talk to the reader

Ⓑ to create sound imagery

Ⓒ to make the poem seem realistic

Ⓓ to show conversation between two people

18 In what way are "I Was Born Today" and "Touching the Earth" similar?

Ⓐ Both are written in free verse.

Ⓑ Both appeal to sight and taste.

Ⓒ Both are separated into stanzas.

Ⓓ Both have regular rhyme schemes.

19 Why does the poet use repetition in Stanza 4 of "I Was Born Today"?

Ⓐ to make the lines flow together smoothly

Ⓑ to help people remember that life is precious

Ⓒ to create visual imagery that describes the speaker's feelings

Ⓓ to emphasize the connection between the speaker and others

COMPREHENSION

20 What is "Touching the Earth" mostly about?

Ⓐ the life of sharecroppers

Ⓑ the author's family history

Ⓒ the way to grow vegetables

Ⓓ the author's connection with the land

21 In the poem "I Was Born Today," one of the speaker's messages is to

Ⓐ appreciate life.

Ⓑ conserve resources.

Ⓒ care for newborn babies.

Ⓓ change as little as possible.

Directions: Read question 22. Write your answer on a separate sheet of paper.

22

> *from* "I Was Born Today"
> And of that yesterday let there remain
>   only the essence,
> The precious gold of what I loved
>   and suffered
> As I walk along the road …
>
> *from* "Touching the Earth"
>   I knew that my grandmother Baba's backyard garden would yield beans, sweet potatoes, cabbage, and yellow squash, that she too would walk with pride among the rows and rows of growing vegetables showing us what the earth will give when tended lovingly.

Compare the structure and style of these two passages. Which passage do you respond to more, and why? Be sure to cite text evidence in your answer.

DONE!

EDGE Level C

UNIT 7

Name _____ Date _____

Student Profile: Cluster Tests

Directions: Use the **Answer Key** and **Scoring Guides** on pages 160, 161, and 162 to score Cluster Tests 1, 2, and 3 respectively. Circle the item number of each correct answer below. Then multiply items correct by points. Include the rubric scores for the constructed-response items. Calculate the overall test score by adding to 100. To gauge mastery for a particular tested skill or Common Core Standard, review the Cluster Test and Unit Test results.

Cluster 1   Date _____

Subtest	Tested Skill	ITEM ANALYSIS		TEST SCORES
		Item Numbers	Mastery	No. Correct x Points = Score
Key Vocabulary	Key Vocabulary L.9-10.6	1 2 3 4 5 6 7 8	6 out of 8 + −	_____ x 4 = _____ /32
Literary Analysis	Analyze Structure: Script RL.9-10.5	9 10 11 12	3 out of 4 + −	_____ x 4 = _____ /16
	Analyze Word Choice RL.9-10.4	16 17 18 19	3 out of 4 + −	_____ x 4 = _____ /16
Comprehension	Comprehension RL.9-10.10	13 14 20 21	3 out of 4 + −	_____ x 4 = _____ /16
Constructed Response	Use Text Evidence RL.9-10.1; RL.9-10.10; W.9-10.9	Rubric Scores Item 15 _____ + Item 22 _____ = _____		= _____ /20

Overall Score (Add Points Earned)   _____ /100

Cluster 2   Date _____

Subtest	Tested Skill	ITEM ANALYSIS		TEST SCORES
		Item Numbers	Mastery	No. Correct x Points = Score
Key Vocabulary	Key Vocabulary L.9-10.6	1 2 3 4 5 6 7 8	6 out of 8 + −	_____ x 4 = _____ /32
Literary Analysis	Analyze Structure: Blank Verse RL.9-10.5	9 10 11 12	3 out of 4 + −	_____ x 4 = _____ /16
	Relate a Story to Its Source RL.9-10.9	16 17 18 19	3 out of 4 + −	_____ x 4 = _____ /16
Comprehension	Comprehension RL.9-10.10	13 14 20 21	3 out of 4 + −	_____ x 4 = _____ /16
Constructed Response	Use Text Evidence RL.9-10.1; RL.9-10.10; W.9-10.9	Rubric Scores Item 15 _____ + Item 22 _____ = _____		= _____ /20

Overall Score (Add Points Earned)   _____ /100

Cluster 3   Date _____

Subtest	Tested Skill	ITEM ANALYSIS		TEST SCORES
		Item Numbers	Mastery	No. Correct x Points = Score
Key Vocabulary	Key Vocabulary L.9-10.6	1 2 3 4 5 6 7 8	6 out of 8 + −	_____ x 4 = _____ /32
Literary Analysis	Analyze Representations: Poetry and Art RL.9-10.7	9 10 11 12	3 out of 4 + −	_____ x 4 = _____ /16
	Analyze Structure and Style RL.9-10.4; RL.9-10.5	16 17 18 19	3 out of 4 + −	_____ x 4 = _____ /16
Comprehension	Comprehension RL.9-10.10	13 14 20 21	3 out of 4 + −	_____ x 4 = _____ /16
Constructed Response	Use Text Evidence RL.9-10.1; RL.9-10.10; W.9-10.9	Rubric Scores Item 15 _____ + Item 22 _____ = _____		= _____ /20

Overall Score (Add Points Earned)   _____ /100

Language Acquisition Rubrics

Cluster 1
JUSTIFY

Group Talk ▶ page 698

Directions: Group students. Give them a few moments to review the selections and consider the task. Students should then share and justify their beliefs about elders.

Language Function | 1 | 2 | 3 | 4 |

What to look for:
how well the student justifies his/her belief by using what he/she knows. Student should use sentence patterns such as *I believe … because …* and *I strongly feel that … because …*

Cluster 2
NEGOTIATE

Role Play ▶ page 722

Directions: Pair students. Give them a few moments to review the selection and decide on a scene. One partner should play Romeo and the other should play Juliet as they try to come to an agreement about their parents.

Language Function | 1 | 2 | 3 | 4 |

What to look for:
how well the student negotiates and reaches an agreement with his/her partner by stating the issue, asking questions, building understanding, compromising, and using direct and persuasive language.

Cluster 3
USE APPROPRIATE LANGUAGE

Formal Introductions ▶ page 744

Directions: Give the students a few moments to review the unit and choose a poet. Each student should then introduce the poet to the class as if he/she were addressing an assembly.

Language Function | 1 | 2 | 3 | 4 |

What to look for:
how well the student uses appropriate language including appropriate choice of words, tone, and volume.

Language Function Rubric	
4	Student effectively performs the function.
3	Student performs the function.
2	Student does not adequately perform the function.
1	Student makes no attempt or offers a non-verbal response.

UNIT 7

Reading and Literary Analysis

Directions: Read each question and choose the best answer.

1 Read the sentence.

> Gina wanted to try on her grandmother's old dress, but the lace was as fragile as a butterfly's wings.

The simile in the sentence compares

A a butterfly and its wings.

B Gina and her grandmother.

C lace and a butterfly's wings.

D her grandmother's dress and lace.

2 Read the sentence.

> A flood of customers poured into the store to buy the latest computer game.

What is the meaning of the sentence?

A Many customers visited the store to buy the computer game.

B The customers looked in every aisle in the store for the new game.

C Eager customers visited the store to buy the game after the store was damaged by high water.

D The customers found that the store stocked its shelves with many copies of the computer game.

3 Read the sentence.

> Sophie was disappointed that her painting did not win the grand prize, but third place is nothing to sneeze at.

The phrase nothing to sneeze at means that third place is

A a worthless award.

B an overwhelming success.

C an important achievement.

D a common accomplishment.

4 Read the sentence.

> Once in a blue moon, my dad dusts off our old tent and camp stove, and we go camping at the lake.

The phrase Once in a blue moon means that the family goes camping

A every year.

B only at night.

C once a month.

D on rare occasions.

GO ON ▶

Reading and Literary Analysis, *continued*

Directions: Questions 5–10 are about "Rebirth." Read the selection. Then read each question and choose the best answer.

Rebirth

Characters:

JAVIER, a teenage boy

MARCUS, a teenage boy

JULIA, a teenage girl

LILY, a teenage girl

SANJAY, an older teenage boy

Scene 1

[*Setting: A park in a rundown city neighborhood. Shabby buildings are crowded into the backdrop. Trash litters the street and sidewalk. A sign on the park entrance reads "City Center Community Garden." The garden is just inside the entrance. There was a bad storm the night before, and the area is littered with debris: fallen tree branches, rocks and mud on the ground, etc. The garden is divided into plots, and all but one plot have flattened, damaged plants. One plot is empty.*]

JAVIER, MARCUS, JULIA, and LILY enter stage left and walk toward the garden.

JAVIER: That was some storm last night.

MARCUS: No joke! I couldn't sleep with the windows banging in the wind. The rain was pouring down the street like a river.

JULIA: I'll bet our garden is going to need a lot of work.

[*They arrive at the garden and look around in dismay.*]

MARCUS: Look at this mess!

JAVIER: Everything is ruined.

LILY: I told you this garden was a stupid idea. You guys did all that work digging and planting and watering and weeding, and look at it now. It looks like I was right!

MARCUS: At least we tried. You didn't do anything!

LILY: I turned the soil like you said, but then I got bored. So what?

JULIA (*bending down to sift through the mess in her garden plot*): I can't believe it. Last week my plants were like rockets, blasting up out of the dirt and growing tall. Now everything is gone.

City Center
Community
Garden

LILY: At least I didn't waste my time.

MARCUS: Nice attitude, Lily. (*To all*) Let's make a resolution to clean this up and start over.

JAVIER: Yeah! It's still early in the spring. I'll bet our plants will grow back again.

JULIA: We can come back tomorrow with our shovels. I still have some seeds left from when we planted the first time.

LILY: You guys are just wasting your time. This whole neighborhood is a mess. Even the plants don't want to stick around. Anything nice here will just <u>perish</u>.

MARCUS: Come on, Lily. The garden made the neighborhood look nicer, and Mr. Zhao said he'd

Reading and Literary Analysis, *continued*

buy the vegetables we grew. We were making a positive effort to change things. It was nice to have a green space in the middle of all this concrete.

JAVIER *(looking up at the trees)*: Hey, look! There's a robin with some sticks in her mouth. I'll bet she's rebuilding her nest.

JULIA: If the birds can start over, so can we.

MARCUS: It's decided then. We'll meet here tomorrow and start over.

LILY: I don't know. I didn't even plant anything in the first place.

MARCUS: Yeah, you were kind of a quitter the first time. Now you've got a second chance. Are you going to take it?

LILY *(angrily)*: I said I don't know. Leave me alone. *[She stalks away.]*

Scene 2

[The garden, the next day. MARCUS and JAVIER are already at work. A pile of brush and debris has been piled off to one side. JULIA enters stage left, carrying packets of seeds and some small plants.]

JULIA: Hi! You guys are amazing. You've done a lot of work already!

JAVIER: We cleaned out all the mess from our plots. We even did yours, too.

JULIA: You guys are so nice! I brought new plants.

JAVIER *(stretching and wiping his forehead)*: This is hard work. Maybe Lily has the right idea to just forget the whole thing.

MARCUS: No way! I'm not quitting now.

JAVIER *(offended)*: Neither am I! It's just…maybe all our hard work doesn't matter. This neighborhood is rotten. Does it really matter if we try to make one green corner where things can grow?

JULIA: You know it does. We get everything from the earth—our food, our water, even the air we breathe. It's up to us to take care of it. And if the earth needs a little help to survive, we have a responsibility to do it.

LILY *(entering stage left)*: Hey, it's the Garden Club! 'How does your garden grow?'

MARCUS: It's getting there. We even cleaned up your plot.

LILY: Why? It's not like I'm going to plant anything.

JULIA *(leaning over and looking closely at the cleared, empty plot)*: Maybe you don't have to, Lily. Come look at this.

[LILY, JAVIER, and MARCUS gather around JULIA.]

JAVIER: I don't believe it!

LILY: Is that a plant?

JULIA: It sure is! One of the plants from our garden must have washed into your plot. It still looks pretty sturdy. I'll bet if you take care of it, it will grow.

LILY: I can't believe the one thing that managed to endure the big storm ended up in my garden!

JULIA: The earth always tries to heal itself. Plants come back, animals come back. They know there's always a second chance.

LILY: I kind of like the idea of second chances. All right, somebody show me how to plant something, and I'll start my garden.

[The others cheer. Then they work in silence for a few minutes.]

MARCUS: We've made a good start today.

JAVIER: It's not much, but at least we're showing respect and making the world a better place.

JULIA: At least in our corner of the world, anyway.

[SANJAY rides by on a bike.]

SANJAY: Hey, I'm glad to see you guys! The Community Club at the high school is going to clean up storm damage in the park this weekend. Do you want to help?

JAVIER: Sure, I'm in.

MARCUS: Me, too.

JULIA: I'll be there.

Reading and Literary Analysis, *continued*

JAVIER: How about you, Lily?

LILY *(smiling)*: Of course! Why stop with just one corner of the world when we can improve the whole thing!

MARCUS: Hey, that's the spirit. It looks like our garden isn't the only thing that has been reborn today.

LILY: Hey, you've got to start somewhere.

---

5 When Marcus says that the "rain was pouring down the street like a river," he means that

   A the rain flooded the street.

   B a river washed away the street.

   C the rain made patterns like a river.

   D a river flooded because of the rain.

6 Read the lines from the play.

> **LILY:** You guys are just wasting your time. This whole neighborhood is a mess. Even the plants don't want to stick around. Anything nice here will just perish.

What does this line reveal about Lily?

   A She is a leader who influences people.

   B She sees the negative side of things.

   C She has other projects she wants to do.

   D She wants to be friends with the others.

7 Read the lines from the play.

> **JAVIER** *(offended)*: Neither am I! It's just… maybe all our hard work doesn't matter. This neighborhood is rotten. Does it really matter if we try to make one green corner where things can grow?

The word inside the parentheses is included to tell the

   A actor how to say the line.

   B audience who is speaking.

   C other characters how to react.

   D director that the line is important.

8 To <u>perish</u> means to

   A die.

   B hide.

   C steal.

   D punish.

9 To <u>endure</u> means to

   A ignore.

   B enable.

   C survive.

   D struggle.

Directions: Read question 10. Write your answer on a separate sheet of paper. ✏️

10 What predictions can you make about how Lily and her friends will change because of what happens in this play? Cite text evidence as you explain your prediction.

UNIT 7

Reading and Literary Analysis, *continued*

Directions: Questions 11 and 12 are about "The Oak." Read the selection. Then read each question and choose the best answer.

The Oak

Some people think the oak tree dignified—
I think that it's all stubbornness and sass,
Impudently raising branches wide
To tempt the wrens and starlings as they pass.

5 The oak infuriates the wilding wind
That seeks to topple its substantial girth;
It cannot see how deep its roots descend,
Anchoring below the fractured earth.
And when the rage has passed, the oak tree shakes

10 The droplets from its branches, shakes a bird
Out from its dappled greening, and awakes.
Leaves rustling? No, it's laughter I just heard.
You're like that oak: when tempests howl and bray
You shelter me, and laugh the storms away.

---

11 Which of the following describes the rhyme scheme in the first four lines of the poem?

A a a b b

B a b a b

C a b c d

D a b c b

12 "The Oak" is an example of

A a script.

B an essay.

C a poem with a rhyme scheme.

D a poem written in free verse.

Reading and Literary Analysis, *continued*

Directions: Questions 13–18 are about "Planting Peas." Read the selection. Then read each question and choose the best answer.

Planting Peas

The earth and I are partners in this endeavor.
I am the one who tills her soil,
sifts away stones and breaks through clods,
bringing black richness up to light.

5 Into my palm I pour dried peas—
hard, round, and <u>dense</u> with waiting life—
and drop them into narrow furrows one by one.
With gentle hands I smooth soil over them,
tucking them into dark, warm blankets

10 where greedy birds can't find them.
And then I leave them there,
to wait, while the earth holds them,
to wait, while the rain nourishes them,
to wait, until the <u>essence</u> inside them wakens.

15 And then how they burst out, reaching in all directions!
Splitting husks to burrow downward into mineral wealth;
shoving grains of dirt aside, wriggling stems upwards
to unfurl their <u>tremulous</u> leaves.
I weed; I watch; I share the watering with
the morning dew;

20 I set out stakes for stems to grasp. But mainly I admire
the earth's wisdom, the age-old knowledge of root and stem,
each plant's <u>resolve</u> to flower and set its fruit.
When emerald half-moons dangle,
fat orbs distending their flesh,

25 I snap a pod from the vine, pop it in my mouth,
and crunch into rain and air and sun,
thanking the earth for this
green perfection.

GO ON ▶

Reading and Literary Analysis, *continued*

13 Which line from the poem includes imagery that appeals to the reader's sense of touch?

A bringing black richness up to light.

B tucking them into dark, warm blankets

C to wait, while the rain nourishes them,

D When emerald half-moons dangle,

14 Read the lines from the poem.

> With gentle hands I smooth soil over them, tucking them into dark, warm blankets where greedy birds can't find them.

"Blankets" refers to the

A cloth that covers the seeds.

B soil the speaker puts on the seeds.

C warm hands that plant the seeds.

D black feathers of birds looking for the seeds.

15 Dense means

A tall.

B bare.

C thick.

D pretty.

16 The essence of something means its

A value when sold.

B source of energy.

C most important quality.

D connection to the earth.

17 Tremulous means

A timid.

B sleepy.

C jealous.

D relieved.

18 To have resolve means to have

A doubt.

B difficulty.

C resources.

D determination.

Directions: Read question 19. Write your answer on a separate sheet of paper.

19 Some people feel that gardening is an activity that gives a gardener a sense of satisfaction and even joy. How does this text support that viewpoint?

GO ON

Reading and Literary Analysis, *continued*

Directions: Questions 20–25 are about "Emily Dickinson," "I'm nobody! Who are you?" and "A bird came down the walk." Read the selections. Then read each question and choose the best answer.

Emily Dickinson

Everyone assumed Emily Dickinson would live a traditional life. Like most women in the 1800s, she would marry. Her work would take her from house to garden and back again. Her life would revolve around her family, church, and neighborhood.

A portrait of Dickinson drawn by an unknown artist.

Instead, Emily Dickinson's life took a mysterious turn. Dickinson was born in 1830 and grew up in Amherst, Massachusetts. She was a lively child who took pleasure in village life. A good student, Dickinson enjoyed singing and attending plays. Then, when Dickinson was in her thirties, she stopped seeing her old friends. She turned down opportunities to travel. When people came to her door, she refused to see them.

No one knows for certain why Emily Dickinson acted this way. Perhaps she had fallen in love with a man she could not marry. One possibility is the Reverend Charles Wadsworth. She called this married minister "my dearest earthly friend." She seems to refer to him in poems such as "If you were coming in the fall." After Wadsworth moved to San Francisco, Dickinson never saw him again.

By the 1860s, Emily Dickinson seldom left her father's house. She rarely had visitors either, although she wrote and received hundreds of letters. Her closest friends were her sister, her brother, and his wife. The tone of her poem "I'm nobody" suggests that Dickinson, while lonely, may have enjoyed her isolation.

Emily Dickinson's adult life was limited to one house in a small town. Her imagination, however, knew no bounds. In poems, she likened a grain of sand to the desert. She saw a relationship between a drop of dew and a flood. With images and metaphors, Emily Dickinson was not limited to what Amherst,

Massachusetts, had to offer. She became one of the greatest poets of her century.

As a poet, Emily Dickinson has been compared to a diamond cutter. Her poems glitter and gleam. Dickinson always chose the right word, the exact phrase. Her language is near perfection. She never wasted a word. Her lean style and rhythm and rhyme schemes were something new to the poetry of her day.

Dickinson's poems show a love of nature, too. She spent hours in her backyard garden. She knew its plants and animals well. "A bird came down the walk," for example, shows her love for a backyard bird and its ability to fly. Dickinson also watched the changing seasons. She saw the cycle of death and rebirth play out in her yard. These observations of nature found their way into her poetry, too.

Dickinson's home on Main Street in Amherst is a popular tourist attraction.

Emily Dickinson died in 1886. At her death, few knew she was a poet. A few of her early poems had appeared in newspapers. After that, however, Dickinson stopped looking for an audience. Poetry for her was a private thing. She revealed her innermost feelings in poems. Perhaps she thought she couldn't publish them respectably, so she tied her poems in bundles and hid them in her room. It was the custom in New England to burn personal papers at the time of someone's death. Fortunately, her family did not follow the tradition. The poems—more than a thousand of them—were saved and published instead. Dickinson's works have been amazing readers ever since!

GO ON ▶

Reading and Literary Analysis, *continued*

I'm Nobody! Who are you?
Emily Dickinson

I'm Nobody! Who are you?
Are you nobody, too?
Then there's a pair of us—Don't tell!
They'd banish us, you know.

5 How dreary to be somebody!
How public, like a frog
To tell your name the livelong day
To an admiring bog!

A bird came down the walk
Emily Dickinson

A bird came down the walk:
He did not know I saw;
He bit an angle-worm in halves
And ate the fellow, raw.

5 And then he drank a dew
From a convenient grass,
And then hopped sidewise to the wall
To let a beetle pass.

He glanced with rapid eyes
10 That hurried all abroad,
They looked like frightened beads, I thought;
He stirred his velvet head

Like one in danger; cautious,
I offered him a crumb,
15 And he unrolled his feathers
And rowed him softer home

Than oars divide the ocean,
Too silver for a seam,
Or butterflies, off banks of noon,
Leap, plashless* as they swim.

*splashless

GO ON

UNIT 7

Reading and Literary Analysis, *continued*

20 Read the lines from "I'm Nobody! Who are you?"

> How dreary to be somebody!
> How public like a frog

These lines reflect Dickinson's decision to

A study singing and perform in plays.

B avoid being in public for most of her life.

C collect her poetry manuscripts in bundles.

D write hundreds of letters to her family and friends.

21 What does the word *banish* in "I'm Nobody! Who are you?" suggest?

A Life as a "Nobody" is a life that is free of fear.

B There are very few people who choose to be a "Nobody."

C People who choose to be "Nobodies" are disliked by society.

D People cannot recognize you as a "Nobody" unless you tell them.

22 In "A bird came down the walk," the poet shares a series of events, concluding with

A the bird's flying away in silence.

B her decision to feed the bird herself.

C her sight of the bird as it hops down the walk.

D the bird's sparing the beetle after eating the worm.

23 Traditional means according to

A age.

B ability.

C chance.

D custom.

24 Perfection means without

A fault.

B hope.

C reason.

D purpose.

Directions: Read question 25. Write your answer on a separate sheet of paper.

25 *Reclusive*, or withdrawn from society, is a word that often is used to describe Emily Dickinson. Support this description with evidence from the biography and from at least one of the poems.

DONE!

Grammar and Writing

Directions: Read each composition. It contains errors. Then read each question and choose the best answer.

The Forest

(1) One warm July afternoon at my father's house my friend Simon and I had nothing to do. (2) My father was going to run an errand, and he suggested we take his old 35mm camera out into the forest behind the house to try our hand at photography. (3) He said he'd tie up the dogs so they wouldn't get in the way. (4) His dogs are Chesapeake Bay Retrievers.

(5) "Be creative!" he said. (6) Then he drove away, waving.

(7) "All right!" I exclaimed. (8) "Let's go take some pictures."

(9) At first, we stopped to shoot some trees and logs. (10) I began to look at the forest differently, paying more attention to the patterns that the shapes and colors of the trees made. (11) I shot a few pictures, and then I passed the camera to Simon. (12) He shot a few more photos, and passed it to me again.

(13) "Let's find something more interesting than logs," he said, and I agreed.

(14) We tramped on further, thinking about what we might find. (15) Whatever it was, it would have to be unique, but easy to shoot. (16) We weren't very good with the camera yet. (17) I didn't want to end up with pictures so boring that no one would want to see them.

(18) The trees gave way to a small clearing of tall grass, <u>bleaches</u> golden by the sun.

(19) "Look!" Simon whispered. (20) He pointed to a chipmunk about 20 yards away, <u>sit</u> on a log at the clearing's edge.

(21) I raised the camera to my eye and peered through the viewfinder at the rodent. (22) I pushed the button to take the picture.

(23) The chipmunk <u>have jumped</u> just as I snapped the picture. (24) Simon thought I <u>had taken</u> the photo just as it was in mid-air. (25) I only hoped that the photo would be in focus. (26) Even though it was only of a chipmunk, the photo could be really great if I had caught the animal "flying."

(27) "Do you want to develop the film now?" I said, the camera to Simon handing. (28) We left the forest and walked the short distance to the store.

(29) "I guess I missed him," I said dejectedly, as we looked at the developed pictures. (30) All we could see was the empty space above the log where the chipmunk had been sitting.

(31) "Yeah, but that was just our first try," said Simon. (32) "We can get more film and try again."

(33) My dad had always loved the forest behind our house, and I had never quite figured out why. (34) Now I think I am beginning to understand.

Grammar and Writing, continued

1 What change, if any, should be made to sentence 1?

   A Change *July* to **july**

   B Put a comma after *house*

   C Change *to* to **too**

   D No change

2 Which sentence is off topic and should be removed from the first paragraph?

   A sentence 1

   B sentence 2

   C sentence 3

   D sentence 4

3 Which of these ideas would most logically follow sentence 12?

   A We considered taking the dogs for a walk.

   B We soon tired of shooting non-moving targets.

   C We wondered if there was a good movie on TV.

   D We talked about the last time we were in the forest.

4 In sentence 18, the word bleaches should be changed to

   A bleach

   B bleached

   C bleaching

   D No change

5 In sentence 20, the word sit should be changed to

   A sat

   B sits

   C sitting

   D No change

6 In sentence 23, the words have jumped should be changed to

   A had jumped

   B has jumped

   C will jump

   D No change

7 In sentence 24, the words had taken should be changed to

   A take

   B will take

   C have taken

   D No change

8 What change, if any, should be made to sentence 27?

   A Put the question mark after the second quotation mark

   B Change *Simon* to **simon**

   C Move *handing* to before **the camera**

   D No change

GO ON

Grammar and Writing, *continued*

Directions: Read each composition. It contains errors. Then read each question and choose the best answer.

Response to "Nothing Gold Can Stay"

(1) In the poem "Nothing Gold Can Stay" by Robert Frost, the author compares the promise and impermanence of youth to the cycle of flowering plants. (2) The poem also explores the value of <u>things that do not last long</u> in life. (3) Though the poem is a mere eight lines in a single stanza, each line contains a metaphor for the passing of youth and the disappointment that accompanies it.

(4) The first half of the poem hints at youth's elusiveness. (5) The poem states in the first and second lines that the color "gold," which is a symbol for youth and newness, is the "hardest hue to hold." (6) The third line mentions youth as an "early leaf." (7) The leaf, <u>imagining</u> here as a flower, suggests the English expression "the flower of youth." (8) Here, as in the poem, the flower signifies the physical beauty of youth. (9) However, the fourth line, "But only so an hour," is a reminder that youth, much like a flower, is a colorful, hopeful stage of life that <u>will have passed</u> before very long. (10) So, the first four lines of the poem <u>will establish</u> youth as a prominent theme.

(11) Frost, <u>describing</u> the feeling of melancholy that accompanies youth's passing, makes a subtle transition in the poem's second half. (12) At this point, the flower of youth is no more when it "subsides to leaf." (13) In other words, beauty and vitality are gone, leaving life in a diminished state that seems plain and incomplete.

(14) Line six contains a reference to the garden of Eden. (15) In this case, Frost compares youth to the peaceful and harmonious time spent in Eden. (16) He links the despair that followed humanity's banishment from this symbolic paradise to the fruitless attempt to hold on to youth. (17) Many people believe Eden was a real place. (18) The final line, "Nothing gold can stay" from which the title is taken, drives this point home. (19) At the end of the poem, gold can be understood metaphorically as representing youth, hope, and idealism as in the first half of the poem; additionally, these qualities are described as gold to underscore they are essential value in the eyes of the poet.

GO ON

EDGE Level C

Grammar and Writing, *continued*

9 In sentence 2, which is the most precise way to write the words things that do not last long?

   A passing times

   B fleeting moments

   C passed moments

   D times that happen fast

10 In sentence 7, the word imagining should be changed to

   A imagine

   B imagines

   C imagined

   D No change

11 In sentence 9, the words will have passed should be changed to

   A passed

   B passing

   C had passed

   D No change

12 In sentence 10, the words will establish should be changed to

   A have established

   B had established

   C established

   D No change

13 In sentence 11, the word describing should be changed to

   A describe

   B describes

   C described

   D No change

14 What change, if any, should be made to sentence 14?

   A Put a comma after *Line six*

   B Change *reference* to **referense**

   C Change *garden* to **Garden**

   D No change

15 Which sentence is **not** related to the main idea of paragraph 4?

   A sentence 14

   B sentence 15

   C sentence 17

   D sentence 18

16 What change, if any, should be made to sentence 19?

   A Change the semicolon to a comma

   B Change *additionally* to **Additionally**

   C Change *they are* to **their**

   D No change

UNIT 7

GO ON

Grammar and Writing, *continued*

Directions: Read the following writing prompt, and write a composition. Use the Writer's Checklist to make sure that you do your best work.

Prompt

In many of the selections in this unit, a character gains or loses respect for something or someone.

Think about a selection you read in this unit or something else you have read in which a character gains or loses respect for something or someone. Write a composition in which you reflect on why this occurs.

Writer's Checklist

☑ Write about all parts of the prompt.

☑ Present a clear central idea, and stay focused on it.

☑ Organize your composition from its introduction to its conclusion.

☑ Use transitions to connect your thoughts for the reader.

☑ Present meaningful ideas, and support them with specific information.

☑ Use appropriate words and a variety of sentence structures.

☑ Proofread and edit your writing for grammar, usage, mechanics, and spelling.

Student Profile: Unit Tests

Directions: Use the **Answer Key** on page 163 to score the multiple-choice items. Circle the item number of each correct answer below. Calculate test scores by assigning one point for each correct answer. Use the scoring guides on page 163 to score the constructed-response items. Use the Good Writing Traits Rubric on page 122 to score the written composition. Total the scores and calculate the % score or use the conversion chart. To gauge mastery for a particular tested skill or Common Core Standard, review the Cluster Test and Unit Test results.

Reading and Literary Analysis

Category	Tested Skill	ITEM ANALYSIS Item Numbers	Mastery	TEST SCORES Points: Earned / Total
Vocabulary	Figurative Language L.9-10.5	1 2 3 4	3 out of 4 + −	_____ / 4
	Key Vocabulary L.9-10.6	8 9 15 16 17 18 23 24	6 out of 8 + −	_____ / 8
Literary Analysis	Analyze Word Choice RL.9-10.4	5 13 14 21	3 out of 4 + −	_____ / 4
	Analyze Structure RL.9-10.5	7 11 12 22	3 out of 4 + −	_____ / 4
	Comprehension RL.9-10.10	6 20	1 out of 2 + −	_____ / 2
Constructed Response	Use Text Evidence RL.9-10.1; RL.9-10.10; W.9-10.9	Rubric Scores Item 10 _____ + Item 19 _____ + Item 25 _____ = _____		_____ / 12

Overall Score (Points Earned ÷ Total Points x 100 = %)   _____ ÷ 34 = _____ %

Grammar and Writing

Category	Tested Skill	ITEM ANALYSIS Item Numbers	Mastery	TEST SCORES Points: Earned / Total
Grammar	Participles and Participial Phrases L.9-10.1	4 5 10 13	3 out of 4 + −	_____ / 4
	Verb Tense L.9-10.1	6 7 11 12	3 out of 4 + −	_____ / 4
Revising and Editing	Writing Traits W.9-10.5	2 3 9 15	3 out of 4 + −	_____ / 4
	Grammar, Mechanics, and Usage L.9-10.2	1 8 14 16	3 out of 4 + −	_____ / 4
Written Composition (Argument) W.9-10.1; W.9-10.4; W.9-10.10	Focus and Unity	Rubric Scores: _____ / 4		_____ / 20
	Organization	_____ / 4		
	Development of Ideas	_____ / 4 =		
	Voice and Style	_____ / 4		
	Written Conventions	_____ / 4		

Overall Score (Points Earned ÷ Total Points x 100 = %)   _____ ÷ 36 = _____ %

Project Rubric: A Literary Anthology

Score	Planning/Preparation	Content of Project	Delivery/Presentation	Collaboration
3 Great	• Reviews a variety of literary anthologies to observe different types of organization, format, etc. • Looks at a wide variety of poems, stories, essays, etc. to choose from.	• Addresses the Essential Question from a variety of angles through the included literature. • Contains at least ten literary selections.	• Includes interesting and relevant illustrations. • Has a format that is neat and legible. • Has a clear organization.	• Works well with others. • Assumes a clear role and related responsibilities.
2 Good	• Reviews several literary anthologies to observe different types of organization, format, etc. • Looks at an adequate amount of poems, stories, essays, etc. to choose from.	• Somewhat addresses the Essential Question through the included literature. • Contains at least five literary selections.	• Includes a few somewhat relevant illustrations. • Has a format that is somewhat neat and legible. • Has a somewhat clear organization.	• Works with others most of the time. • Sometimes has difficulty sharing decisions and responsibilities.
1 Needs Work	• Reviews one or no literary anthologies to observe different types of organization, format, etc. • Does not look at many poems, stories, essays, etc. to choose from.	• Does not address the Essential Question through the included literature. • Contains less than five literary selections.	• Includes no illustrations or irrelevant illustrations. • Has a format that is not neat or legible. • Does not seem to have any organization.	• Cannot work with others in most situations. • Cannot share decisions or responsibilities.

EDGE Level C

Self-Assessment

Directions: Circle the numbers that show how much you agree or disagree with each sentence.
Then answer the question below. If necessary, use the back of the page.

	Not Yet	With Help	Most of the Time	Very Well
1 I know how to identify elements of drama and poetry and how to analyze the structure and word choices in a script or poem.	1	2	3	4
2 When I read a story adapted from an earlier source, I know how to relate the two readings.	1	2	3	4
3 When I read an illustrated poem, I know how to compare the verbal and visual representations.	1	2	3	4
4 I know how to visualize images and how to identify emotional responses and sensory images while reading.	1	2	3	4
5 I know how to interpret non-literal language such as idioms, similes, and metphors.	1	2	3	4
6 I know how to enrich my sentences using verb tenses and participial phrases.	1	2	3	4

7 Think of one thing you learned really well in this unit. Tell how you will use this the next time you read or write.

_____

_____

_____

_____

_____

_____

_____

_____

_____

_____

_____

Measures for Reading

Measures for Writing

EDGE Level C

Personal Connections to Reading

Directions: Circle one answer for each question.

How often do you read . . .	Never	Rarely	Sometimes	Often
❶ for pleasure?	1	2	3	4
❷ to learn how to do something (for example, from a manual or instruction book)?	1	2	3	4
❸ to locate information on a schedule or a map?	1	2	3	4
❹ to search on the Internet?	1	2	3	4
❺ to learn about current events?	1	2	3	4
❻ to communicate with friends and family (for example, with letters, notes, or e-mails)?	1	2	3	4
❼ in a language other than English?	1	2	3	4

AFFECTIVE & METACOGNITIVE

Directions: Put a ✔ next to all of the statements that apply to you.

☐ ❽ I sometimes read aloud to family members, such as younger children or grandparents.

☐ ❾ If I like what I'm reading, it is easier to understand.

☐ ❿ My reading has improved since last year.

☐ ⓫ I am good at following written instructions.

☐ ⓬ I only read books when they are assigned at school.

☐ ⓭ I would rather read an article on the Internet than in a magazine or newspaper.

☐ ⓮ I have a library card.

GO ON ▶

Personal Connections to Reading, *continued*

Directions: Briefly answer each question.

15 What do you consider when choosing something to read?_____

_____

_____

16 If you are choosing a book to read, how do you find one at the right level of difficulty—not too hard and not

too easy? _____

_____

17 Do you read other languages besides English? ☐ Yes   ☐ No

If yes, which languages can you read?_____

If yes, which language is most comfortable for you to read? _____

18 In general, do you find reading easy or difficult? If it is difficult for you, what are the

hardest parts?_____

_____

19 Are there things you would like to read that are too difficult for you? ☐ Yes   ☐ No

If yes, what are they? _____

_____

20 What would you like to learn to do better as a reader?_____

_____

_____

21 If you were asked to give suggestions to a younger person who was having trouble reading,

what would they be? _____

_____

_____

AFFECTIVE & METACOGNITIVE

EDGE Level C

Name _____ Date _____

What Interests Me: Reading Topics

A. What interests me?

Directions: Put a ✔ next to all the topics that interest you. There are many, many other things that might interest you, of course—too many to list. If your interests are not on the list, write them on the blank lines.

❏ Acting	❏ Electronics	❏ Photography
❏ Animals	❏ Fashion	❏ Poetry
❏ Arts and crafts	❏ Gardening	❏ Politics
❏ Auto mechanics	❏ Golf	❏ Psychology
❏ Auto racing	❏ Hiking	❏ Puzzles
❏ Baseball	❏ Hockey	❏ Rock climbing
❏ Basketball	❏ Languages	❏ Rock collecting
❏ Camping	❏ Math	❏ Sailing
❏ Cheerleading	❏ Motorcycles	❏ Sewing
❏ Chemistry	❏ Mountain biking	❏ Skateboarding
❏ Chess	❏ Movies: watching	❏ Skiing
❏ Coin collecting	❏ Movies: making	❏ Swimming
❏ Computer animation	❏ Music: listening	❏ Travel
❏ Cooking and baking	❏ Music: playing	❏ Video games
❏ Dancing	❏ Nature	❏ Weight lifting
❏ Ecology	❏ Painting/Drawing	❏ Woodworking

Additional interests not included on the list:

_____   _____

_____   _____

_____   _____

B. Which interests would I like to read about?

A person who enjoys playing basketball may read books or magazines that provide tips to help improve passing and shooting skills. He or she may also enjoy reading about the history of the sport or the lives of professional basketball players.

Look at the interests you checked and listed. Circle the ones you have read about or would like to read about.

Name _____ Date _____

What I Do: Reading Strategies

Before starting to read a book, how often do you . . .	Never	Rarely	Sometimes	Often
1 look inside to get an idea of what the book is about?	1	2	3	4
2 check to see what genre it is?	1	2	3	4
3 think about why the author may have written the book?	1	2	3	4
4 set a purpose for your reading?	1	2	3	4
5 choose a graphic organizer to hold your thinking?	1	2	3	4

When reading a book, how often do you . . .	Never	Rarely	Sometimes	Often
6 make sure you understand the text?	1	2	3	4
7 do something to help you better understand what you are reading? (for example, put ideas in your own words, reread the text, or use a slower reading rate)	1	2	3	4
8 think about the main ideas?	1	2	3	4
9 pause to sum up what you have read so far?	1	2	3	4
10 reflect on what you have learned and if it has changed your thinking in any way?	1	2	3	4
11 ask yourself what the book reminds you of?	1	2	3	4

AFFECTIVE & METACOGNITIVE

GO ON ▶

What I Do: Reading Strategies, *continued*

When reading a book, how often do you . . .	Never	Rarely	Sometimes	Often
12 write down questions?	1	2	3	4
13 try to think the way the writer thinks?	1	2	3	4
14 make mental pictures from the descriptions?	1	2	3	4
15 use all your senses to imagine the people, places, and events?	1	2	3	4
16 make connections between what you are reading and your own life?	1	2	3	4
17 make connections between what you are reading and other things you have read?	1	2	3	4
18 make connections between what you are reading and the rest of the world?	1	2	3	4
19 make inferences by combining what the writer tells you with what you already know?	1	2	3	4
20 put new information together with old information to come up with big ideas?	1	2	3	4

AFFECTIVE & METACOGNITIVE

DONE!

What I Do: Vocabulary Strategies

Directions: Answer questions 1–5.

1 When you read your school assignments, how many of the words do you usually know?

Check one.

☐ all or almost all

☐ most

☐ about half

☐ less than half

☐ none or almost none

2 Do you think you would be a better reader if you knew more words? ☐ Yes ☐ No

3 People learn new words in different ways. One person might decide to draw a picture related to a new word. Another person might use the word in a sentence. Someone else might learn the word by saying it out loud over and over again.

When you learn a new word, do you use any "memory tips" or strategies to help you remember it? ☐ Yes ☐ No

If yes, what do you do?

_____

_____

_____

_____

4 If you see a word you don't know while reading, what do you usually do?

☐ I keep reading even if I don't know what the word means.

☐ Sometimes I stop to figure out what the word means, and sometimes I keep reading.

☐ I try to figure out what the word means or look it up before going on.

GO ON

What I Do: Vocabulary Strategies, *continued*

5 If you are trying to figure out the meaning of a word you don't know, what do you usually do? Check all the strategies you use. If you use other strategies, please list them.

☐ I say the word out loud to see if it sounds familiar.

☐ I think about other words that might be related to it.

☐ I check to see if there is a word part, such as a prefix or root, that looks familiar.

☐ I try to figure out what the word means by looking at the words and sentences around it.

☐ I ask a friend, teacher, or parent what the word means.

☐ I look up the word in a dictionary or glossary.

☐ Other _____

_____

_____

_____

_____

AFFECTIVE & METACOGNITIVE

DONE!

EDGE Level C

Name _____ Date _____

Personal Connections to Writing

Directions: Read the sentences about writing. Circle the numbers that show how much
you agree or disagree with each sentence.

	Strongly Disagree	Disagree	Agree	Strongly Agree
1 I like to write.	1	2	3	4
2 I think I am a good writer.	1	2	3	4
3 My teachers think that my writing is good.	1	2	3	4
4 I write better about things that interest me.	1	2	3	4
5 I like to share my writing with others.	1	2	3	4
6 I like to help other people with their writing.	1	2	3	4
7 Writing is easy for me.	1	2	3	4
8 My writing is better than it used to be.	1	2	3	4
9 I am trying to improve my writing.	1	2	3	4
10 It is important to know how to write.	1	2	3	4

AFFECTIVE & METACOGNITIVE

GO ON

Name _____ Date _____

Personal Connections to Writing, *continued*

Directions: For many people, some stages of the writing process are easier to do than others. Read the list of things people do when they write. Circle the numbers that show how hard or how easy you think each stage is.

	Hard	Somewhat Hard	Somewhat Easy	Easy
❶ Deciding what I want to write about	1	2	3	4
❷ Organizing my thoughts for writing	1	2	3	4
❸ Thinking of enough things to say in my writing	1	2	3	4
❹ Getting feedback on my writing from others	1	2	3	4
❺ Changing my writing to make it better	1	2	3	4
❻ Correcting little mistakes in my writing	1	2	3	4
❼ Deciding when my writing is finished	1	2	3	4
❽ Sharing my writing with others	1	2	3	4

AFFECTIVE & METACOGNITIVE

Directions: Answer questions 9 and 10. If you need more room, use the back of the page.

❾ Which stage of the writing process do you think is the easiest? Explain why. _____

_____

_____

❿ Which stage of the writing process do you think is the hardest? Explain why. _____

_____

_____

DONE!

EDGE Level C

Name _____   Date _____

What Interests Me: Writing

Directions: This survey will help you discover who you are as a writer. Answer parts A–D.

A. What interests me?

Directions: Put a ✔ next to all the topics that interest you. If you do not see your interests, add them to the list.

My Self
- ❑ hopes
- ❑ dreams
- ❑ strengths
- ❑ personality
- ❑ other: _____

My Family
- ❑ parents
- ❑ brothers/sisters
- ❑ memories
- ❑ vacations
- ❑ other: _____

My Friends
- ❑ best friends
- ❑ funny moments
- ❑ helpful friends
- ❑ spending time together
- ❑ other: _____

My Community
- ❑ the neighborhood
- ❑ neighborhood people
- ❑ doing things together
- ❑ things to improve
- ❑ other: _____

My Country
- ❑ history
- ❑ government
- ❑ laws
- ❑ states/cities/towns
- ❑ other: _____

My World
- ❑ the environment
- ❑ travel/exploration
- ❑ history
- ❑ countries/cultures
- ❑ other: _____

My Beliefs
- ❑ values
- ❑ religion
- ❑ philosophy
- ❑ holidays
- ❑ other: _____

My Feelings
- ❑ fear
- ❑ excitement
- ❑ love
- ❑ wonder
- ❑ other: _____

My Hobbies
- ❑ games/sports
- ❑ cars
- ❑ music/dance
- ❑ cooking
- ❑ other: _____

My School
- ❑ teachers
- ❑ activities
- ❑ classmates
- ❑ classes
- ❑ other: _____

My Future
- ❑ job/college
- ❑ relationships
- ❑ apartment/house
- ❑ children
- ❑ other: _____

Add to the List
- _____
- _____
- _____
- _____
- _____

AFFECTIVE & METACOGNITIVE

Now list 3 topics that most interest you. Write why you are interested in them.

1 _____ Why? _____

2 _____ Why? _____

3 _____ Why? _____

What Interests Me: Writing, *continued*

B. For whom do I write?

Directions: Read the list of people you may write for. Circle the number that shows how often you write for these people.

How often do you write for . . .	Never	Rarely	Sometimes	Often
1 yourself?	1	2	3	4
2 friends?	1	2	3	4
3 family?	1	2	3	4
4 teachers?	1	2	3	4
5 employers?	1	2	3	4
6 strangers?	1	2	3	4
7 someone else: _____?	1	2	3	4

For whom do you most like to write? _____

C. Why do I write?

Directions: Read the list of reasons you may write. Circle the number that shows how often you write for these reasons.

How often do you write to . . .	Never	Rarely	Sometimes	Often
1 teach people something?	1	2	3	4
2 explain something to people?	1	2	3	4
3 entertain people?	1	2	3	4
4 make people feel emotion?	1	2	3	4
5 persuade people to believe something?	1	2	3	4
6 persuade people to do something?	1	2	3	4
7 express how you feel?	1	2	3	4
8 express what you think?	1	2	3	4
9 do something else: _____?	1	2	3	4

For what reason do you most like to write? _____

AFFECTIVE & METACOGNITIVE

What Interests Me: Writing, continued

D. What do I write?

Directions: Put a ✔ next to all the writing forms that you use, and answer the questions.

❏ I write lists.
What types of lists do you write? _____
_____

❏ I write emails or letters.
What types of emails or letters do
you write? _____
_____

❏ I write directions.
What types of directions do
you write? _____
_____

❏ I write song or rap lyrics.
What types of lyrics do you write? _____
_____

❏ I write diary or journal entries.
What types of diary or journal entries
do you write? _____
_____

❏ I write notes to myself.
What types of notes do you write? _____
_____

❏ I write a job application or resume.
What types of applications or resumes
do you write? _____
_____

❏ I write poetry.
What types of poetry do you write? _____
_____

❏ I write stories.
What types of stories do you write? _____
_____

❏ I write screenplays.
What types of screenplays do
you write? _____
_____

❏ I write reviews.
What types of reviews do
you write? _____
_____

❏ I write speeches.
What types of speeches do you write? _____
_____

❏ I write essays.
What types of essays do you write? _____
_____

❏ I write reports.
What types of reports do you write? _____
_____

❏ I write articles.
What types of articles do you write? _____
_____

❏ I write cartoons, comic strips,
or graphic novels.
What types of cartoons, comic strips, or graphic
novels do you write? _____
_____

In which form do you most like to write? _____

AFFECTIVE & METACOGNITIVE

What I Do: Writing Strategies

Directions: Reflect on the process you used to write your composition titled _____

Prewriting

1 What did you do that helped you brainstorm and plan your composition? _____

_____

2 What will you do differently when you brainstorm and plan your next composition? _____

_____

Drafting

3 What did you do that helped you draft your composition? _____

_____

4 What will you do differently when you draft your next composition? _____

_____

Revising

5 What did you do that helped you revise your composition? _____

_____

6 What will you do differently when you revise your next composition? _____

_____

Editing and Proofreading

7 What did you do that helped you edit your composition? _____

_____

8 What will you do differently when you edit your next composition? _____

_____

Publishing

9 What did you do that helped you publish your composition? _____

_____

10 What will you do differently when you publish your next composition? _____

_____

AFFECTIVE & METACOGNITIVE

Name _____ Date _____

Class Tally for Self-Assessments

Directions: Use this generic chart to tally class results for self-assessments. Write the questions in the left column of the chart. Then plot student responses by writing each student's initials in the cell with the corresponding rating.

Self-Assessment _____ Date _____ Period _____

Questions	1	2	3	4

EDGE Level C

AFFECTIVE & METACOGNITIVE

Writing Rubrics

Writing Forms

EDGE Level C

Good Writing Traits Rubric

Score	Focus and Unity	Organization	Development of Ideas	Voice and Style	Written Conventions	Extension (see next page)
4	**Focus:** Clearly establishes and consistently maintains a central idea or claim. **Unity:** All facts, ideas, examples, details are relevant and clearly connected to the central idea or claim.	**Structure:** The organizational pattern is appropriate to the audience, purpose, and task. **Coherence:** Includes a strong introduction and conclusion and leads the reader through a logical progression of ideas with varied and appropriate transitions.	**Content Quality:** Consistently presents meaningful ideas or claims in a logical way that is appropriate to the task, purpose, and audience. **Elaboration:** Includes relevant, clear reasoning, details, evidence, and/or description: that are effective and comprehensive.	**Style and Voice:** Fully establishes and effectively maintains a voice that is appropriate to the audience, purpose, and task. **Words and Sentences:** Consistently chooses precise words and varied sentences that are appropriate to the audience and purpose and clearly convey the writer's meaning.	**Grammar and Usage:** Demonstrates strong command of English grammar and usage conventions. All sentences are formed correctly. **Mechanics and Spelling:** Demonstrates strong command of mechanics and spelling. Use of punctuation, capitalization, and spelling is effective and consistent.	All or most of the features of the type of writing are present.
3	**Focus:** Adequately establishes and mostly maintains a central idea or claim. **Unity:** Most facts, ideas, examples, details are relevant and mostly connected to the central idea or claim.	**Structure:** The organizational pattern is mostly appropriate to the audience, purpose, and task. **Coherence:** Includes an introduction and conclusion and leads the reader through a progression of ideas with some transitions.	**Content Quality:** Mostly presents adequate ideas or claims that are appropriate to the task, purpose, and audience. **Elaboration:** Includes reasoning, details, evidence, and/or description that are adequate but incomplete.	**Style and Voice:** Mostly establishes and maintains a voice that is appropriate to the audience, purpose, and task. **Words and Sentences:** Mostly chooses precise words and a variety of sentences that are appropriate to the audience and purpose and adequately convey meaning.	**Grammar and Usage:** Demonstrates adequate command of English grammar and usage conventions. Errors are limited and do not impede understanding. Most sentences are formed correctly. **Mechanics and Spelling:** Demonstrates adequate command of mechanics and spelling. Use of punctuation, capitalization, and spelling is generally consistent.	Some of the features of the type of writing are present.
2	**Focus:** Partially establishes a central idea or claim. **Unity:** Some facts, ideas, examples, details are relevant and somewhat connected to the central idea or claim.	**Structure:** The pattern is inconsistent or less appropriate to the audience, purpose, or task. **Coherence:** Has an introduction and conclusion but leads the reader through loosely connected ideas that may be incomplete or not obvious to the reader.	**Content Quality:** Presents adequate ideas or claims that are less appropriate to the task, purpose, and audience. **Elaboration:** Includes weak reasoning, details, evidence, and/or description and may include extraneous or loosely related material.	**Style and Voice:** Inconsistently establishes and maintains a voice appropriate to the audience, purpose, and task. **Words and Sentences:** Demonstrates uneven word choice and limited sentence variety or chooses language mostly inappropriate to the audience and purpose. Meaning is vague or imprecise.	**Grammar and Usage:** Demonstrates partial command of English grammar and usage conventions. Frequent errors may impede understanding. Some sentences are formed incorrectly. **Mechanics and Spelling:** Demonstrates partial command of mechanics and spelling. Use of punctuation, capitalization, and spelling is inconsistent.	Few of the features of the type of writing are present.
1	**Focus:** Lacks a central idea or claim. **Unity:** Few facts, ideas, examples, details are relevant. Most do not support the central idea or claim or connections are unclear.	**Structure:** Lacks any organizational pattern. **Coherence:** Lacks an introduction or conclusion. Ideas are hard to understand.	**Content Quality:** Presents inappropriate or irrelevant ideas or claims. **Elaboration:** Lacks reasoning, details, evidence, and/or description.	**Style and Voice:** Does not establish and maintain a voice or uses a voice that is inappropriate to the audience, purpose, and task. **Words and Sentences:** Demonstrates little or no word choice and no sentence variety. Chooses language inappropriate to the audience, purpose, and task, hindering meaning.	**Grammar and Usage:** Demonstrates little or no command of English grammar and usage conventions. **Mechanics and Spelling:** Demonstrates little or no command of mechanics and spelling.	Very few, if any, of the features of the type of writing are present.

Good Writing Traits Rubric: Extension

Type of Writing	Focus and Unity	Organization	Development of Ideas	Voice and Style	Written Conventions
Argumentative	Focuses on and defends a position or argument.	Uses one or a combination of organizational patterns in an appropriate way for the purpose and intended audience. Some Organizational Patterns: · Spatial · Chronological · General to specific	Elaborates with logical reasons, explanations, details, examples, facts, and statistics; establishes credibility; and appeals to the logic and emotion of the reader. Anticipates and addresses reader questions, concerns, expectations, biases, and counter-arguments.	Uses a voice and style that are appropriate to the purpose and intended audience.	Uses standard English conventions.
Informative/ Explanatory	Focuses on and explains a central idea or thesis.	· Specific to general · Most important to least important · Least important to most important · Enumeration · Classification · Illustration · Definition	Elaborates with explanations, details, examples, facts, statistics, and reasons. Anticipates and addresses reader questions and expectations.		
Narrative	Focuses on and relates a sequence of events.	· Analysis · Comparison and contrast · Question and answer · Cause and effect · Problem and solution · Hypothesis and results	Elaborates with elements of imaginative text such as plot, character, setting, dialogue, conflict, and suspense to engage the reader. Elaborates with concrete sensory details and figurative language to help the reader form a mental picture.		

WRITING RUBRICS & FORMS

EDGE Level C

Good Writing Trait: Focus and Unity Rubric

Directions: Use this rubric to score a composition for Focus and Unity.

Score	Focus and Unity	
	How clearly does the writing present a central idea or claim?	**How well does everything go together?**
4 Wow!	The writing expresses a <u>clear</u> central idea or claim about the topic.	<u>Everything</u> in the writing goes together. • The main idea of each paragraph goes with the central idea or claim of the paper. • The main idea and details within each paragraph are related. • The conclusion is about the central idea or claim.
3 Aaah.	The writing expresses a <u>generally</u> clear central idea or claim about the topic.	<u>Most</u> parts of the writing go together. • The main idea of most paragraphs goes with the central idea or claim of the paper. • In most paragraphs, the main idea and details are related. • Most of the conclusion is about the central idea or claim.
2 Hmmm.	The writing includes a topic, but the central idea or claim is <u>not</u> clear.	<u>Some</u> parts of the writing go together. • The main idea of some paragraphs goes with the central idea or claim of the paper. • In some paragraphs, the main idea and details are related. • Some of the conclusion is about the central idea or claim.
1 Huh?	The writing includes many topics and <u>does not</u> express one central idea or claim.	The parts of the writing <u>do not</u> go together. • Few paragraphs have a main idea, or the main idea does not go with the central idea or claim of the paper. • Few paragraphs contain a main idea and related details • None of the conclusion is about the central idea or claim.

Good Writing Trait: Organization Rubric

Directions: Use this rubric to score a composition for Organization.

Score	Organization	
	Does the writing have a clear structure, and is it appropriate for the writer's audience, purpose, and type of writing?	**How smoothly do the ideas flow together?**
4 Wow!	The writing has a structure that is <u>clear</u> and appropriate for the writer's audience, purpose, and type of writing.	The ideas progress in a smooth and orderly way. • The introduction is strong. • The ideas flow well from paragraph to paragraph. • The ideas in each paragraph flow well from one sentence to the next. • Effective transitions connect ideas. • The conclusion is strong.
3 Aaah.	The writing has a structure that is <u>generally</u> clear and appropriate for the writer's audience, purpose, and type of writing.	<u>Most</u> of the ideas progress in a smooth and orderly way. • The introduction is adequate. • Most of the ideas flow well from paragraph to paragraph. • Most ideas in each paragraph flow from one sentence to the next. • Effective transitions connect most of the ideas. • The conclusion is adequate.
2 Hmmm.	The structure of the writing is <u>not</u> clear or <u>not</u> appropriate for the writer's audience, purpose, and type of writing.	<u>Some</u> of the ideas progress in a smooth and orderly way. • The introduction is weak. • Some of the ideas flow well from paragraph to paragraph. • Some ideas in each paragraph flow from one sentence to the next. • Transitions connect some ideas. • The conclusion is weak.
1 Huh?	The writing is not clear or organized.	<u>Few or none</u> of the ideas progress in a smooth and orderly way.

EDGE Level C

WRITING RUBRICS & FORMS

Good Writing Trait: Development of Ideas Rubric

Directions: Use this rubric to score a composition for Development of Ideas.

Score	Development of Ideas	
	How thoughtful and interesting is the writing?	**How well are the ideas or claims explained and supported?**
4 Wow!	The writing engages the reader with meaningful ideas or claims and presents them in a way that is interesting and appropriate to the audience, purpose, and type of writing.	**The ideas or claims are fully explained and supported.** · The ideas or claims are well developed with important details, evidence, and/or description. · The writing feels complete, and the reader is satisfied.
3 Aaah.	<u>Most</u> of the writing engages the reader with meaningful ideas or claims and presents them in a way that is interesting and appropriate to the audience, purpose, and type of writing.	<u>Most</u> of the ideas or claims are explained and supported. · Most of the ideas or claims are developed with important details, evidence, and/or description. · The writing feels mostly complete, but the reader still has some questions.
2 Hmmm.	<u>Some</u> of the writing engages the reader with meaningful ideas or claims and presents them in a way that is interesting and appropriate to the audience, purpose, and type of writing.	<u>Some</u> of the ideas or claims are explained and supported. · Only some of the ideas or claims are developed. Details, evidence, and/or description are limited or not relevant. · The writing leaves the reader with many questions.
1 Huh?	The writing does <u>not</u> engage the reader. It is not appropriate to the audience, purpose, and type of writing.	The ideas or claims are <u>not</u> explained or supported. The ideas or claims lack details, evidence, and/or description, and the writing leaves the reader unsatisfied.

WRITING RUBRICS & FORMS

Good Writing Trait: Voice and Style Rubric

Directions: Use this rubric to score a composition for Voice and Style.

Score	Voice and Style	
	Does the writing have a clear voice and is it the best style for the type of writing?	**Is the language interesting and are the words and sentences appropriate for the purpose, audience, and type of writing?**
4 Wow!	The writing <u>fully</u> engages the reader with its individual voice. The writing style is best for the type of writing.	The words and sentences are interesting and appropriate to the purpose and audience. • The words are precise and engaging. • The sentences are varied and flow together smoothly.
3 Aaah.	<u>Most</u> of the writing engages the reader with an individual voice. The writing style is mostly best for the type of writing.	<u>Most</u> of the words and sentences are interesting and appropriate to the purpose and audience. • Most words are precise and engaging. • Most sentences are varied and flow together.
2 Hmmm.	<u>Some</u> of the writing engages the reader, but it has no individual voice and the style is not best for the writing type.	<u>Some</u> of the words and sentences are interesting and appropriate to the purpose and audience. • Some words are precise and engaging. • Some sentences are varied, but the flow could be smoother.
1 Huh?	The writing does <u>not</u> engage the reader.	<u>Few or none</u> of the words and sentences are appropriate to the purpose and audience. • The words are often vague and dull. • The sentences lack variety and do not flow together.

WRITING RUBRICS & FORMS

EDGE Level C

Good Writing Trait: Written Conventions Rubric

Directions: Use this rubric to score a composition for Written Conventions.

Score	Written Conventions	
	Are the sentences written correctly?	**Does the writing show correct punctuation, capitalization, and spelling?**
4 Wow!	The sentences are complete and correct. Fragments may be used on purpose to achieve an effect.	The writing is free of major errors in punctuation, capitalization, and spelling.
3 Aaah.	<u>Most</u> of the sentences are complete and correct.	The writing has <u>some</u> errors in punctuation, capitalization, and spelling.
2 Hmmm.	<u>Few</u> of the sentences are complete and correct, but the reader can understand the meaning.	The writing has <u>many</u> errors in punctuation, capitalization, and spelling.
1 Huh?	The sentences are <u>not</u> complete and correct. The writing is difficult to read and understand.	The errors in punctuation, capitalization, and spelling make the writing difficult to read and understand.

WRITING RUBRICS & FORMS

Good Writing Traits: Class Profile

Directions: Use the **Good Writing Traits Rubric** on page 122 to score students' written compositions. Then plot the scores on the Rubric below by writing each student's initials in the appropriate cell. Identify the trait(s) with which the most students need practice.

Scale	Focus & Unity	Organization	Development of Ideas	Voice & Style	Written Conventions
4					
3					
2					
1					

WRITING RUBRICS & TOOLS

EDGE Level C

Writing Portfolio: Coversheet

Name:

Directions: Students, use this coversheet to keep track of the compositions in your writing portfolio. In the chart, write the titles of your compositions and the dates of your drafts.

Unit	Writing Project	Title of Your Composition	Draft 1 Date	Draft 2 Date	Draft 3 Date
1	Short Story				
2	Autobiographical Narrative				
3	Position Paper				
4	Research Report				
5	Literary Research Report				
6	Persuasive Essay				

Writing Portfolio: Record of Scores

Name: _____

Directions: Teachers, use this record to keep track of your student composition scores. Use the **Good Writing Traits Rubric** on page 122 to score the compositions.

Unit	Writing Project	Date	Focus and Unity	Organization	Development of Ideas	Voice and Style	Written Conventions	Overall Score
1	Short Story							
2	Autobiographical Narrative							
3	Position Paper							
4	Research Report							
5	Literary Research Report							
6	Persuasive Essay							

EDGE Level C

WRITING RUBRICS & TOOLS

Name: _____

Writing Portfolio: Strengths and Needs Summary

Directions: Teachers, use this chart to summarize the strengths and needs of your students. This information will be valuable during student conferences and for instructional planning.

Writing Traits	Consistent Strengths	Some Successes	Greatest Needs
Focus and Unity			
Organization			
Development of Ideas			
Voice and Style			
Written Conventions			

Name _____ Date _____

Self-Assessment: Written Composition

Directions: Put a ✔ next to the form of writing that you used. Read your composition, and answer questions 1–4.

Writing Form

❏ short story   ❏ research report

❏ autobiographical narrative   ❏ literary research report

❏ position paper   ❏ persuasive essay

1. What did you like best about your composition?

_____

_____

_____

2. What did you do well?

_____

_____

_____

3. What could you improve about your composition?

_____

_____

_____

4. What should you remember to do when writing the next composition?

_____

_____

_____

_____

EDGE Level C

WRITING RUBRICS & TOOLS

Name _____ Date _____

Peer-Assessment: Written Composition

Directions: Put a ✔ next to the form of writing that your partner used. Read your partner's composition, and answer questions 1–4.

Writing Form

❏ short story   ❏ research report

❏ autobiographical narrative   ❏ literary research report

❏ position paper   ❏ persuasive essay

1. What did you like best about your partner's composition?

_____

_____

_____

2. What did your partner do well?

_____

_____

_____

3. What could your partner improve about his or her composition?

_____

_____

_____

4. What should your partner remember to do when writing the next composition?

_____

_____

_____

WRITING RUBRICS & TOOLS

"THE MOUSTACHE" AND "WHO WE REALLY ARE"

1–8. KEY VOCABULARY
(4 points each/32 points total)

1. D	2. A	3. C	4. B
5. A	6. A	7. C	8. B

9–12. LITERARY ANALYSIS
(4 points each/16 points total)

9. B	10. A	11. B	12. B

13–14. COMPREHENSION
(4 points each/8 points total)

13. D	14. D

15. CONSTRUCTED RESPONSE
(10 points total)

15. What to look for: Student cites strong and thorough evidence to support what the text says.

Points	Performance
10	Complete answer with relevant evidence
5	Partial answer with some evidence
0	No response or off topic

16–18. LITERARY ANALYSIS
(4 points each/12 points total)

16. D	17. B	18. B

19–21. COMPREHENSION
(4 points each/12 points total)

19. C	20. A	21. C

22. CONSTRUCTED RESPONSE
(10 points total)

22. What to look for: Student draws valid inferences about people's misunderstandings and cites strong and thorough evidence from the text to support this analysis.

Points	Performance
10	Valid inferences with relevant evidence
5	Partial inferences with some evidence
0	No response or off topic

"TWO KINDS" AND "NOVEL MUSICIAN"

1–8. KEY VOCABULARY
(4 points each / 32 points total)

1. C 2. D 3. A 4. D
5. D 6. B 7. B 8. C

9–11. LITERARY ANALYSIS
(4 points each / 12 points total)

9. C 10. B 11. C

12–14. COMPREHENSION
(4 points each / 12 points total)

12. D 13. C 14. C

15. CONSTRUCTED RESPONSE
(10 points total)

15. What to look for: Student draws a valid inference about this turning point in the mother-daughter relationship and cites strong and thorough evidence from the text to support this analysis.

Points	Performance
10	Valid inference with relevant evidence
5	Partial inferences with weak evidence
0	No response or off topic

16–18. LITERARY ANALYSIS
(4 points each / 12 points total)

16. D 17. B 18. D

19–21. COMPREHENSION
(4 points each/12 points total)

19. A 20. A 21. A

22. CONSTRUCTED RESPONSE
(10 points total)

22. What to look for: Student presents a valid analysis that relates the caption to the author's purpose.

Points	Performance
10	Valid analysis
5	Partial analysis
0	No response or off topic

"SKINS" AND "NICOLE"

1–8. KEY VOCABULARY
(4 points each/32 points total)

1. A   2. C   3. D   4. B
5. B   6. C   7. D   8. C

9–11. LITERARY ANALYSIS
(4 points each/12 points total)

9. D   10. A   11. B

12–14. COMPREHENSION
(4 points each/12 points total)

12. D   13. A   14. B

15. CONSTRUCTED RESPONSE
(10 points total)

15. What to look for: Student presents a valid analysis that relates Randolph's character to the theme of the story and cites strong and thorough evidence from the text to support this analysis.

Points	Performance
10	Complete answer with relevant evidence
5	Partial answer with some evidence
0	No response or off topic

16–19. LITERARY ANALYSIS
(4 points each/16 points total)

16. D   17. B   18. B   19. B

20–21. COMPREHENSION
(4 points each/8 points total)

20. B   21. C

22. CONSTRUCTED RESPONSE
(10 points total)

22. What to look for: Student presents a valid analysis that relates the mother's statement to Nicole's own viewpoint.

Points	Performance
10	Valid analysis
5	Partial analysis
0	No response or off topic

Answer Keys and Scoring Guides

READING AND LITERARY ANALYSIS UNIT TEST

1–20. MULTIPLE-CHOICE *(1 point each/22 points total)*

1. C	**2.** C	**3.** B	**4.** B	**5.** A	**6.** D	**7.** B	**8.** B	**9.** C	**11.** C
12. B	**13.** C	**14.** D	**15.** A	**17.** C	**18.** D	**19.** D	**20.** B	**21.** B	**22.** A

10., 16., & 23.. CONSTRUCTED RESPONSE *(4 points each/12 points total)*

Points	Criteria
4	Full answer; provides extensive support with relevant examples
3	Partial answer; provides several relevant examples
2	Partial answer; provides one relevant example
1	Partial answer; no example provided
0	No response or off topic

Conversion Chart: Points Earned to Percent Score

Points	0	1	2	3	4	5	6	7	8	9	10	11	12	13	14	15	16	17	18	19	20	21	22	23	24	25	26	27	28	29	30	31	32
%	0	3	6	9	13	16	19	22	25	28	31	34	38	41	44	47	50	53	56	59	63	66	69	72	75	78	81	84	88	91	94	97	100

GRAMMAR AND WRITING UNIT TEST

1–16. MULTIPLE-CHOICE *(1 point each/16 points total)*

1. C	**2.** C	**3.** C	**4.** A	**5.** B	**6.** A	**7.** D	**8.** B
9. C	**10.** D	**11.** C	**12.** A	**13.** A	**14.** C	**15.** D	**16.** A

WRITTEN COMPOSITION *(20 points total)*

Use the Good Writing Traits rubric on page 122 to score the written composition.

Conversion Chart: Points Earned to Percent Score

Points	0	1	2	3	4	5	6	7	8	9	10	11	12	13	14	15	16	17	18	19	20	21	22	23	24	25	26	27	28	29	30	31	32	33	34	35	36
%	0	3	6	8	11	14	17	19	22	25	28	31	33	36	39	42	44	47	50	53	56	58	61	64	67	69	72	75	78	81	83	86	89	92	94	97	100

ANSWER KEYS & ANSWER SHEET

© National Geographic Learning, a part of Cengage Learning, Inc.

EDGE Level C

"LA VIDA ROBOT" AND "READING, WRITING, AND...RECREATION?"

1–8. KEY VOCABULARY
(4 points each / 32 points total)

1. B   2. A   3. A   4. A
5. B   6. C   7. A   8. D

9–12. LITERARY ANALYSIS
(4 points each / 16 points total)

9. D   10. C   11. C   12. B

13–14. COMPREHENSION
(4 points each / 8 points total)

13. C   14. D

15. CONSTRUCTED RESPONSE
(10 points total)

15. What to look for: Student provides a valid analysis of the text feature and cites strong evidence from the text to support this analysis.

Points	Performance
10	Valid analysis with relevant evidence
5	Partial analysis with some evidence
0	No response or off topic

16–18. LITERARY ANALYSIS
(4 points each / 12 points total)

16. C   17. C   18. B

19–21. COMPREHENSION
(4 points each / 12 points total)

19. D   20. D   21. D

22. CONSTRUCTED RESPONSE
(10 points total)

22. What to look for: Student identifies the information addressed by the "5Ws + H" and presents a clear analysis of the relationship between that information, other information in the passage, and the main idea of the passage.

Points	Performance
10	Complete answer with relevant evidence
5	Partial answer with some evidence
0	No response or off topic

"MY LEFT FOOT" AND "SUCCESS IS A MIND-SET"

1–8. KEY VOCABULARY
(4 points each / 32 points total)

1. B	2. A	3. A	4. B
5. A	6. D	7. D	8. B

9–11. LITERARY ANALYSIS
(4 points each / 12 points total)

9. B   10. C   11. C

12–14. COMPREHENSION
(4 points each / 12 points total)

12. D   13. C   14. B

15. CONSTRUCTED RESPONSE
(10 points total)

15. What to look for: Student provides a valid analysis of the importance of the details to the autobiography as a whole and cites strong evidence from the text to support this analysis.

Points	Performance
10	Valid analysis with relevant evidence
5	Partial analysis with some evidence
0	No response or off topic

16–18. LITERARY ANALYSIS
(4 points each / 12 points total)

16. C   17. C   18. B

19–21. COMPREHENSION
(4 points each / 12 points total)

19. C   20. C   21. C

22. CONSTRUCTED RESPONSE
(10 points total)

22. What to look for: Student clearly explains the importance of Dr. Carson's mother and correctly identifies the other people he mentions in the same discussion.

Points	Performance
10	Complete explanation with correct details
5	Partial explanation with one correct detail
0	No response or off topic

"THE FREEDOM WRITERS DIARY" AND "STRENGTH, COURAGE, AND WISDOM"

1–8. KEY VOCABULARY
(4 points each/32 points total)

1. A	2. D	3. D	4. C
5. C	6. C	7. D	8. D

9–11. LITERARY ANALYSIS
(4 points each/12 points total)

9. B   10. A   11. D

12–14. COMPREHENSION
(4 points each/12 points total)

12. B   13. C   14. D

15. CONSTRUCTED RESPONSE
(10 points total)

15. What to look for: Student provides a valid analysis of the important idea in the diary entry and cites strong evidence from the text to support this analysis.

Points	Performance
10	Valid analysis with relevant evidence
5	Partial analysis with some evidence
0	No response or off topic

16–18. LITERARY ANALYSIS
(4 points each/12 points total)

16. B   17. B   18. A

19–21. COMPREHENSION
(4 points each/12 points total)

19. D   20. C   21. B

22. CONSTRUCTED RESPONSE
(10 points total)

22. What to look for: Student accurately identifies relevant word choices in the song lyrics and clearly explains their importance.

Points	Performance
10	Accurate identification with clear explanation
5	Fair identification with weak explanation
0	No response or off topic

READING AND LITERARY ANALYSIS UNIT TEST

1–24. MULTIPLE-CHOICE *(1 point each/22 points total)*

1. A	**2.** C	**3.** C	**4.** B	**5.** D	**6.** A	**7.** D	**8.** A	**9.** D	**10.** C
12. A	**13.** D	**14.** B	**15.** A	**17.** D	**18.** C	**19.** D	**20.** B	**21.** A	**22.** C	**23.** B	**24.** B

11., 16., & 25. CONSTRUCTED RESPONSE *(4 points each/12 points total)*

Points	Criteria
4	Full answer; provides extensive support with relevant examples
3	Partial answer; provides several relevant examples
2	Partial answer; provides one relevant example
1	Partial answer; no example provided
0	No response or off topic

Conversion Chart: Points Earned to Percent Score

Points	0	1	2	3	4	5	6	7	8	9	10	11	12	13	14	15	16	17	18	19	20	21	22	23	24	25	26	27	28	29	30	31	32	33	34
%	0	3	6	9	12	15	18	21	24	26	29	32	35	38	41	44	47	50	53	56	59	62	65	68	71	74	76	79	82	85	88	91	94	97	100

GRAMMAR AND WRITING UNIT TEST

1–16. MULTIPLE-CHOICE *(1 point each/16 points total)*

1. B	**2.** C	**3.** B	**4.** A	**5.** D	**6.** D	**7.** D	**8.** A
9. B	**10.** B	**11.** A	**12.** D	**13.** C	**14.** A	**15.** A	**16.** D

WRITTEN COMPOSITION *(20 points total)*

Use the Good Writing Traits rubric on page 122 to score the written composition.

Conversion Chart: Points Earned to Percent Score

Points	0	1	2	3	4	5	6	7	8	9	10	11	12	13	14	15	16	17	18	19	20	21	22	23	24	25	26	27	28	29	30	31	32	33	34	35	36
%	0	3	6	8	11	14	17	19	22	25	28	31	33	36	39	42	44	47	50	53	56	58	61	64	67	69	72	75	78	81	83	86	89	92	94	97	100

"AMIGO BROTHERS" AND "LEAN ON ME"

1–8. KEY VOCABULARY
(4 points each / 32 points total)

1. A	2. C	3. A	4. B
5. D	6. D	7. D	8. B

9–11. LITERARY ANALYSIS
(4 points each / 12 points total)

9. A   10. C   11. A

12–14. COMPREHENSION
(4 points each/12 points total)

12. B   13. C   14. B

15. CONSTRUCTED RESPONSE
(10 points total)

15. What to look for: Student provides a valid analysis of the influence of word choices upon style in the passage and cites strong evidence from the text to support this analysis.

Points	Performance
10	Valid analysis with relevant evidence
5	Partial analysis with some evidence
0	No response or off topic

16–18. LITERARY ANALYSIS
(4 points each / 12 points total)

16. A   17. A   18. A

19–21. COMPREHENSION
(4 points each/12 points total)

19. C   20. C   21. A

22. CONSTRUCTED RESPONSE
(10 points total)

22. What to look for: Student accurately identifies the rhyme scheme in the lines and provides a valid analysis of the role of rhyme scheme in the structure of the verse.

Points	Performance
10	Accurate identification with clear explanation
5	Fair identification with weak explanation
0	No response or off topic

ANSWER KEYS & ANSWER SHEET

"MY BROTHER'S KEEPER" AND "WHAT PRICE LOYALTY?"

1–8. KEY VOCABULARY
(4 points each / 32 points total)

1. B	2. C	3. D	4. D
5. A	6. C	7. B	8. D

9–11. LITERARY ANALYSIS
(4 points each / 12 points total)

9. A 10. C 11. C

12–14. COMPREHENSION
(4 points each / 12 points total)

12. A 13. B 14. B

15. CONSTRUCTED RESPONSE
(10 points total)

15. What to look for: Student provides a valid analysis of the effect of the sentence structure in the passage and cites strong evidence from the text to support this analysis.

Points	Performance
10	Valid analysis with relevant evidence
5	Partial analysis with some evidence
0	No response or off topic

16–19. LITERARY ANALYSIS
(4 points each / 16 points total)

16. A 17. D 18. B 19. D

20–21. COMPREHENSION
(4 points each / 8 points total)

20. A 21. D

22. CONSTRUCTED RESPONSE
(10 points total)

22. What to look for: Student accurately identifies the author's viewpoint and cites text evidence when explaining the author's methods of making the viewpoint clear.

Points	Performance
10	Accurate identification with text-based explanation
5	Fair identification with weak explanation
0	No response or off topic

"THE HAND OF FATIMA" AND "OLD WAYS, NEW WORLD"

1–8. KEY VOCABULARY
(4 points each/32 points total)

1. A 2. B 3. B 4. D
5. C 6. A 7. C 8. A

9–12. LITERARY ANALYSIS
(4 points each/16 points total)

9. D 10. D 11. C 12. A

13–14. COMPREHENSION
(4 points each/8 points total)

13. C 14. D

15. CONSTRUCTED RESPONSE
(10 points total)

15. What to look for: Student provides a valid analysis of the viewpoints in the passage and relates the analysis to the text to support this analysis.

Points	Performance
10	Valid analysis with clear relationship to the text
5	Partial analysis with some relationship to the text
0	No response or off topic

16–18. LITERARY ANALYSIS
(4 points each/12 points total)

16. B 17. C 18. B

19–21. COMPREHENSION
(4 points each/12 points total)

19. A 20. D 21. C

22. CONSTRUCTED RESPONSE
(10 points total)

22. What to look for: Student provides a valid analysis of the reporter's viewpoint and refers to the text when explaining this analysis.

Points	Performance
10	Valid analysis with clear reference to the text
5	Partial analysis with vague reference to the text
0	No response or off topic

READING AND LITERARY ANALYSIS UNIT TEST

1–24. MULTIPLE-CHOICE *(1 point each/22 points total)*

1. D	**2.** B	**3.** D	**4.** B	**5.** B	**6.** A	**7.** A	**8.** A	**9.** B	**10.** C	**11.** B
12. D	**14.** B	**15.** B	**16.** A	**17.** C	**18.** C	**20.** D	**21.** C	**22.** A	**23.** C	**24.** B

13., 19., & 25. CONSTRUCTED RESPONSE *(4 points each/12 points total)*

Points	Criteria
4	Full answer; provides extensive support with relevant examples
3	Partial answer; provides several relevant examples
2	Partial answer; provides one relevant example
1	Partial answer; no example provided
0	No response or off topic

Conversion Chart: Points Earned to Percent Score

Points	0	1	2	3	4	5	6	7	8	9	10	11	12	13	14	15	16	17	18	19	20	21	22	23	24	25	26	27	28	29	30	31	32	33	34
%	0	3	6	9	12	15	18	21	24	26	29	32	35	38	41	44	47	50	53	56	59	62	65	68	71	74	76	79	82	85	88	91	94	97	100

GRAMMAR AND WRITING UNIT TEST

1–16. MULTIPLE-CHOICE *(1 point each/16 points total)*

1. B	**2.** B	**3.** B	**4.** D	**5.** A	**6.** D	**7.** B	**8.** A
9. C	**10.** B	**11.** D	**12.** D	**13.** A	**14.** A	**15.** A	**16.** C

WRITTEN COMPOSITION *(20 points total)*

Use the Good Writing Traits rubric on page 122 to score the written composition.

Conversion Chart: Points Earned to Percent Score

Points	0	1	2	3	4	5	6	7	8	9	10	11	12	13	14	15	16	17	18	19	20	21	22	23	24	25	26	27	28	29	30	31	32	33	34	35	36
%	0	3	6	8	11	14	17	19	22	25	28	31	33	36	39	42	44	47	50	53	56	58	61	64	67	69	72	75	78	81	83	86	89	92	94	97	100

EDGE Level C

"FACE FACTS" AND "SILENT LANGUAGE"

1–8. KEY VOCABULARY
(4 points each/32 points total)

1. C	2. B	3. A	4. D
5. C	6. C	7. A	8. D

9–12. LITERARY ANALYSIS
(4 points each/16 points total)

9. D	10. C	11. B	12. C

13–14. COMPREHENSION
(4 points each/8 points total)

13. B	14. B

15. CONSTRUCTED RESPONSE
(10 points total)

15. What to look for: Student accurately identifies the two causes and effects in the paragraph and explains the relationship clearly.

Points	Performance
10	Accurate identification of both relationships with clear explanation
5	Identification of one relationship with weak explanation
0	No response or off topic

16–18. LITERARY ANALYSIS
(4 points each/12 points total)

16. B	17. D	18. B

19–21. COMPREHENSION
(4 points each/12 points total)

19. A	20. D	21. C

22. CONSTRUCTED RESPONSE
(10 points total)

22. What to look for: Student accurately identifies the problem and solution in the paragraph and explains the relationship clearly.

Points	Performance
10	Accurate identification with clear explanation
5	Fair identification with weak explanation
0	No response or off topic

"THEY SPEAK FOR SUCCESS" AND "BREAKING THE ICE"

1–8. KEY VOCABULARY

(4 points each/32 points total)

1. D   2. D   3. B   4. B
5. D   6. A   7. D   8. C

9–11. LITERARY ANALYSIS

(4 points each/12 points total)

9. A   10. B   11. C

12–14. COMPREHENSION

(4 points each/12 points total)

12. B   13. B   14. B

15. CONSTRUCTED RESPONSE

(10 points total)

15. What to look for: Student accurately states the main idea of the paragraph and clearly explains how the example details support it.

Points	Performance
10	Accurate statement of main idea and clear explanation of supporting details
5	Weak statement of main idea and vague explanation of supporting details
0	No response or off topic

16–18. LITERARY ANALYSIS

(4 points each/12 points total)

16. D   17. A   18. B

19–21. COMPREHENSION

(4 points each/12 points total)

19. D   20. B   21. A

22. CONSTRUCTED RESPONSE

(10 points total)

22. What to look for: Student provides a valid analysis of the humorous techniques used in the paragraph and cites strong evidence from the text to support this analysis.

Points	Performance
10	Valid analysis with relevant evidence
5	Partial analysis with some evidence
0	No response or off topic

EDGE Level C

ANSWER KEYS & ANSWER SHEET

"MY ENGLISH" AND "HOW I LEARNED ENGLISH"

1–8. KEY VOCABULARY
(4 points each/32 points total)

1. D	2. C	3. A	4. D
5. A	6. B	7. A	8. A

9–12. LITERARY ANALYSIS
(4 points each/16 points total)

9. A   10. A   11. B   12. C

13–14. COMPREHENSION
(4 points each/8 points total)

13. D   14. A

15. CONSTRUCTED RESPONSE
(10 points total)

15. What to look for: Student provides a valid analysis of the chronological structure of the paragraph and refers to signal words in supporting this analysis.

Points	Performance
10	Valid analysis with clear reference to signal words
5	Partial analysis with vague reference to signal words
0	No response or off topic

16–19. LITERARY ANALYSIS
(4 points each/16 points total)

16. D   17. B   18. C   19. B

20–21. COMPREHENSION
(4 points each/8 points total)

20. A   21. C

22. CONSTRUCTED RESPONSE
(10 points total)

22. What to look for: Student provides a valid analysis of the relationship between free verse elements used in the lines and the poet's ideas and cites strong evidence from the text to support this analysis.

Points	Performance
10	Valid analysis with relevant evidence
5	Partial analysis with some evidence
0	No response or off topic

EDGE Level C

Answer Keys and Scoring Guides

READING AND LITERARY ANALYSIS UNIT TEST

1–24. MULTIPLE-CHOICE *(1 point each/22 points total)*

1. C	**2.** C	**3.** A	**4.** D	**5.** B	**6.** C	**7.** A	**8.** A	**9.** D	**11.** C	**12.** A
13. B	**14.** B	**15.** B	**16.** C	**18.** D	**19.** B	**20.** C	**21.** B	**22.** B	**23.** D	**24.** A

10., 17., & 25. CONSTRUCTED RESPONSE *(4 points each/12 points total)*

Points	Criteria
4	Full answer; provides extensive support with relevant examples
3	Partial answer; provides several relevant examples
2	Partial answer; provides one relevant example
1	Partial answer; no example provided
0	No response or off topic

Conversion Chart: Points Earned to Percent Score

Points	0	1	2	3	4	5	6	7	8	9	10	11	12	13	14	15	16	17	18	19	20	21	22	23	24	25	26	27	28	29	30	31	32	33	34
%	0	3	6	9	12	15	18	21	24	26	29	32	35	38	41	44	47	50	53	56	59	62	65	68	71	74	76	79	82	85	88	91	94	97	100

GRAMMAR AND WRITING UNIT TEST

1–16. MULTIPLE-CHOICE *(1 point each/16 points total)*

1. A	**2.** D	**3.** C	**4.** C	**5.** D	**6.** D	**7.** B	**8.** B
9. B	**10.** C	**11.** A	**12.** C	**13.** A	**14.** C	**15.** C	**16.** B

WRITTEN COMPOSITION *(20 points total)*

Use the Good Writing Traits rubric on page 122 to score the written composition.

Conversion Chart: Points Earned to Percent Score

Points	0	1	2	3	4	5	6	7	8	9	10	11	12	13	14	15	16	17	18	19	20	21	22	23	24	25	26	27	28	29	30	31	32	33	34	35	36
%	0	3	6	8	11	14	17	19	22	25	28	31	33	36	39	42	44	47	50	53	56	58	61	64	67	69	72	75	78	81	83	86	89	92	94	97	100

ANSWER KEYS & ANSWER SHEET

"SAY IT WITH FLOWERS" AND "THE JOURNEY"

1–8. KEY VOCABULARY
(4 points each/32 points total)

1. A	2. B	3. B	4. A
5. D	6. C	7. D	8. B

9–11. LITERARY ANALYSIS
(4 points each/12 points total)

9. B   10. C   11. B

12–14. COMPREHENSION
(4 points each/12 points total)

12. C   13. B   14. A

15. CONSTRUCTED RESPONSE
(10 points total)

15. What to look for: Student provides a valid analysis of the passage's contribution to the story's conflict and refers to text details in supporting this analysis.

Points	Performance
10	Valid analysis with clear reference to text details
5	Partial analysis with vague reference to text details
0	No response or off topic

16–18. LITERARY ANALYSIS
(4 points each/12 points total)

16. C   17. D   18. D

19–21. COMPREHENSION
(4 points each/12 points total)

19. B   20. A   21. C

22. CONSTRUCTED RESPONSE
(10 points total)

22. What to look for: Student provides a valid analysis of the metaphor and clearly relates its meaning to the overall meaning of the poem.

Points	Performance
10	Valid analysis with relevant evidence
5	Partial analysis with some evidence
0	No response or off topic

"JUST LATHER, THAT'S ALL" AND "THE WOMAN WHO WAS DEATH"

1–8. KEY VOCABULARY
(4 points each/32 points total)

1. A   2. B   3. A   4. A
5. C   6. A   7. B   8. B

9–11. LITERARY ANALYSIS
(4 points each/12 points total)

9. A   10. D   11. D

12–14. COMPREHENSION
(4 points each/12 points total)

12. B   13. B   14. A

15. CONSTRUCTED RESPONSE
(10 points total)

15. What to look for: Student provides a valid analysis of the author's use of the narrator's thoughts to convey suspense and cites text evidence in supporting this analysis.

Points	Performance
10	Valid analysis with adequate text evidence
5	Partial analysis with little text evidence
0	No response or off topic

16–19. LITERARY ANALYSIS
(4 points each/12 points total)

16. C   17. A   18. D   19. C

20–21. COMPREHENSION
(4 points each/8 points total)

20. D   21. C

22. CONSTRUCTED RESPONSE
(10 points total)

22. What to look for: Student provides a valid analysis of the cultural beliefs, values, and experiences reflected in the quotation and refers to text details in the analysis.

Points	Performance
10	Valid analysis with relevant text details
5	Partial analysis with some text details
0	No response or off topic

"BE-ERS AND DOERS" AND "MY MOMENT OF TRUTH"

1–8. KEY VOCABULARY
(4 points each/32 points total)

1. B	2. D	3. D	4. C
5. B	6. D	7. C	8. B

9–11. LITERARY ANALYSIS
(4 points each/12 points total)

9. A   10. B   11. A

12–14. COMPREHENSION
(4 points each/12 points total)

12. D   13. D   14. A

15. CONSTRUCTED RESPONSE
(10 points total)

15. What to look for: Student provides a valid analysis of the foreshadowing that is suggested in the passage and includes text evidence in the analysis.

Points	Performance
10	Valid analysis with adequate text evidence
5	Partial analysis with some text evidence
0	No response or off topic

16–18. LITERARY ANALYSIS
(4 points each/12 points total)

16. C   17. B   18. B

19–21. COMPREHENSION
(4 points each/12 points total)

19. D   20. C   21. A

22. CONSTRUCTED RESPONSE
(10 points total)

22. What to look for: Student provides a valid analysis of the purpose of the paragraph and its role in the overall purpose of the article and refers to the text in doing so.

Points	Performance
10	Valid analysis with relevant text references
5	Partial analysis with some text references
0	No response or off topic

EDGE Level C

READING AND LITERARY ANALYSIS UNIT TEST

1–24. MULTIPLE-CHOICE *(1 point each/22 points total)*

1. B	**2.** D	**3.** D	**4.** A	**5.** D	**6.** C	**7.** C	**8.** B	**9.** A	**10.** B	**11.** D
13. A	**14.** C	**15.** D	**16.** C	**17.** C	**18.** B	**19.** B	**21.** A	**22.** C	**23.** A	**24.** C

12., 20., & 25. CONSTRUCTED RESPONSE *(4 points each/12 points total)*

Points	Criteria
4	Full answer; provides extensive support with relevant examples
3	Partial answer; provides several relevant examples
2	Partial answer; provides one relevant example
1	Partial answer; no example provided
0	No response or off topic

Conversion Chart: Points Earned to Percent Score

Points	0	1	2	3	4	5	6	7	8	9	10	11	12	13	14	15	16	17	18	19	20	21	22	23	24	25	26	27	28	29	30	31	32	33	34
%	0	3	6	9	12	15	18	21	24	26	29	32	35	38	41	44	47	50	53	56	59	62	65	68	71	74	76	79	82	85	88	91	94	97	100

GRAMMAR AND WRITING UNIT TEST

1–16. MULTIPLE-CHOICE *(1 point each/16 points total)*

1. C	**2.** B	**3.** A	**4.** C	**5.** B	**6.** C	**7.** A	**8.** D
9. B	**10.** C	**11.** B	**12.** B	**13.** A	**14.** C	**15.** D	**16.** B

WRITTEN COMPOSITION *(20 points total)*

Use the Good Writing Traits rubric on page 122 to score the written composition.

Conversion Chart: Points Earned to Percent Score

Points	0	1	2	3	4	5	6	7	8	9	10	11	12	13	14	15	16	17	18	19	20	21	22	23	24	25	26	27	28	29	30	31	32	33	34	35	36
%	0	3	6	8	11	14	17	19	22	25	28	31	33	36	39	42	44	47	50	53	56	58	61	64	67	69	72	75	78	81	83	86	89	92	94	97	100

"TOO YOUNG TO DRIVE?" AND "RULES OF THE ROAD"

1–8. KEY VOCABULARY
(4 points each/32 points total)

1. A   2. B   3. C   4. D
5. B   6. B   7. B   8. D

9–11. LITERARY ANALYSIS
(4 points each/12 points total)

9. D   10. C   11. B

12–14. COMPREHENSION
(4 points each/12 points total)

12. B   13. C   14. B

15. CONSTRUCTED RESPONSE
(10 points total)

15. What to look for: Student clearly and correctly identifies the argument in the passage and the evidence given in the text to support it.

Points	Performance
10	Clear, correct identification of argument and text evidence
5	Unclear or inaccurate identification of argument and text evidence
0	No response or off topic

16–19. LITERARY ANALYSIS
(4 points each/12 points total)

16. A   17. A   18. A   19. D

20–21. COMPREHENSION
(4 points each/12 points total)

20. A   21. A

22. CONSTRUCTED RESPONSE
(10 points total)

22. What to look for: Student provides a valid analysis of the development of the idea stated in the subhead of the paragraph and refers to the text in doing so.

Points	Performance
10	Valid analysis with relevant text references
5	Partial analysis with some text references
0	No response or off topic

"PIRACY BITES!" AND "DOONESBURY ON DOWNLOADING"

1–8. KEY VOCABULARY
(4 points each / 32 points total)

1. C	**2.** B	**3.** D	**4.** A
5. C	**6.** C	**7.** B	**8.** B

9–12. LITERARY ANALYSIS
(4 points each / 16 points total)

9. D	**10.** A	**11.** D	**12.** C

13–14. COMPREHENSION
(4 points each / 8 points total)

13. A	**14.** B

15. CONSTRUCTED RESPONSE
(10 points total)

15. What to look for: Student provides a valid analysis and evaluation of the persuasive support provided in the paragraph and refers to text details in the response.

Points	Performance
10	Valid analysis/evaluation with relevant text details
5	Partial analysis/ evaluation with some text details
0	No response or off topic

16–19. LITERARY ANALYSIS
(4 points each / 12 points total)

16. D	**17.** D	**18.** A	**19.** C

20–21. COMPREHENSION
(4 points each / 12 points total)

20. B	**21.** C

22. CONSTRUCTED RESPONSE
(10 points total)

22. What to look for: Student clearly and accurately identifies the central idea and provides a valid analysis of the dialogue's role in pointing to that idea.

Points	Performance
10	Correct identification of central idea and valid analysis of the role of dialogue
5	Adequate identification of central idea and partial analysis of the role of dialogue
0	No response or off topic

"LONG WALK TO FREEDOM" AND "WE HOLD THESE TRUTHS"

1–8. KEY VOCABULARY
(4 points each/32 points total)

1. C	**2.** B	**3.** B	**4.** B
5. A	**6.** C	**7.** D	**8.** D

9–12. LITERARY ANALYSIS
(4 points each/16 points total)

9. C	**10.** D	**11.** D	**12.** B

13–14. COMPREHENSION
(4 points each/8 points total)

13. C	**14.** A

15. CONSTRUCTED RESPONSE
(10 points total)

15. What to look for: Student gives examples of word choices from the text and provides a valid analysis of their purpose.

Points	Performance
10	Valid analysis with clear examples from the text
5	Partial analysis with vague reference to the text
0	No response or off topic

16–19. LITERARY ANALYSIS
(4 points each/16 points total)

16. B	**17.** C	**18.** A	**19.** A

20–21. COMPREHENSION
(4 points each/8 points total)

20. D	**21.** A

22. CONSTRUCTED RESPONSE
(10 points total)

22. What to look for: Student accurately and clearly explains the similarities and differences in the two statements and refers to the texts in the explanation.

Points	Performance
10	Accurate, clear explanation with appropriate text references
5	Fair explanation with weak text references
0	No response or off topic

READING AND LITERARY ANALYSIS UNIT TEST

1–24. MULTIPLE-CHOICE *(1 point each/22 points total)*

1. C	2. A	3. C	4. D	5. B	6. B	7. D	8. B	9. B	11. D	12. D
13. A	14. C	15. C	16. C	18. D	19. B	20. B	21. A	22. D	23. D	24. B

10., 17., & 25. CONSTRUCTED RESPONSE *(4 points each/12 points total)*

Points	Criteria
4	Full answer; provides extensive support with relevant examples
3	Partial answer; provides several relevant examples
2	Partial answer; provides one relevant example
1	Partial answer; no example provided
0	No response or off topic

Conversion Chart: Points Earned to Percent Score

Points	0	1	2	3	4	5	6	7	8	9	10	11	12	13	14	15	16	17	18	19	20	21	22	23	24	25	26	27	28	29	30	31	32	33	34
%	0	3	6	9	12	15	18	21	24	26	29	32	35	38	41	44	47	50	53	56	59	62	65	68	71	74	76	79	82	85	88	91	94	97	100

GRAMMAR AND WRITING UNIT TEST

1–16. MULTIPLE-CHOICE *(1 point each/16 points total)*

1. D	2. D	3. D	4. A	5. B	6. C	7. B	8. C
9. A	10. C	11. A	12. B	13. D	14. B	15. B	16. D

WRITTEN COMPOSITION *(20 points total)*

Use the Good Writing Traits rubric on page 122 to score the written composition.

Conversion Chart: Points Earned to Percent Score

Points	0	1	2	3	4	5	6	7	8	9	10	11	12	13	14	15	16	17	18	19	20	21	22	23	24	25	26	27	28	29	30	31	32	33	34	35	36
%	0	3	6	8	11	14	17	19	22	25	28	31	33	36	39	42	44	47	50	53	56	58	61	64	67	69	72	75	78	81	83	86	89	92	94	97	100

"THE JEWELS OF THE SHRINE" AND "REMEMBERED"

1–8. KEY VOCABULARY
(4 points each/32 points total)

1. B	2. D	3. D	4. C
5. C	6. B	7. D	8. B

9–12. LITERARY ANALYSIS
(4 points each/16 points total)

9. B 10. C 11. C 12. B

13–14. COMPREHENSION
(4 points each/8 points total)

13. A 14. D

15. CONSTRUCTED RESPONSE
(10 points total)

15. What to look for: Student provides a valid analysis of Okorie's words and their effect and presents text evidence to support it.

Points	Performance
10	Valid analysis with relevant text evidence
5	Partial analysis with some text evidence
0	No response or off topic

16–19. LITERARY ANALYSIS
(4 points each/16 points total)

16. A 17. A 18. D 19. C

20–21. COMPREHENSION
(4 points each/8 points total)

20. B 21. B

22. CONSTRUCTED RESPONSE
(10 points total)

22. What to look for: Student correctly identifies the new information and relates it to the theme of the poem, referring to the text in doing so.

Points	Performance
10	Correct identification and valid analysis with relevant text references
5	Weak identification and analysis with little text reference
0	No response or off topic

ANSWER KEYS & ANSWER SHEET

"ROMEO AND JULIET" AND "WEST SIDE STORY"

1–8. KEY VOCABULARY
(4 points each/32 points total)

1. B	2. C	3. B	4. A
5. B	6. C	7. A	8. B

9–12. LITERARY ANALYSIS
(4 points each/16 points total)

9. D	10. D	11. B	12. D

13–14. COMPREHENSION
(4 points each/8 points total)

13. A   14. C

15. CONSTRUCTED RESPONSE
(10 points total)

15. **What to look for:** Student provides an appropriate interpretation and analysis of the dialogue, referring to the text in doing so.

Points	Performance
10	Valid interpretation and analysis with relevant text references
5	Weak interpretation and analysis with some text reference
0	No response or off topic

16–19. LITERARY ANALYSIS
(4 points each/16 points total)

16. B	17. C	18. A	19. A

20–21. COMPREHENSION
(4 points each/8 points total)

20. D   21. B

22. CONSTRUCTED RESPONSE
(10 points total)

22. **What to look for:** Student provides a clear, thoughtful comparison of the two scenes and uses text details to support ideas.

Points	Performance
10	Clear and thoughtful comparison with appropriate use of text details
5	Vague comparison with little use of text details
0	No response or off topic

EDGE Level C

ANSWER KEYS & ANSWER SHEET

"POEMS FOR THE EARTH" AND "I WAS BORN TODAY" / "TOUCHING THE EARTH"

1–8. KEY VOCABULARY
(4 points each/32 points total)

1. D	2. C	3. C	4. D
5. A	6. D	7. C	8. A

9–12. LITERARY ANALYSIS
(4 points each/16 points total)

9. A   10. C   11. B   12. A

13–14. COMPREHENSION
(4 points each/8 points total)

13. C   14. A

15. CONSTRUCTED RESPONSE
(10 points total)

15. What to look for: Student provides a valid analysis of the presentation of "strength" in each poem and refers to each text to support that analysis.

Points	Performance
10	Valid analysis with relevant text references
5	Weak analysis with little text reference
0	No response or off topic

16–19. LITERARY ANALYSIS
(4 points each/16 points total)

16. B   17. A   18. B   19. D

20–21. COMPREHENSION
(4 points each/8 points total)

20. D   21. A

22. CONSTRUCTED RESPONSE
(10 points total)

22. What to look for: Student provides a valid comparison of the poems' structure and style and analysis of their effect, citing text evidence in doing so.

Points	Performance
10	Valid comparison and analysis with relevant text evidence
5	Vague comparison and analysis with some text evidence
0	No response or off topic

READING AND LITERARY ANALYSIS UNIT TEST

1–24. MULTIPLE-CHOICE *(1 point each/22 points total)*

1. C	**2.** A	**3.** C	**4.** D	**5.** A	**6.** B	**7.** A	**8.** A	**9.** C	**11.** B	**12.** C
13. B	**14.** B	**15.** C	**16.** C	**17.** A	**18.** D	**20.** B	**21.** C	**22.** A	**23.** D	**24.** A

10., 19., & 25. CONSTRUCTED RESPONSE *(4 points each/12 points total)*

Points	Criteria
4	Full answer; provides extensive support with relevant examples
3	Partial answer; provides several relevant examples
2	Partial answer; provides one relevant example
1	Partial answer; no example provided
0	No response or off topic

Conversion Chart: Points Earned to Percent Score

Points	0	1	2	3	4	5	6	7	8	9	10	11	12	13	14	15	16	17	18	19	20	21	22	23	24	25	26	27	28	29	30	31	32	33	34
%	0	3	6	9	12	15	18	21	24	26	29	32	35	38	41	44	47	50	53	56	59	62	65	68	71	74	76	79	82	85	88	91	94	97	100

GRAMMAR AND WRITING UNIT TEST

1–16. MULTIPLE-CHOICE *(1 point each/16 points total)*

1. B	**2.** D	**3.** B	**4.** B	**5.** C	**6.** A	**7.** D	**8.** C
9. B	**10.** C	**11.** D	**12.** A	**13.** D	**14.** C	**15.** C	**16.** C

WRITTEN COMPOSITION *(20 points total)*

Use the Good Writing Traits rubric on page 122 to score the written composition.

Conversion Chart: Points Earned to Percent Score

Points	0	1	2	3	4	5	6	7	8	9	10	11	12	13	14	15	16	17	18	19	20	21	22	23	24	25	26	27	28	29	30	31	32	33	34	35	36
%	0	3	6	8	11	14	17	19	22	25	28	31	33	36	39	42	44	47	50	53	56	58	61	64	67	69	72	75	78	81	83	86	89	92	94	97	100

EDGE Level C

ANSWER KEYS & ANSWER SHEET

Name _____ Date _____

Answer Sheet

Directions: Fill in the circle beside your Level, Unit, and Test Type. Then mark your answers in column **1** if you are taking a Cluster Test, in column **2** if you are taking a Unit Test for Reading and Literary Analysis, or in column **3** if you are taking a Unit Test for Grammar and Writing. Use a separate sheet of paper for your written responses.

Level	Unit		Test Type	
○ A	○ 1	○ 5	○ Cluster Test 1	○ Unit Test: Reading & Literary Analysis
○ B	○ 2	○ 6	○ Cluster Test 2	○ Unit Test: Grammar & Writing
○ C	○ 3	○ 7	○ Cluster Test 3	
	○ 4			

Cluster Test

1. Ⓐ Ⓑ Ⓒ Ⓓ
2. Ⓐ Ⓑ Ⓒ Ⓓ
3. Ⓐ Ⓑ Ⓒ Ⓓ
4. Ⓐ Ⓑ Ⓒ Ⓓ
5. Ⓐ Ⓑ Ⓒ Ⓓ
6. Ⓐ Ⓑ Ⓒ Ⓓ
7. Ⓐ Ⓑ Ⓒ Ⓓ
8. Ⓐ Ⓑ Ⓒ Ⓓ
9. Ⓐ Ⓑ Ⓒ Ⓓ
10. Ⓐ Ⓑ Ⓒ Ⓓ
11. Ⓐ Ⓑ Ⓒ Ⓓ
12. Ⓐ Ⓑ Ⓒ Ⓓ
13. Ⓐ Ⓑ Ⓒ Ⓓ
14. Ⓐ Ⓑ Ⓒ Ⓓ
15. Write Response
16. Ⓐ Ⓑ Ⓒ Ⓓ
17. Ⓐ Ⓑ Ⓒ Ⓓ
18. Ⓐ Ⓑ Ⓒ Ⓓ
19. Ⓐ Ⓑ Ⓒ Ⓓ
20. Ⓐ Ⓑ Ⓒ Ⓓ
21. Ⓐ Ⓑ Ⓒ Ⓓ
22. Write Response

Unit Test:
Reading and Literary Analysis
NOTE: In addition to item 25, there are two other written response items. Check your test for the item number.

1. Ⓐ Ⓑ Ⓒ Ⓓ
2. Ⓐ Ⓑ Ⓒ Ⓓ
3. Ⓐ Ⓑ Ⓒ Ⓓ
4. Ⓐ Ⓑ Ⓒ Ⓓ
5. Ⓐ Ⓑ Ⓒ Ⓓ
6. Ⓐ Ⓑ Ⓒ Ⓓ
7. Ⓐ Ⓑ Ⓒ Ⓓ
8. Ⓐ Ⓑ Ⓒ Ⓓ
9. Ⓐ Ⓑ Ⓒ Ⓓ
10. Ⓐ Ⓑ Ⓒ Ⓓ
11. Ⓐ Ⓑ Ⓒ Ⓓ
12. Ⓐ Ⓑ Ⓒ Ⓓ
13. Ⓐ Ⓑ Ⓒ Ⓓ
14. Ⓐ Ⓑ Ⓒ Ⓓ
15. Ⓐ Ⓑ Ⓒ Ⓓ
16. Ⓐ Ⓑ Ⓒ Ⓓ
17. Ⓐ Ⓑ Ⓒ Ⓓ
18. Ⓐ Ⓑ Ⓒ Ⓓ
19. Ⓐ Ⓑ Ⓒ Ⓓ
20. Ⓐ Ⓑ Ⓒ Ⓓ
21. Ⓐ Ⓑ Ⓒ Ⓓ
22. Ⓐ Ⓑ Ⓒ Ⓓ
23. Ⓐ Ⓑ Ⓒ Ⓓ
24. Ⓐ Ⓑ Ⓒ Ⓓ
25. Write Response

Unit Test:
Grammar and Writing

1. Ⓐ Ⓑ Ⓒ Ⓓ
2. Ⓐ Ⓑ Ⓒ Ⓓ
3. Ⓐ Ⓑ Ⓒ Ⓓ
4. Ⓐ Ⓑ Ⓒ Ⓓ
5. Ⓐ Ⓑ Ⓒ Ⓓ
6. Ⓐ Ⓑ Ⓒ Ⓓ
7. Ⓐ Ⓑ Ⓒ Ⓓ
8. Ⓐ Ⓑ Ⓒ Ⓓ
9. Ⓐ Ⓑ Ⓒ Ⓓ
10. Ⓐ Ⓑ Ⓒ Ⓓ
11. Ⓐ Ⓑ Ⓒ Ⓓ
12. Ⓐ Ⓑ Ⓒ Ⓓ
13. Ⓐ Ⓑ Ⓒ Ⓓ
14. Ⓐ Ⓑ Ⓒ Ⓓ
15. Ⓐ Ⓑ Ⓒ Ⓓ
16. Ⓐ Ⓑ Ⓒ Ⓓ
17. Ⓐ Ⓑ Ⓒ Ⓓ
18. Ⓐ Ⓑ Ⓒ Ⓓ
19. Ⓐ Ⓑ Ⓒ Ⓓ
20. Ⓐ Ⓑ Ⓒ Ⓓ

TEACHER USE ONLY Record your scores for the written responses.

Cluster Test Constructed-Response Items

15. ⓪ ⑤ ⑩
22. ⓪ ⑤ ⑩

Unit Test Constructed-Response Items

⓪ ① ② ③ ④
⓪ ① ② ③ ④
⓪ ① ② ③ ④

Unit Test Written Composition Scores

Focus & Unity ① ② ③ ④
Organization ① ② ③ ④
Development of Ideas ① ② ③ ④
Voice & Style ① ② ③ ④
Written Conventions ① ② ③ ④
No Response ○